Spiritual Adventures

Spiritual Adventures

A Traveler's Guide to Extraordinary Vacations

STEPHANIE OCKO

Stephanie Ocko (signature)

CITADEL PRESS
Kensington Publishing Corp.
www.kensingtonbooks.com

CITADEL PRESS BOOKS are published by

Kensington Publishing Corp.
850 Third Avenue
New York, NY 10022

All Kensington titles, imprints, and distributed lines are available at special
quantity discounts for bulk purchases for sales promotions, premiums, fund-
raising, educational, or institutional use. Special book excerpts or customized
printings can also be created to fit specific needs. For details, write or phone
the office of the Kensington special sales manager: Kensington Publishing
Corp., 850 Third Avenue, New York, NY 10022, attn: Special Sales
Department, phone 1-800-221-2647.

CITADEL PRESS and the Citadel logo are Reg. U.S. Pat. & TM Off.

First printing: January 2003

10 9 8 7 6 5 4 3 2 1

Printed in the United States of America

Library of Congress Control Number: 2002113379

ISBN 0-8065-2369-7

Contents

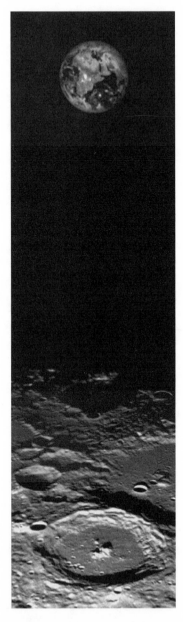

Earth from the Moon surveyor *Clementine,* as it orbits the
Moon's north pole, 1994. (*NASA*)

Preface

The purpose of this book is to describe some of the most popular spiritual "adventures" available today. Many of them have been around for a long time, but none with such current popularity. Although often described as pilgrimages or sacred travel, they remain, nevertheless, a form of tourism, which is how this book addresses them. As long as a product is being sold that involves introducing a stranger to a new area, it should be subject to standards that can be defined and described. This basic consideration is intended to enhance the buyer's spiritual experience, whether it is a physical journey to a sacred site or an inner journey to a new place within.

The book does not aspire to give advice about which adventure is right for the reader, because one's spiritual journey is fundamentally private. But the opportunity for exploration is rich, and the facilitators are ready to help. Most of the companies included in this book have an abundance of ideas and places for interesting adventures, and years of experience dealing with a constituency of sensitive and sensible travelers. They are able to make you feel a true part of the spiritual adventure.

The choices can be challenging: hiking in the Himalayas;

swimming in the wild ocean; sleeping alone in the desert; or winding your way through Andean passes or dense Amazonian jungle. Other adventures include luxury accommodations and first-class cruises, as well as activities with lots of time for meditation and reflection. You will meet local people willing to introduce you to their ways of spiritual connection. Or, you can take inner journeys through meditation or prayer with groups and create new states of peace and harmony; or sit under starry skies and wait for signs of life from other parts of the universe. In many cases, the spiritual territory has yet to be mapped.

Quantum discoveries govern a lot of spiritual adventures, especially the theory of nonlocality, in which twinned photons behave in identical ways even though they have been separated. This new perspective has had an impact on spiritual leaders who believe in the interconnectedness of all living things.

"Saving the earth" is also the dynamic message from shamans, alien abductees, people who work with nature "devas," and those who swim with dolphins. They report in unison that earth health is jeopardized by manmade abuse as well as by natural occurrences, some of which—big volcanic eruptions, huge storms—will be devastating.

Nothing is easy about these adventures. Spiritual growth relies on rigorous daily self-discipline, constant attention to the moment, and spiritual workouts. But you will not be alone. Many tour leaders are part of the culture they will introduce to you. Local guides enhance the understanding of the place and the experience.

Some individual adventures listed may not be offered every year, but serve as a sample of the type of adventure a company organizes. The list is offered in good faith, without bias or preference, and does not pretend to be complete. Neither the author nor the publisher takes responsibility for any travel provider's incompetence, or for any accident or injury to any participant incurred on an adventure. Every effort has been made to ensure that contact information is current and accurate. However, the reader should be aware of the volatility of web addresses, telephone numbers, and E-mail addresses.

At this writing the world appears to be in turmoil, generally. "The tourist comes in peace," said former UNEP director Noel Brown at a recent conference of the International Institute of Peace through Tourism (www.iipt.org). Tourism is an important source of revenue in most countries; for some, it is the principal source of foreign currency. Travel that encourages knowledge and respect for sacred and ancient cultural expression fosters understanding between and among people.

"The traveler develops a stake in the host's prosperity, and forms new respect for its culture and a greater affection for *place*, in effect becoming more at home on earth. In turn," Brown said, "the world becomes a more hospitable and familiar place, with much that should be protected, cherished, and enhanced."

I signed the contract to write this book two days before September 11, 2001, shortly after the sudden death of a close friend. I am grateful for the opportunity to visit communities of people for whom discussion of spiritual matters is a natural outgrowth of their lives. Thanks especially to: Bruce Bender and Ann La Farge at Citadel; Toni Neuberger; Stacy Bell; Jy and Gail Chiperzak; Steve Armstrong; Jack Sheremetoff; Cindy Weaver at Sacred Traditions; John Milton; Sparrow Hawk; Ron Russell; Barry Wood, modern-day Merlin; agent Jane Jordan Browne; everyone who answered questions and especially those who asked them. For the pictures, a special gratitude goes to photographer Roger Archibald, my partner, whom I also thank for his exquisite patience.

Introduction

The most beautiful thing we can experience is the mysterious.

—Albert Einstein

A good book on the spirit opens doors to other worlds. This book offers several invitations to you to risk what you know and to cross the threshold into brave new ways of thinking and feeling. It's a gift to yourself that only you can give.

Spiritual adventures are not chocolate-coated. You will need all the inner strength you can muster. Sometimes they simultaneously evoke opposite feelings: humiliation and love, terror and delight. This is the tough-love hallmark of spiritual growth. The learning process is hard-nosed, indifferent, sometimes messy and chaotic. It takes practice and focus. But it is breathtakingly uplifting.

If you have the courage to go into the unknown and are willing to map brand new territory, and if you feel you are already a personal warrior fighting the daily dragons of fear and uncertainty, the spiritual adventures in this book will take you away and bring you back changed. You will be awakened and aware of a divine direction. You will be able to uncover new internal zones from which you can access peace, happiness, and understanding.

But on another level, the push to a broader and deeper spiritual involvement in life seems to be part of our evolution as human beings. Ready or not, we might be programmed to evolve to a higher consciousness that translates into a different identity of ourselves as humans, more adapted to silent communication, more caring for others and our place in the world, and better able to incorporate invisible worlds into our daily reality.

Revelations from other fields of science break the molds of our beliefs. Physicists describe the startling similarities between subatomic particles and the movement of the universe. Anthropologists witness unusual healing by shamans; zoologists study how animals think and display self-awareness and a sense of humor; psychiatrists investigate, with alien abductees, the other dimensions abductees believe they have visited.

The late Willis Harman, one of the founders of the Institute of Noetic Sciences, said, "When other profound change took place [in history], those living through it tended to be unaware of its historical significance, and aware mostly of the transitional pains and difficulties. We're fortunate enough not only to watch major change take place within a lifetime, but also to possess enough knowledge to have a good picture of what's going on. Our part in it can be exhilarating and fun."

Others before us have lived in an ever-shifting, unpredictable quantum world. But we *know* we do. If that doesn't add a thrill, nothing will.

Whatever you choose to do, you bring yourself to it and you bring yourself back, fulfilled. Your encounter with the spirit is uniquely yours. And it will be astonishing.

Lion and lioness, Kenya. (*Stephanie Ocko*)

Chapter 1
Meditation

My own view is that as long as we're breathing, we have lots of options.

—Jon Kabat-Zinn

If spiritual change has a boot camp, it is meditation. Learning how to stay still in one place while not thinking the thoughts your mind *wants* to think takes practice and rigorous self-discipline. Although it is counter-intuitive to connect to life by not being a part of it, meditation underlies all of the adventures mentioned in this book. It deepens your experience of the moment and, over time, opens doors to places you didn't even know existed.

The main purpose of meditation is to minimize or temporarily eliminate your conscious state. Although meditation comes in many forms, there are two main types: *detaching* from your thoughts by consciously clearing your mind; and *focusing* on one thing, a candle, a picture, or repeated phrase or word.

"QUIET" CHI GONG MEDITATION

Stand, arms at your side. Clear your mind. Close your eyes and lower your head.

1

Concentrate on your navel. Touch your navel 3 times (men use left hand, women use right hand).

Breathe deeply 12 times.

Imagine that you are looking at your eyes.

Imagine that you are looking at the space between your eyes for one second.

For three breaths, imagine that your chi (life force) is traveling from the point between your eyes to your navel.

Now, breathe through your navel 5 times.

Imagine that your navel sticks to the corresponding point on your back on each exhale.

Now inhale through that point.

Focus on your navel, listen to yourself inhaling and exhaling for ten or fifteen minutes.

Then tell yourself you are bringing your meditation to a close. Open your eyes and lift your head, gazing at something in the distance.

Use your left hand (women: right) to rub your navel 24 times in ever-increasing circles.

Rub 24 times in the opposite direction.

Rub your hands together until they are warm. Wipe your face with them 36 times.

Use the right hand to pat the left shoulder 3 times. Use the left hand to pat the right shoulder 3 times.

Tap your left hand top and bottom 3 times with the right hand. Do the same with the opposite hands.

Bending over, use your right hand to tap your left foot, top to bottom, 3 times. Do the same with the left hand on the right foot.

Straighten up.

This is a good meditation for people who have trouble just sitting and breathing. It is also effective for lapsed meditators who want to meditate again. Usually, Chi Gong is a series of movements that stimulate the flow of Chi, or vital energy, through invisible channels in the body. This Quiet or Relaxed

Chi Gong meditation, from China dating about the first century, is intended to control the seven emotions: joy, pleasure, anger, love, hatred, sadness, and desire. It takes about twenty to thirty minutes.

VIPASSANA MEDITATION

Sit comfortably for twenty minutes in the lotus position or in a chair. Keep your back straight, eyes closed. Breathe in. Breathe out. Breathe in. Breathe out. Say to yourself at each breath, "I am breathing in. I am breathing out." When a thought comes in, watch it. As it leaves, just observe it. Breathe in. Breathe out. Listen to noises as they fall away outside of you, near you, inside you. Breathe in. Breathe out.

This meditation was practiced two thousand years ago by monks in India following the Theravada Buddhist path. Its intention is to produce a detached awareness through mindfulness. Unlike the Chi Gong meditation, it focuses on the breath and visualizes nothing.

Mindfulness is paying attention to the moment and to the process, rather than the goal. Smell the carrots you are slicing; feel the soap bubbles on your hands under the running water; hear the leaves being lifted by the wind. Studies have found that mindfulness meditation is a powerful coping strategy for dealing with stress from chronic pain or the sense that your life is out of your control. In other words, it grounds you in the moment.

ZEN MEDITATION, OR ZAZEN

Sit on the floor and place your legs and feet in whatever position is comfortable; or kneel; or sit in a chair. Keep your spine straight and your nose in line with your navel. With your mouth closed, breathe through your nose and place your tongue on the roof of your mouth. Lower your eyelids, looking at nothing.

Palms up, support one hand with your dominant hand, and lightly touch the two thumbs. Breathe.

Concentrate on your hara, the point two inches below your navel. As you rock your torso back and forth to find your center of gravity, visualize your breath reaching deep into the hara, then returning.

Count each time you breathe in and each time you breathe out, until you reach ten; then begin again.

As you breathe more slowly, count one for each inhalation and exhalation. Counting keeps you focused. Count and come back to the moment if thoughts intervene. Imagine your mind as the surface of a quiet pool; thoughts break the stillness. Smooth, the pool reflects perfect images of the sun and the clouds; broken, the images are distorted.

As your concentration deepens, stop counting.

Be the breath.

Let the breath breathe.

The aim of practicing Zen is to empty the mind of all the personal, psychological, and cultural baggage that we've managed to stuff into our personalities, and to begin to see for the first time who we really are and what life is all about. Masters teach their students *koans*—questions with answers that make you feel as if you missed the lecture. For example:

Q: "If everything is reducible to the One, where is the One to be reduced?"

A: "When I was in the district of Ch'ing Hai, I had a robe made that weighed seven *chin.*"

A *koan* empties the mind by mocking rational thinking. "The idea is not to reduce the human mind to a moronic vacuity," explains Alan Watts in *The Way of Zen,* "but to bring into play its innate and spontaneous intelligence by using it without forcing it."

For a playful and challenging introduction to Zen, see www.do-not-zzz.com.

RELAXATION RESPONSE MEDITATION

Get comfortable wherever you are and put away whatever you were doing. Relax and breathe deeply and slowly. Then breathe through your nose, and, as you breathe out, repeat a phrase such as, *The Lord is my shepherd, I shall not want,* or a sound like *Om* that reverberates throughout the chest cavity. Continue until you feel it is time to come back, usually after ten to twenty minutes. You can peek at the clock, but don't set the alarm.

Keep Breathing

How you meditate is up to you. You can sit, stand, walk, lie down; do it in your closet or under a tree; recite a mantra or not recite anything; stare at a candle or a picture or keep your eyes closed.

The key to meditating is to keep your back straight in order to open your lungs. Meditation is all about breathing and opening channels for the unobstructed flow of air. Count the number of times you breathe in a minute (one breath=inhalation and exhalation). The average is fifteen to seventeen times. Daily meditation will reduce that number by half. Longtime meditators breathe two or three times a minute.

If you have trouble getting started, try these suggestions:

- Tense all your muscles. Relax them gradually to see how tense you really are.
- Count your breaths. Count 1 to 10, then repeat. Count 1 to 100, then repeat.

- Visualize something beautiful, relaxing, or peaceful—a calm memory, warmth, comfort, love.
- Place your hand on your belly and feel your stomach moving with each breath. Your stomach *should* move in and out. This guarantees that your entire lung capacity is involved.
- Concentrate on your breath when thoughts come. They will keep moving if you don't pay attention to them. On the other hand, if you have something that you *should* be thinking about or analyzing or resolving, do it, and *then* meditate.

Is it for me?

Not everybody is a happy meditator. Several surveys indicate that about a third of the people polled said they meditate every

Tori Arch, entrance to sacred place, Nikko, Japan. (*Roger Archibald*)

day. Another third say they meditate occasionally. The final third was split between those who had tried and failed and those who had never tried.

Huston Smith, professor of philosophy and comparative religions at Massachusetts Institute of Technology, University of California, Berkeley, and Syracuse University, and longtime student of the mystical, said he faithfully "paid his dues" by sitting for an hour each morning and each evening for two decades—"with disappointing results."

Yoga, Tai Chi, and Chi Gong are mind/body practices that are done in a semi-meditative state, and may work for you if you are unable to meditate otherwise.

If all else fails, just sitting and staring at nothing is not so bad. It's a behavior we share with animals, especially cats, the Olympic champions of the empty gaze.

Meditation Has Come a Long Way

The practice of meditation in the United States has grown over the last three or four decades and has undergone various adaptations. In the 1970s the Maharishi Mahesh Yogi brought Transcendental Meditation (TM) to this country where some people paid a handsome sum to learn how to meditate and to be given a secret mantra (see: www.tm.org). TM, still popular, was the first to bring meditation into the mainstream. At the same time, Dr. Herbert Benson, president of the Mind/Body Medical Institute, published the book *The Relaxation Response,* which taught that concentrated slow, deep breathing was the primary tool in the war against stress.

In the past twenty years, Buddhism has set up shop in the United States, establishing retreat centers not only for the use of Buddhists but also as teaching centers for Westerners. The practice of meditation is generally attributed to Buddha in the sixth century before the common era (B.C.E), but it is probably older.

Meditation techniques come in all shapes and sizes these days, from ritually relaxing every part of your body; to creatively visualizing concepts like love and peace; to controlling your sexual energy in Kundalini chakras, or energy points. Kundalini is a yoga derivative, in which you concentrate on raising your energy from the first chakra, between your anus and sexual organ, through the four torso chakras to the crown of your head.

Mini-meditations, a product of Benson's *Relaxation Response*, are five- or ten-minute practices that can be done anywhere. Many companies that allow meditation breaks encourage the practice to create a more relaxed atmosphere and benefit production.

Why meditate?

In an interview in *New Age* magazine (Sept/Oct 2001), Jon Kabat-Zinn, founder of the Stress Reduction Clinic at the Uni-

Shinto priest, Japan. (*Roger Archibald*)

versity of Massachusetts Medical Center in Worcester, and Andrew Weil, director of the Program in Integrative Medicine and clinical professor at the University of Arizona, (each of whom has spent an extended retreat at a Vipassana center) agreed that meditation does not have to be part of a philosophical system.

"The essence of meditation practice is universal," said Kabat-Zinn, "it has to do with the quality of awareness and attention." Meditation helps you be in the present. "It's the risk that your whole life could go by and you would miss it," said Kabat-Zinn, "because you were absorbed in what you thought you needed to be doing."

Without meditation, Weil said he probably would have given in to escapism activities—distractions like travel, drugs, or sex. "For me, one of the insights from meditation is that I am here and that I take myself everywhere—that I have to sit down and face myself," said Weil.

Weil, who teaches breath work to his students of internal medicine, says that meditation is the only function in which the conscious mind actually controls the autonomic nervous system.

The Benefits

Many studies have found that any kind of meditation improves your cardiovascular health and creates statistically significant changes in perception, sense of time, vividness of imagination, increased joy, creativity, and capacity for love. Several studies done in India found that prolonged meditative states produced "phenomenological experiences of consciousness," or "thoughtless awareness."

To trace exactly what happens in the brain during "peak" moments in long periods of meditation, professor of radiology Andrew Newberg and psychiatrist Eugene d'Aquili of the University of Pennsylvania injected radioactive liquid into the veins of their subjects, Franciscan nuns and Tibetan meditators, when the subjects indicated they had reached moments of "bliss." Using a Single Photon Emission Computed Tomography (SPECT) imaging tool that traces radioactivity in the brain, Newberg and d'Aquili studied their subjects' brain circuits and discovered interesting changes during both mind-emptying meditation and single-focused prayer.

In both cases, neural activity created by "the willful intention to quiet the conscious mind" subdued activity in the prefrontal cortex, the area of the brain that controls bodily movement and will; and the posterior parietal lobe, the seat of the orientation association area, where the self orients itself in space and time. Newberg and d'Aquili write in *Why God Won't Go Away* that subduing activity in these areas would lead to changes in the brain in which the self appeared to dissolve, and the sense of place and time, disappeared, leading to an "absolute sense of unity" with infinity. In the case of the subjects who focused on a single image, there was an experience of being "mystically absorbed" into the image.

In other words, they concluded, God is hardwired in our brains. Or, you could say, we cocreate with God our moments of bliss.

What is enlightenment?

> While on the shop and street I gazed
> My body of a sudden blazed,
> And twenty minutes more or less
> It seemed, so great my happiness,
> That I was blessèd and could bless.
>
> —W.B. Yeats, *Vacillation*

D.T. Suzuki, a modern interpreter of Zen, explains enlightenment as like ordinary experience, except you feel as if you are two inches off the ground. "Logically stated," he wrote, "all [the world's] opposites and contradictions are united and harmonized into a consistent organic whole. This is a mystery and a miracle."

In 400 B.C.E., Lieh-tzu, a Taoist who was famous for his ability to "ride the wind," wrote that after nine years of training, "internal and external were blended into unity . . . I was borne this way and that on the wind like dry chaff or leaves falling from a tree. In fact, I knew not whether the wind was riding on me or I, on the wind."

More recently, Paul Dong, a Chi Gong teacher for two decades, says he reached "unity of person and heaven" only after four years of training with a teacher. Now when he practices Chi Gong at night, he sometimes experiences the highest stage, and "the self merges with the Milky Way, the cosmos, and the stars."

After enlightenment, what?

With faithful practice, you probably will experience a state of universal blending or bliss. But where do you go with that? If you live in a world with daily demands—overwork, mistakes in your phone bill, road rage—a constant state of bliss might be inappropriate. And you might lose your edge.

Paul Townsend, a software writer who spent twelve years in a Tibetan monastery, says "don't accept idle bliss as success." Writing in *Qi: The Journal of Traditional Eastern Health and Fitness,* Townsend reminds us not to forget that the purpose of meditation is to focus your mind and that if you meditate all day, you can put your "goals on the fast track."

His method, he says, is to identify your centers: first, focus on your breathing (which is like controlling your thoughts in meditation); then focus on your goal (which is like focusing on a candle or a sound in meditation). Switching back and forth throughout the day, Townsend says, produces amazing results in your daily life.

Remember that the purpose of meditation is to turn down the noise so you can hear the music.

SPIRITUAL RETREATS

Buddhist

Insight Meditation Society 1230 Pleasant Street, Barre, MA 01005. 978-355-4378 (tel); 978-355-6398 (fax). Web site: www. dharma.org

Located in the midst of eighty wooded acres in central Massachusetts, the Insight Meditation Society, founded in 1975, welcomes individual and group retreats in Vipassana meditation. The daily schedule (begins at 5:00 A.M., ends at 10:00 P.M.) is spent in sitting and walking meditation. Single rooms are spartan. About $40 a day; some scholarships are available.

Shambhala International 1084 Tower Road, Halifax, Nova Scotia, B3H 2Y5, Canada. 902-420-1118 (tel). E-mail: info@shambhala. org; Web site: www.shambhala.org

At centers located in the United States, Canada, and France, Shambhala offers a variety of solitary, weekend, and month-long retreats, as well as intensive study programs and extended stays for serious students of Buddhism. Costs vary depending on location and length of stay.

Cloud Mountain Retreat Center 373 Agren Road, Castle Rock, WA 98611. 888-465-9118 (toll free); 360-274-4859 (tel); 360-274-9119 (fax). E-mail: info@cloudmountain.org; Web site: www.cloudmountain.org

Voted one of the premier Dharma centers in the United States by *Time* magazine, Cloud Mountain offers retreats in Vipassana meditation ranging in length from three to twenty-seven days. The center is located in a rural area in southern Washington State. Prices vary; the average is about $50 a night.

Zen Buddhist

Zen Mountain Monastery   P.O. Box 197 PC, South Plank Road, Mt. Tremper, NY 12457. 845-688-2228 (tel); 845-688-2415 (fax). E-mail: registrar@dharma.net; Web site: www.mro.org

Located in the foothills of the Catskill Mountains in New York, Zen Mountain Monastery offers a different kind of retreat. Interweaving Zen with daily activities, each retreat is structured around a program as varied as Zen Archery to Knowing How to Be Satisfied Among Our Inexhaustible Desires. After instruction is given in *zazen,* or Zen meditation, the day begins and ends with meditation. Prices vary; three days, about $175. "Everyone is asked to come prepared for a challenging experience, to participate fully—with the whole body and mind . . ." and to stay until the conclusion.

Ram Sangha Retreats   319 West 18th Street, #6G, New York, NY 10011. 212-645-6070 (tel). E-mail: yogaijp@earthlink.net; Web site: www.ramsangha.com

Part of the Zen Studies Society, Ram Sangha Retreats is located three hours north of New York City in the Catskill Mountains at Dai Bosatsu Zendo Kongo-ji. Three retreats a summer, each three or four days, offer walking meditation, daily yoga, swimming in Beecher Lake, and chanting. Cost: about $450 to $700.

The Zen Studies Society was established in 1956 by D.T. Suzuki, one of the first practitioners to introduce Zen to the West. Since 1965, the society has been under the leadership of a Japanese Zen monk, Eido Tai Shimano. The society also runs New York Zendo Shobo-ji, on Manhattan's Upper East Side. Web site: www.zenstudies.org; to receive the newsletter, send your name and address to: mailinglist@zenstudies.org.

Green Gulch Farm & Zen Center   1601 Shoreline Highway, Sausalito, CA 94965. 415-383-3134 (tel); 415-383-3128 (fax). Web site: www.sfzc.org

Green Dragon Temple, as it is also known, was established in 1972 and is a thriving organic farm and Zen center. A typical retreat includes meditation and classes in organic gardening or the Japanese tea ceremony. Rooms are in a cedar lodge with shared bath; vegetarian meals; about $100 a night.

Tassajara Zen Mountain Center   300 Page Street, San Francisco, CA 94102. 415-431-3771 (tel). Web site: www.zendo. com

Deep in the Los Padres National Forest near Monterey, California, Tassajara Zen Mountain Center is up a steep dirt road accessible by Tassajara's shuttle ("the Stage"). Retreatants will stay in Japanese-style stone and pine redwood cabins lit by kerosene lamps. Five-day Zen retreats include meditation, discussions, classes with a Zen teacher. Costs: $100 for the retreat; $50 a night for lodging. Rate includes three gourmet vegetarian meals and use of the Japanese bathhouse. Tassajara also has

Detail, Buddha: thumbs and first digits together, one position of hands in meditation. (*Roger Archibald*)

workshops, as well as weekend and longer work programs. Reserve after April 1; spaces fill quickly.

Monasteries

Mepkin Abbey 1098 Mepkin Abbey Road, Moncks Corner, SC 29461. 843-761-8509 (tel); 843-761-6719 (fax). E-mail: guestmaster@ mepkinabbey.org; Web site: www.mepkinabbey.org

Mepkin Abbey is a working Trappist monastery which follows the Liturgy of the Hours, a "dialogue of listening and response" during which "the monks gather to give voice to that inner song of God's praise found in every human heart." Men and women of any religion are welcome to spend one to six nights, respecting and practicing the code of silence, the Rule of Saint Benedict. A monk assists visitors with the order of prayer. Most simple rooms have a private bath. Donation requested.

Dominican Retreat House 7103 Old Dominion Drive, McLean, VA 22101-2799. 703-356-4243 (tel). E-mail: info@dominicanretreat.org; Web site: www.dominicanretreat.org

Four miles from Washington, D.C., this twelve-acre "oasis of tranquility" retreat center for men and women is run by the Dominican Sisters of Saint Catherine de Ricci. Individuals seeking solitude and rest are invited for one to several days. They offer special all male or female weekend retreats and spiritual direction, if requested. Weekend: the nuns quote $230, but will consider less, for those in financial need.

New Camaldoli Hermitage 62475 Coast Highway 1 at Lucia, Big Sur, CA 93920-9656. 831-667-2456 (tel); E-mail: vocations@ contemplation.com; Web site: www.contemplation.com

Thirteen hundred feet above the Pacific Ocean, New Camaldoli was created in 1958 by Italian monks from the order of Saint Romuald. Men and women are invited to spend time in silent meditation and reflection. The Hermitage has single rooms with lavatories and gardens overlooking the ocean, shared shower room, and kitchen, where you "pick up your meals." Five trailers located on the hillside below the Hermitage have full bath and housekeeping facilities. Reserve well in advance. Suggested donation: $60 per night for room; $70 per night for trailers.

Mount Calvary Retreat House P.O. Box 1296, Santa Barbara, CA 93102. 805-962-9855, ext. 10 (tel). Web site: www. mount-calvary.org

The Benedictine Retreat House and Monastery, established in 1947 by the Anglican Order of the Holy Cross, is a Spanish-style mission overlooking Santa Barbara and the Pacific Ocean. Men and women of any denomination are invited to find solitude, study, or work. Groups are welcome. Reserve in advance. Rooms with bath: $70 per night.

East West Retreat Center Santa Maria delle Rose, 2C, 06081 Assisi, Italy. +39 (0) 349-499-1293 (tel); 801-459-4035 (U.S. fax). E-mail: info@sacredtravel.org; Web site: www.sacredtravel.org

Retreats in honor of Saint Francis and Saint Clare are offered to those who want to spend time in "contemplative spirituality" in Assisi. Bruce and Ruth Davis guide group meditations at the center, as well as at places in the area sacred to the saints. Special individual and family retreats are offered throughout the year, including one that spends half of an autumn week in the Rieti Valley vineyards. Ruth Davis offers a private movement retreat for dancers and non-dancers. E-mail: ruth@sacredtravel. org. Prices vary. The Davises also run a retreat center in Bali.

Migliara Retreats (Summer): Loc. Migliara 64, Madonnuccia, 52030 Pieve Santo Stefano (AR), Italy. +39 (0) 575-795-105 (tel/ fax). (Winter): No.7, 94 Crescent Road, Toronto, Ontario, Canada M4W 1T5. 416-323-1133 (tel); 416-323-020 (fax). E-mail: lucem@ican. net; Web site: www.dallaluce.com

Lucinda Vardey has been offering pilgrimage retreats in a five-hundred-year-old Tuscany farmhouse since 1995. A maximum of seven retreatants stay in spacious rooms surrounded by wildflowers, and spend the week focusing on various aspects of Christian history and meaning. For example, readings may include: "In the Footsteps of Saint Francis"; "The Development of Gregorian Chants"; "The Holy Women of Tuscany and Umbria." Cost includes all ground transport, room and board: $1,000 to $1,200.

Transdenominational Jewish Retreat

Elat Chayyim 99 Mill Hook Road, Accord, NY 12404. 800-398-2630 (toll free); 845-626-0157 (tel); 845-626-2037 (fax). E-mail: info@elatchayyim.org; Web site: www.elatchayyim.org

This Jewish spiritual retreat center, located in the foothills of the Catskill Mountains, offers a place for meditation and silence, as well as prayer services, for individuals and families. Men and women of all denominations are invited to spend a weekend, week, or the holidays in an atmosphere of spiritual Judaism. Special programs for artists. Weekend: about $200 to $300, includes all meals and lodging.

Quaker Retreat Center

Pendle Hill 338 Plush Mill Road, Wallingford, PA 19086. 800-742-3150 (toll free); 610-566-4507 (tel). Web site: www.pendlehill. org

You are invited to bring your cares and spend a weekend on several quiet acres planted with flowering trees, talking about your fears and concerns, and leaving lighter and happier. Weekend, about $225, includes room and board. Other programs are available.

Chi Gong or Healing Tao Retreats

Silent Ground P.O. Box 28, Surge Narrows, BC, V0P 1W0 Canada, 250-830-7212 (tel). E-mail: siground@island.net; Web site: www. silentground.com

Located on Read Island in the Strait of Georgia, British Columbia, this meditation retreat center encourages "mindfulness of breath, body, feeling, and mind." Rising at 5:30 A.M. for meditation and breathing, you spend the day doing Chi Gong, Tao Yoga, and meditation, and end the day with dinner, Six Healing Sounds and Bone Breathing. Three-week winter program teaches basic, intermediate, and advanced courses. About $95 a day; $490 a week includes lodging and all meals. Possibility of long stays. Add 7 percent GST.

Healing Tao USA c/o Jeronimo, 3 Hotel Road, Walker Valley, NY 12588. 888-999-0555 (toll free); 201-457-1983 (tel); 201-343-8511 (fax). E-mail: info@HealingDao.com; Web site: www.HealingDao.com

At two retreat centers, one in the Catskill Mountains in New York and the other at Mount Madonna, south of San Francisco, California, instructors offer all aspects of Tao basics and Chi Gong. Week-long retreats run through the summer and include integrated healing techniques, whole body breathing, and yoga. One-week retreat from about $800 to $1,000, including room and board.

Nondenominational Meditation Retreat Centers

Hollyhock Retreat Center P.O. Box 127, Manson's Landing, Cortés Island, BC V0P 1K0, Canada. 800-933-6339 (toll free); 250-935-6576 (tel. outside North America). E-mail: registration@hollyhock.ca; Web site: www.hollyhock.ca

This nondenominational retreat center in British Columbia is an upscale place of "peace, personal growth, and restoration." Meals are gourmet vegetarian; the hot tub overlooks the ocean. Hollyhock's wide variety of programs and broad interpretation of spiritual expression welcomes people with open hearts and minds. Dancers, painters, musicians, calligraphers, and singers appreciate the ability to incorporate meditation with their arts.

Non-artists go to renew their spirits. Tuition prices vary; single room and bath, about $170 a night. Some scholarships available for certain programs.

Omega Institute 150 Lake Drive, Rhinebeck, NY 12572-3252. 800-944-1001 (toll free); 845-266-8691 (fax). Web site: www.eomega.org

Omega sponsors week-long retreats at Maho Bay, Saint John, Virgin Islands; Mount Madonna, California; and Costa Rica, each with a special focus and speakers. Seven days about $1,200 to $1,500.

Shantigar Village 63 Davenport Road, Rowe, MA 01367. 413-339-4332 (tel). E-mail: email@shantigar.org; Web site: www.shantigar.org

This green expanse in the northern Berkshires, "where apple trees . . . whisper when the moon is full," is the summer home of a theater healing and meditation retreat, conceived and run by playwright Jean-Claude van Itallie. His unique Writing on Your Feet workshop recognizes that writing starts in the belly and "is a physical process carried on the breath." Sponsors programs on performance and theater, plus special programs for women and gay men. Non-profit; suggested donation about $250, vegetarian meals extra, under $50.

Rowe Camp and Conference Center P.O. Box 273, Kings Highway Road, Rowe, MA 01367. 413-339-4954 (tel). E-mail: info@rowecenter.org; Web site: www.rowecenter.org

The Rowe Center, located in the Berkshires of northwestern Massachusetts, hosts weekend conferences and yearlong retreats. This quiet, vegetarian, healing place inspires graceful contemplation. Conference fees range from $160 to $240, using a sliding scale based on your annual household income. Food and lodging are between $80 and $190. The Rowe Center also considers barter and exchanging work for fees.

Nirarta Centre for Living Awareness Br Tabola, Sidemen, Karangasem, Bali 80864 Indonesia. +62 (0)366-24122 (tel); +62 366 21444 (fax; mark clearly: *Attn. Nirarta 24122*). E-mail: pwrycza@telkom.net; Web site: www.awareness-Bali.com

Nirarta's lush gardens are nestled among green hills and terraced rice fields and cooled by sweet Bali breezes that provide a deeply relaxing environment. Living Awareness: The Direct Approach to Awakening is a weeklong meditation retreat that explores the subtleties of change. Other offerings include personal development seminars, nature walks, hikes, and Balinese dance. Or, you can do a private retreat and join the staff for a twice-daily awareness meditation. Interesting international visitors. Living Awareness retreat: seven days, $625 shared room; $725 single.

Nature Retreats

Now is the time to integrate the inner and outer world. We are not separate.

—Laurie Monroe, The Monroe Institute

El Santuario Retreat Baja California Sur, Mexico. 805-541-7921 (tel). E-mail: baja@el-santuario.com; Web site: www. el-santuario. com

If getting away from it all is your primary concern, this place is thirty miles south of Loreto and a two-day drive from San Diego. Located on Ensenada Blanca, a bay with a long beach, islands, dolphins, and kayaks, El Santuario will facilitate your retreat with a resident psychotherapist/meditation teacher. *Casitas* (bungalows) are simple: showers are solar-heated, and the composting toilets are ecologically correct. The food is fresh, some of which is organic; you can help cook the evening meal if you want. A week: $400 single, $600 couple with everything, including kayak.

Pacific beach. For some people, the rhythm of the ocean encourages meditation. (*Roger Archibald*)

The Findhorn Foundation   The Park, Findhorn, IV36 3TZ, Scotland. +44 (0)1309-690311 (tel); +44 (0) 1309-691301 (fax). E-mail: vcentre@findhorn.org; Web site: www.findhorn.org

Findhorn's retreat house is on the island of Iona, a spectacular site for contemplation and meditation. Findhorn runs three summer retreats, one at the Celtic celebration of Beltane that marks the passing of spring to summer; one in June when you can work in the garden if you like; and one in late August for gay men. Lodging and food, one week: £350 to £195, according to your circumstances.

Northern Edge Algonquin   #17 Isabella Street, P.O. Box 329, South River, ON, P0A 1X0, Canada.

Northern Edge Algonquin offers a banquet of innovative programs year-round. Algonquin DreamQuest is a paddling adventure with media personality, physicist, and *Magical Blend* contributing editor Craig Webb, an expert in applied and lucid dreaming. Paddle by day; then, after a campfire dinner, learn how to "navigate the inner world of dreams." Seven days: $310 (plus excursion fees).

Xenia Creative Development Centre   RR1, P.O. Box N59, Bowen Island, BC, V0N 1G0, Canada. 604-947-9816 (tel); 604-947-9076 (fax). E-mail: xeniatlc@direct.ca; Web site: www.xenia centre.com

This thirty-eight-acre sanctuary nestled between two lakes, has two eleven-circuit labyrinths, a one-thousand-year-old Douglas fir tree named Opa, and an outdoor wood-burning sauna. Create your own silent retreat when you stay in one of the cottages; prepare your own meals in the kitchen at the lodge. Writers and artists are welcome. Rates per night: $85 to $115.

Circles of Air, Circles of Stone   P.O. Box 48, Putney, VT 05346. 802-387-6624 (tel). E-mail: Sparrow@together.net; Web site: www.circles-of-air.com

Rituals for the Earth, held in the early fall in Vermont's Green Mountains, is a weeklong event for men and women that includes a medicine walk, rituals of purification, access to animal allies, as well as understanding the presence of earth, wind, and water. Seven days: $550, includes food.

Rose Mountain Retreat Center   P.O. Box 355, Las Vegas, NM 87701. 505-425-5728 (tel). E-mail: rosemount@newmexico.com; Web site: www.buzzarte.org

Rose Mountain is located in the Sangre de Cristo Mountains at an elevation of 8,000 feet. Andy Gold offers a variety of summer programs with guest leaders. Eric Kolvig leads a Vipassana Meditation Retreat for beginners and advanced meditators (five days: $320). Rabbi Rami Shapiro gives a six-day story-telling workshop, Our Stories, Our Selves, which explores the Jewish Mystical Teaching Tradition (six days: $550). Many other interesting programs. Gourmet vegetarian meals; camping facilities with hot showers.

Sacred Passage   Drawer CZ, Bisbee, AZ 85603. 520-432-7353 (tel/fax). E-mail: sacred@primenet.com; Web site: www.sacred way. com

John Milton's Way of Nature's Special Trainings are designed to open communion with "Mother Earth, Great Spirit, and one's true nature." Gaia-Flow Moving Meditation, Chi Gong, Tai Chi intensives; geomancy, the study of Earth's ancient meridians, and lots more are offered. Locations, prices vary; two to twelve days.

Native Tours and Travel   Contact: Sonja Tanner, 6875 Highway 65 NE, Minneapolis, MN 55432. 866-404-9102 (toll free); 763-571-8184 (tel); 763-571-7889 (fax). E-mail: boozhoo@nativetours. com; Web site: www.nativetours.com

This company works only with Native American tribal- or tribal member-owned tour companies, and offers a variety of nature and tribal experiences. Their Women's Sacred Journey spends five summer days in Glacier National Park, Montana, participating in Blackfoot ceremonies, horseback riding, hiking, fishing, and swimming. Lodging in tepees on the edge of the lake; gourmet camp meals. Limit: ten women, about $1,000 per person.

Ojai Foundation   9739 Ojai-Santa Paula Road, Ojai, CA 93023. 805-646-8343 (tel). Web site: www.ojaifoundation.org

The Ojai Foundation is a "nondenominational educational sanctuary" located at the foot of the Los Padres Mountains north of Los Angeles. Part of the foundation is on a site formerly owned by mystic Annie Besant, who formed the Happy Valley Association in 1927. It is dedicated to fostering a "caring, mindful culture" by bringing the Way of Council to business, educational, and therapeutic communities on its forty peaceful acres of ancient oak and sagebrush.

Design your own retreat, bring your spouse or family, or go

alone; use the outdoor ceramics studio; fast, meditate, and do body work. Guests stay in wooden-floored, canvas-walled domes and yurts.

Their Work Retreat/Life Transitions program is a four-week work program for people seeking to change their lives by interweaving work and contemplation. Daily meditation; work in the garden, kitchen, or maintenance. Fee: $150, plus twenty-five hours of work per week.

Web Sites

RETREATS
www.learningmeditation.com

www.meditationcenter.com

Peaceful pond, with carp and lily pads. (*Roger Archibald*)

Pre-season quiet. (*Roger Archibald*)

www.meditationsociety.com

www.aspire.org

www.retreatsonline.com

www.spirituality.com

www.nicabm.com, the site of the National Institute for the Clinical Application of Behavioral Medicine gives weekend, six-day, and six-month programs in learning to use intuition.

BREATHING

www.pranayama.org Pranayama is a form of hatha yoga that uses breathing to induce certain healing reactions in the body.

www.breathwork.com is the Web site of Holotropic breath-work, a breathing therapy designed by psychiatrists Christina and Stanislav Grof (see: *Psychology of the Future*).

www.sundoor.com is the Web site of Peggy Dylan, who gives workshops in fire walking. She also teaches a Breathwork Intensive, a conscious breathing technique that promotes vitality, clarity, and creativity.

www.breathwalk.com is the Web site of Breathwalk, and provides information on a combination of meditative walking and breathing.

Chapter 2

Questions and Answers

What is a spiritual adventure?

A spiritual adventure is a planned trip in which you focus on overcoming the limitations that keep you from incorporating your spiritual self into your daily life. This is not to say that solo sailors on long voyages or backpackers on extensive treks don't encounter themselves and God in the same place. Nor does it exclude a moment you might experience ballooning over the desert at dawn or soaking up the rays on a beach. A spiritual adventure, pilgrimage, voyage, whatever you call it, has the *intention* of focusing on an internal change that will charge you with the responsibility of maintaining a spiritual path.

Do I need a spiritual guide?

A good guide is probably the most important part of your life's adventure. Sociologist and author Robert Wuthnow (*After Heaven: Spirituality in America Since the 1950s*) says that you need a spiritual guide in the same way you need a fishing guide, someone who knows the territory and the fish. You may meet him or her on a spiritual adventure, or in your local community center.

Finding a good one may take trial and error; don't settle for any-one less than the best person for *you*.

Psychotherapist and former Catholic monk Thomas Moore warns against being taken in by sweet talk, what Moore calls "lukewarm spiritual baby food." Be suspicious of leaders who promise "easy inspiration and surface personal development." Make sure your spiritual teacher is a few steps ahead of you and sincerely qualified to teach; otherwise, says psychotherapist Rick Gossett, you risk losing your spirit in "banality."

Some advise starting with your own religion to find a spiri-tual director or teacher. If that doesn't feel right, drop in at a dif-ferent house of worship, and tell the priest, rabbi, minister, or imam that you need a spiritual guide. When you have found someone you can talk to about issues that are neither psycho-logical nor sociological, but spiritual, make sure you are not "being made over in another's image," writes Margaret Guen-ther in *Holy Listening*. This person should be comfortable with God, and be able to host you and God. Some people have more than one spiritual guide.

Former physicist Russell Targ advises finding "a group of like-minded people who will support your path." Then take it from there. Moore says reading the *Tao Te Ching* will teach you how to "survive and thrive boldly." Also, he advises just standing in a medieval cathedral or temple or mosque or at a "pagan holy well—anywhere," he says, "you're placed in a sublime setting where you're challenged to transcend yourself." The guide might then come to you.

How do I know which experience is right for me?

Some people try them all. The old familiar saying, "When the pupil is ready, the teacher will come," applies. Events in your life will point you in one direction over another. Sometimes geogra-phy determines your choice: You can imagine being alone in Death Valley in the spring more comfortably than you might imagine being in close quarters with others on a boat in the summer. One person said he didn't care what he did as long as he was near the ocean. Another said she automatically chose the American Southwest, because "that's where the spirituality is in this country."

What are the advantages of group travel? Who goes on a spiritual adventure?

You generally meet others who are on the same wavelength. Most groups are kept small (except for a legendary trip to Peru with a famous speaker, which so the story goes, took four hundred people, most of whom barely knew that the famous speaker actually spoke). The groups comprise people of all ages, generally mid-thirties and older. Teenagers can join special programs—vision quests, for example. One company described its participants as, "Everybody. They're just interesting."

A surprising number of people create their own groups, go off together to visit shamans or shrines, and find that the experience deepens their friendship. Others go alone intentionally. One vision quester said that of the four others on the trip, one he never knew, one he stays in touch with, and two he will never see again.

Is there any kind of quality control?

The best quality indicator is how long the company has been doing what it does. Ask to talk to past participants, and read all the literature. If the directors seem more adept at visiting the Pleiades, you may want to shop around. Companies' directors share an infectious enthusiasm, but make sure they are comfortable with the nuts-and-bolts aspects of group travel, from making good hotel reservations to having a list of restaurants. A clean bed and good food should be a top priority; ask the nitty-gritty questions. One key indicator of how responsive they will be to your needs is how fast they return your initial phone call or E-mail. You should feel that you are important to them.

How long is the ideal spiritual adventure?

Apparently, according to providers, it's not so much *where* you go, but *how much time* you spend and *real experience* you have. A weekend workshop can leave you feeling high, but unless you work hard at continuing it, it will remain as predigested as a pop tart. Ready-to-wear concepts—becoming an overnight shaman or finding your true inner purpose—are too easy to put in the basket. Nurturing your spirit takes work, discipline, constant focus, daily attention. And you may not always be cheery in the process.

Some providers believe you need *at least* a week for anything substantive to sink in, whether it's a meditation retreat or a dolphin swim. Your own private spiritual journey will last the rest of your life.

Are there any advantages to traveling to an underdeveloped country?

Absolutely. Nothing will open your mind or heart faster than experiencing the world as most of the world's populations do. Learn something about the culture you plan to visit before you go—not just the ancient or spiritual aspects that you find interesting, but also how the local people live today. Eat where the locals eat; learn a few words of the language; understand what life is like for them in the twenty-first century. Your spirit will do the rest.

Just bear in mind: not all of *them* will be spiritual. In fact, some of them might be crooks if they sense you are vulnerable. Tour director Alan Leon of Sacred Heritage Travel says of the

Camel rider, Petra, Jordan. (*Roger Archibald*)

"false gurus" operating in the Andes: "Just because someone has psychic abilities and the power to call spirits does not mean we should blindly follow him. Psychic powers do not necessarily mean one is spiritually evolved."

Is it necessary to travel at all?

No. But travel is a powerful psychological organizer: you have to explain who you are, where you're coming from, and where you're going. Plus, you have to show up on time. New challenges in another place often induce sea changes, or provide the push you need to get rolling again.

Where you continue your path is up to you. It's like moving

to another house in another community, except that you're making a place inside yourself for that community to come to you.

Are spiritual adventures for couples?

This is an individual decision that depends on the strength and direction of your relationship. If you feel your spirit is taking you barreling down I-95, and your beloved wants to amble along the back roads, consider embarking on separate experiences. Many companies offer all-women pilgrimages; some do trips exclusively with men. When you find a spiritual experience that strengthens you, you can bring new strength to your relationship.

What's the most important thing about a tour?

Probably the tour guide. Depend on the guide not only to know the territory and when to put you in touch with local guides, but also to sense your spiritual mood and needs. Many guides will give you private time to be alone at a sacred site, to keep a journal, or just let the experience resonate. "He who leads others with simplicity is the source of blessing," said Lao Tzu.

Can I do any of these alone?

Some, yes. You can visit sacred sites alone, walk ley lines, or do a meditation retreat. But you really need a group for a vision quest, because it provides an important follow-up after a solo experience. You are much safer with a group in shaman country or swimming with wild dolphins.

Otherwise, it depends on you. Some people start with a group tour because it's a safe way to take a first step; and, if they

Sometimes you have to go it alone. (*Roger Archibald*)

are lucky, to find a compatible support group. It's harder and not always advisable to go alone because without a follow-up, you can have the experience but miss the point. One day you may find you are ready for a solitary experience. Or, you may go through the dark night of the soul and find you must be alone.

Spiritual growth usually means a change. How can I handle this?

Providers emphasize that you can expect change if you spend at least seven days doing something focused on the spirit. Change is a given. How long it lasts and what you do with it, is up to you. That's why it's important to aim high. A guide or teacher helps. Pray or meditate daily, which is what Wuthnow calls "the practice of spirituality." Popular writer Caroline Myss advises finding your spiritual purpose by defining your personal archetype—whether it's a goddess or a warrior—and riding the mythical path to self-understanding.

Read books on higher consciousness. "Always keep your eyes and ears open, waiting to hear from the Divine," advises New York Seminary theology professor Elizabeth Koenig.

People in the know believe the whole human race is about to chunk up a notch; they are using phrases like "interconnect-edness of every living thing," and "self-transformation." Go for compassion, go for altruism, go for global understanding; but make it a part of your daily life, not just a sometime thing.

How will I know if I am having a spiritual experience?

The daily discipline of meditation or prayer is fundamental. Over a period of a few weeks, most people report changes. For some, it comes out of the blue, like the final descent on a roller coaster: you feel safe, but the forces around you are overpower-ing. Voices come out of nowhere, bringing messages of comfort, or just calling your name. You may experience feelings of being in the company of invisible advisers who suggest wise actions.

The presence of spirit guides—all these things—are there for you, if you let them in. People who know say it rarely happens in a linear way: spiritual experiences are chaotic, sometimes very funny, unpredictable, unreliable, and changeable.

Gay Norton Edelman, a former editor at *McCall's*, described her spiritual path in *Spirituality and Health*, as "an up-and-down kind of thing." With her spiritual director, a nun at Trinity Church in New York City, she would glide from feeling she was "the one person God's going to forget" to having "big spiritual highs." Ultimately she came to realize that relaxing in her "true nature was exactly the same as coming closer to God."

Every adviser has the same mantra: Each day discipline your-self to pray or meditate.

Netmaker, Venezuela. Fisherman mends the net he depends on for his livelihood. (*Roger Archibald*)

A friend of mine has been having nightmares and says peculiar things are happening to her. She thinks it's spiritual, and that she might be being called to be a shaman, or something like that. Where can she go for help? Her therapist says she's having psychotic episodes.

Read Lucy Tart's commentary on this at www.opus-net.org. Tell your friend her experience is not that unusual these days; more and more psychotherapists report cases of people who have unusual and incomprehensible experiences. For some it is tiny

Roman temple ruins, The Citadel, Amman, Jordan. (*Roger Archibald*)

and baffling miracles: problems are resolved without intervention; things disappear and reappear in unlikely places. Others, who consider themselves "rational," experience lost time or, out of the corner of their eye, encounter people who resemble insects.

Precognition—what Russell Targ defines as, "How the future you experience can affect your life at an earlier time"—seems to be happening more often and more widely.

If your friend's problem is serious, Tart advises avoiding the standard psychotherapy route, and, instead, becoming a real explorer. Also try www.ehe.org, the site for Exceptional Human Experience, and www.ciis.edu/comserv/sen.html, the Spiritual Emergence Network.

What is synchronicity and where can I get some?

Synchronicity is when beautiful things come together at the same time. Psychologist Carl Jung used the term to explain the condition that occurs when change is ready to bloom: everything points in one direction, and miracles seem to happen. James Redfield, author of *The Celestine Prophecy,* says it takes courage to rely on your intuition, or your higher self; but if you do, you can often encourage synchronicity. He advises, "Make a fool of yourself gracefully. Be bold. Create miracles."

The point is "to electrify the spiritual impulse that animates all of life," says Wuthnow. When you fall in love, the erotic pulls open doors to new worlds, and draws you to new galaxies; your love is everywhere at once. Spiritual attraction rides the same path. In your heightened state, you begin to see God in others. And there's no turning back.

Trust yourself. "In the greater picture," says Alan Leon, "the universe is much more benevolent than many of us think."

Chapter 3
Group Tours to Sacred Sites

When you begin your journey to Ithaka,
Then pray that the road is long,
full of adventure, full of knowledge.
—C.P. Cavafy, *Ithaka*

For want of a better term, travel that answers the needs of spiritual seekers could be called "the new paradigm of travel." It's not that spiritual pilgrimages are new: ancient Greeks walked to Eleusis, a few miles north of Athens, every September to pay homage to the goddess Demeter. In medieval England, cooks, nuns, merchants, and at least one knight (as recorded by Chaucer) rode horses to Canterbury Cathedral for the adventure and time off, as well as for religious reasons.

The difference, now, is that the demand for spiritual travel has spawned a growth industry: small-group specialty travel to diverse ancient sacred sites, like the Egyptian pyramids, or to places that mark milestones in the life of a religious figure, such as Buddha. As in previous eras, travel is still a quest of the spirit; but now, the traveler seeks a spiritual dimension that will encompass and satisfy a new restlessness. It's exploratory and adventurous.

Why travel at all?

Some would argue that you do not need to leave home to go on a pilgrimage. The act of deciding to investigate something will

Pilgrims made difficult annual voyages to cathedrals spread over Europe and England, such as Mont Saint Michel, in Normandy, France—still a destination for pilgrims. (*Stephanie Ocko*)

take you there spiritually. Perhaps the biggest personal benefits derived through travel actually come from being with descendants of the people whose sites you are visiting. Talking with them, eating the same food, riding their camels or horses, singing their songs, and protecting yourself from the same sun or sudden rain can ignite in you a deep understanding of how other people live—then and now.

Sarah York, a Unitarian-Universalist minister, who went on pilgrimages to Thailand and Scotland, said, "I recommend leaving. As long as you are in your home, something in your space will lure you into ordinary time."

York emphasizes the importance of performing the ceremony of separation. Writing in *New Age* magazine, she advises announcing to your friends and family that you are leaving. But be aware of the risk of change: your home, your relationships, and especially *you* may not be the same when you return. Gayle Lawrence, owner of Journeys of Discovery, says, "Taking this type of risk can be an emotionally scary time as we transform from who we have been into who we are destined to become."

The Benefits of a Spiritual Group

Aside from learning about a particular place or belief system, spiritual group travel also allows you to be with like-minded people. While expert local guides fill in the historical facts and sociological texture of the place, your own tour guides weave meditation, prayer, and ritual throughout the fabric of each day. Some trips include a motivational speaker or author who will help further deepen your understanding.

Sacred Sites

There are thousands, maybe hundreds of thousands, of known sacred sites, and hundreds more that we don't know. Scattered around the world, sacred islands, waterfalls, battlefields, groves in which saintly apparitions materialize signify areas where our ancestors might have made *their* spiritual changes. Caves preserve the sacred power and beauty of the animals painted by prehistoric hunters. The terrible gulf left by the fallen twin towers at the World Trade Center immortalizes a space sacred to those whose lives were changed on September 11, 2001.

Some believe that sacred sites physically exert a special magnetic force. The Mexican Mayan elder and time-keeper Hunbatz Men says that sacred sites emit altered radio waves—higher frequencies and lower electromagnetism—that create a disorientation in the human psyche. This, says Men, will help us "to enter dimensions that are timeless and nonlinear to prepare our body and spirit for the shift of the ages."

Whether it is very personal or very public, sacred space—where we link dreams with reality, the divine with the human, the past with the future—is endemic to being human. Ideally, you will be able to experience the spirit that is imbued in the structures, places, or paths that you visit, some of which exert an unnatural power.

Ancient Sites

Archaeologists often ask what happens to the gods and goddesses when the people who worshiped them move away. Do they stay in the temples built for their worship? Does their presence linger in the fields or lie sleeping in the hills, waiting for someone to call their names?

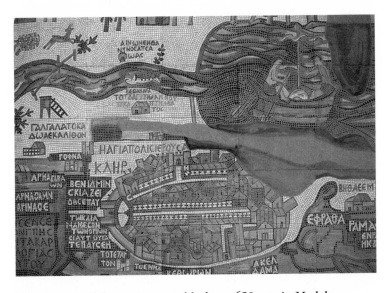

Mosaic map of the ancient world, about 650 C.E., in Madeba, Jordan, includes the entire area from the Lebanon coast to the desert, south of the Nile delta. (Reconstruction, south of Amman.) (*Roger Archibald*)

EGYPT: THE GREAT PYRAMID

One of the biggest mysteries in the Western world is Cheops'
pyramid—the most massive of the three on the Egyptian Gizeh
Plateau, a few miles south of Cairo. Seven city blocks square,
built of huge limestone blocks and about 360 feet high at its
apex, the pyramid is thought to have been built about 4500
B.C.E., and maybe earlier. Within the four sides are central chambers, the largest of which is called the King's Chamber, reached
by a narrow shaft about three feet high, three feet wide, and
about 129 feet long. Here sits an empty sarcophagus, carved out
of stone, which scholars believe never held the king's coffin,

Tour director Ruth Whiting stands in front of Khefren's Pyramid,
surrounded by her aura. (*Courtesy of Ruth Whiting, One World
Tours,* www.1worldtours.com)

but which might have been the site of initiation ceremonies rumored for many centuries.

In addition to early writings about secret ceremonies, the uniqueness of the architecture has prompted interested travelers, mystics, scientists, and pseudo scientists to do geometrical and mathematical analyses formed on the theory that the pyramid design was based on a sacred circle inscribed on the plateau, since most of its measurements relate to a value for pi. According to some, the purity of its numbers and its alignment with certain stars link it directly to beings from higher civilizations whose spaceship landed on the truncated top of the Great Pyramid. Others, who believe the Egyptians were scientists in their own right, wonder what happened to the ancient builders' extraordinary astronomical and mathematical knowledge: Was it lost? Was it passed on through the Knights Templar and Freemasons?

Sparks?

A powerful belief for at least a hundred years is that the pyramid sits on a kind of vortex which renders it an electrical conduit. Several years ago, as reported by Peter Tompkins, an Egyptian guide who led climbers up the outside of the pyramid, pointed out that raising an open hand above his head while standing on the top of the pyramid produced a ringing sound. A British inventor took it one step further; he wrapped a wet newspaper around a wine bottle (so the story goes), held it above his head as he stood on the top, and produced a conductor that actually sent out sparks from the bottle.

All of this has contributed to Egypt's popularity among New Age travelers, to the great pleasure of the Egyptian Ministry of Tourism, but to the dismay of the Council of Antiquities. Climbing the outside of the Great Pyramid—a sport in the 1900s—was forbidden in the early 1970s. Since then, the huge number of tourists eager to revive and perform their own ceremonies inside the pyramid caused the Egyptian government in

1999 to limit the number of daily visitors. Now only 120 people are allowed to stoop and squeeze into the passage each morning and each afternoon for the walk up to the King's Chamber. Some spiritual tours get special permission—for a fee—to enter the chamber for small group meditation and rituals before or after the official hours.

Ancient Egypt is more than gods, goddesses, lost knowledge, hidden powers of the dead, and temples. Some of the artifacts of the lively civilization that thrived for centuries on the banks of the Nile are displayed in the Cairo Museum: intricate gold and faience jewelry worn by both men and women; whimsical friezes of cats chasing waterfowl and playing among the reeds; toys; musical instruments; and magnificent boats, all traces of a lyrical and lovely spirit. Your local guide will open this world, while your tour guide will enable you to make space for your spirit.

You need both a passport and a visa to visit Egypt, which you can get in advance or at Cairo airport when you arrive, for $15 cash. The special fee to enter the King's Chamber before or after visiting hours depends on the number in your group; usually it is between $50 and $100. The following tour companies will inform you of the extra price.

All One World's Spiritual Egypt Tours with Ruth Shilling
860-742-5685 (tel). E-mail: info@1worldtours.com; Web sites: www.BelovedEgypt.com and www.1worldtours.com

Ruth Shilling, an instructor at the University of Connecticut, runs tours exclusively to Egypt and is accompanied in Egypt by Mohamed Hafez Hassan, a local Egyptologist. Together, they make sure you have an opportunity to meditate seven times at sacred sites, as well as visit the most important sites twice. You also have time on your own to develop your personal rhythm to connect with the sites. Ten- to sixteen-day tours (one with a Nile cruise) cost between $3,000 and $4,000 and include luxury hotel in Cairo and airfare from New York.

Luminati, Inc. P.O. Box 2162, Carefree, AZ 85377. 888-488-1151 (Toll Free). E-mail: luminatiaz@aol.com; Web site: www.luminati.net

Every year Luminati runs several women-only spiritual pilgrimages to Egypt, which are hosted by seventh-level channel Sheila Reed. One is accompanied by Sherry Anshara, a medical intuitive and healer; another by LeiLani Schmidt, a spiritual counselor. All trips visit major sites as well as out-of-the-way places, include ceremonies, first-class accommodations, and a luxury cruise on the Nile. Luminati also will design a custom trip for your company. Twelve days: $3,995, includes airfare from New York City. Luminati offers a special travel savings plan: if you pay $500 down (which most tour companies require), and agree to pay in full (in seven monthly installments) before you go, they will give you a $450 discount on the trip.

Purple Mountain Tours 34 Purple Mountain Road, Putney, VT 05346. 802-387-4753 (tel/fax). E-mail: hshik@sover.net; Web site: www.purplemountaintours.com

Pilgrimage to the Gods and Goddesses of Egypt is a mystical tour with a seven-day Nile cruise. Helene Shik, your guide, has arranged private time for rituals, meditation, and ceremonies in the Temples of Isis, Sekhmet, Hathor, and Horus, culminating with private meditation during the spring equinox in the Great Pyramid. About $5,000, including airfare from New York City.

Mystical Destinations Andrea Mikana-Pinkham, Director, 800-231-9811 (Toll free); 928-770-7060 (tel). E-mail: info@mysticaldestinations.com; Web site: www.mysticaldestinations.com

Guided by a "metaphysical" Egyptologist, Mystical Destinations offers a Nile cruise to Luxor with stops along the way at temples, many of which were healing sites. Twelve days, about $2,800 including airfare from New York City. Private time in the King's Chamber in late afternoon is optional; an extra fee is charged.

Mind Body Travel P.O. Box 1535, Nevada City, CA 95959. 888-888-0717 (toll free). Web site: www.mindbodytravel.com

Mind Body offers several tours to Egypt. The Sacred Chakra tour is accompanied by author Kevin Ryerson and Dr. Gabriel Cousens, both of whom guide you through temples corresponding to chakras as you cruise down the Nile to the Great Pyramid, the Crown Chakra. This tour mixes the exotic with the esoteric. Also included during the cruise are spiritual discussions on the Kaballah, Kali-Ray Tri Yoga, ancient Hebrew Yoga, and Ruah Ha Kodesh meditation. Ten days, about $2,900, including airfare from New York City.

Spirit Journeys P.O. Box 3046, Asheville, NC 28802. 800-490-3684 (toll free). E-mail: info@spiritjourneys.com; Web site: www. spiritjourneys.com

Egyptian Mysteries is a five-star, seven-day cruise from Giza to Upper Egypt for visits to temples, then back to Giza on the spring equinox for an exclusive private ceremony inside the King's Chamber of the Great Pyramid. Your guides are Steve Thomson, a teacher and psychic, Eugene Donaldson, and a local Egyptologist. About $4,300, including airfare from New York City.

Power Place Tours & Conferences, Inc. 116 King Street, Frederiksted, Virgin Islands 00840. 800-234-8687 (toll free); 340-772-2030 (tel); 340-772-1392 (fax).

In business for twenty-six years, Power Place Tours invites authors and spiritual leaders Neale Donald Walsch, Robert Bauval, Matthew Fox, Rabbi Michael Lerner, and Gregg Braden (among others) as speakers on a variety of tours that visit the Great Pyramid and Sphinx. Each speaker agrees to give one workshop or lecture per tour; further interaction can be worked out between individuals or the group and the speaker. Psychics and intuitives usually accompany the tours for private consultation. Price: about $3,000 for seven days. Additional optional week visiting other sites available for about the same price.

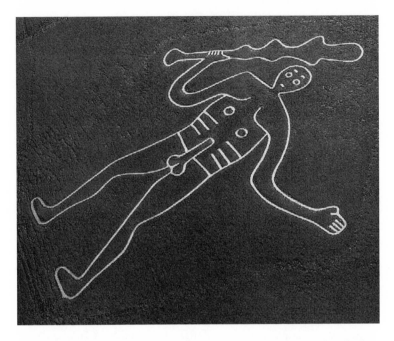

The Warrior God or Giant, Cerne, England. Carved into the chalk approximately 2,000 years ago, the Giant, which measures about 180 feet long by 167 feet across, has long been the site of maypole dances and fertility rituals. (*tourist photo*)

Visions Travel & Tours, Inc. 5250 West Century Boulevard, Suite 301, Los Angeles, CA 90045. 800-888-5509 (toll free); 310-568-0138 (tel); 310-568-0246 (fax). E-mail: visionstravel@aol.com; Web site: www.visionstravel.com

Best known, they claim, for "integrity, creativity, and value," Visions Travel provides metaphysical and spiritual tours to Egypt with informed guides who share with you what they have found. Some tour guides are well-known psychics; others focus on healing. Several tours a year. A fifteen-day mystical tour to Egypt, with a seven-day cruise, about $4,000; includes airfare from New York City.

ENGLAND

King Arthur and the Holy Grail

Like Homer's *Iliad* and *Odyssey*, the *Legends of King Arthur*, the story of a sixth century Celtic king who drove the invading Saxons out of Great Britain, were recited for centuries around winter fires and under the stars of summer skies. The myths and legends reveal quests and trials with savage dragons and sea monsters; a blind singer; seven cities that must be won; nine beautiful maidens, seven handsome brothers, and twelve loyal knights; magic swords in lakes and stones; tales of love won and betrayed; a round table; a city called Camelot; the Isle of Avalon; a magician named Merlin; a beautiful blonde queen named Gwynevere; and Arthur, the once and future King.

Woven throughout this tale is the arrival in Great Britain of the Holy Grail—according to one legend, the cup in which Joseph of Arimathea captured a few drops of blood from the crucified Christ. At a site not far from Camelot in Glastonbury, Joseph built the kingdom's first Christian church in order to house the Grail. In the sixth century, Benedictine monks established an abbey there, which became the largest in Great Britain by the Middle Ages and a major destination for pilgrims.

During this period the Grail disappeared; and legends changed the Grail from a cup into a cauldron, a stone, or a shining apparition, which Arthur and his Knights of the Round Table went on quests to find. Did they? According to one legend, they did, and buried it (as a chalice) under an unusual conical hill named Glastonbury Tor or in the well, now called the Chalice Well, at the base of the tor.

Southwestern England is full of sites sacred to the Arthurian legends—from stones out of which he might have pulled the sword Excalibur, to lakes where the mysterious lady might have offered him the sword. But the center of the legends is in Glastonbury, a small town that has been called the center of the New Age in Europe.

Glastonbury Abbey still exists, although in ruins (dating from the rout by troops of Henry VIII, who closed it in 1537). The thorn tree that Joseph of Arimathea is said to have planted in the first century still thrives. Gone are King Arthur's bones, and those of his fair-haired wife, found by the monks in a deep grave after a fire in 1184; all that remains is a plaque.

The Isle of Avalon, now called Glastonbury Tor, was also thought to have been Arthur's resting place, according to legend. Archaeological digs have produced some fifth century Mediterranean artifacts, but no bones.

Nevertheless, Glastonbury Tor is a magical place rising out of the wetlands. During World War II, when Nazi bombers flew over Glastonbury, the tor became fogged in, isolating its pinnacle with the ruined tower of Saint Michael, and disoriented the pilots, making them think they were flying over the sea. Archae-

Glastonbury Tor in Glastonbury, England, the possible site of King Arthur's Avalon. The outline of the labyrinthine walk culminating in the lone tower of the ruined church of Saint Michael is visible in the snow. (*Courtesy of Merlin Tours,* www.merlintours.co.uk)

ologists believe that Glastonbury Tor was an island when Arthur and his men held court not far away, and therefore deserves to be called the Isle of Avalon.

Tintagel, on the coast in Cornwall, a sea-torn craggy collection of rocks and ragged beaches, is the site of the wall of a ruined, ancient church. Legends place Arthur's birth at Tintagel, where, it is said, the sea washed him up and the magician Merlin rescued him and kept him in a sea cave.

Whether your quest is for the Holy Grail or the presence of King Arthur or earlier Celtic deities, the search itself will lead you to places that exert change. A story is told of two knights who meditated in the Chapel of the Grail, and came out feeling different. Their friends noticed the change and asked them what caused it. "Go where we went," was the reply, "and you will see."

Gothic Image Tours 7 High Street, Glastonbury, Somerset BA6 9DP, England. +44(0)1458-831281 (tel); +44(0)1458-833385 (fax). E-mail: tours@gothicimage.co.uk; Web site: www.gothic imagetours.co.uk/questtour.htm

Avalon to Camelot, a Journey Through the Mists of Time, is a ten-day tour that covers the main Arthur sites, the Abbey and Glastonbury Tor, the remains of Camelot and Tintagel, plus visits to Neolithic stone circles and Celtic sanctuaries such as Saint Nectan's Fairy Glen, where you can swim in the healing waters. Guides and authors include Hamish Miller and Paul Broadhurst (*The Sun and the Serpent*), Arthurian authority Geoffrey Ashe, Druid priestess Emma "Bobcat" Restall-Orr, and John Michell, "mystic antiquarian." About £1,500.

Mind Body Travel P.O. Box 1535, Nevada City, CA 95959; 888-888-0717 (toll free). E-mail: info@mindbodytravel.com; Web site: www.mindbodytravel.com

Shawna Carol's Goddess Chant is an eleven-day music trip to Glastonbury. Perform the goddess chant at the sacred well beneath the tor, and celebrate the Celtic springtime Beltane ritual fire on top of the tor. Trip includes Goddess Chant concerts and

Merlin, with guests, lifts the cover of the sacred Chalice Well in Glastonbury, where one legend claims the Holy Grail is hidden. (*Courtesy of Merlin Tours,* www.merlintours.co.uk)

opportunities for individual counseling and healing. Cost: about $2,800, including airfare from New York City.

Merlin Tours Cross Keys Motors, Lydford on Fosse, Somerset, TA11 7EZ, England. +44(0)1963-240613 (tel). E-mail: merlin@ merlintours.co.uk; Web site: www.merlintours.co.uk

The Archdruid of Glastonbury and Stonehenge, under a special agreement with Merlin Tours, acts as your guide on the Merlin Trail, a ten-day tour of major sites, mostly in western England, associated with the famous Arthurian magician, Merlin. Rollo Maughfling shares his knowledge of ancient druidic spirituality both formally and informally as you travel by minibus with a maximum of ten passengers. Stay at bed-and-breakfasts. Ten days, £990.

Purple Mountain Tours 34 Purple Mountain Road, Putney, VT 05346. 802-387-4753 (tel/fax). E-mail: hshik@sover.net; Web site: www.sover.net/~hshik

Initiation into the Earth Mysteries of England and Scotland travels from London to the island of Iona off the Scottish coast, and includes ceremonies and rituals at most of the sites. You will walk up Glastonbury Tor, for example, before the sun is up to connect "with the Goddess energy"; search for the true meaning of the Holy Grail in a purification rite at the Chalice Well; meditate for two hours in the inner circle at Stonehenge; experience fairy power in the Neolithic stone formations on the way to Scotland; and finally, spend time with the Divine Feminine in the Celtic sanctuary on Iona, once the home of priestesses. Thirteen days, about $3,600, first-class accommodation, plus airfare.

Stonehenge

The small circle of stones that appears in the Salisbury Plain as you pull over the hill in Wiltshire, in the south of England, looks as if it were built by fairies. Maybe it was. Now in a state of dis-

Stonehenge during a solar eclipse. (*NASA*)

array, the huge megalithic ring includes a partial circle of stones within which is a horseshoe of five gigantic trilithons geometrically aligned with the midsummer sunrise and midwinter sunset.

Who built it? Nobody knows for sure. How? Lots of discussion on this. When? Probably in three phases, beginning in 3050 B.C.E. and ending about 1600 B.C.E. Was it a religious center? Druids think so. And it seems to be part of a network of 450 other megalithic monuments. How can you relate to it? If Stonehenge is important to you, take a tour that allows you to enter at least the stone circle inside the perimeter when it is closed to other visitors.

Modern Realities

The sad fact is that Stonehenge, standing for at least four millennia, has wearied recently from too many visitors eager to leave offerings or carve their names, or to take away tiny chips of stone as mementos. Increased road traffic pollutes the air and threatens the underpinnings of the megaton stones. The British Heritage Society closed the circle to foot traffic about five years ago, and erected a rope fence to keep tourists a safe distance away. Stonehenge is now part of a World Heritage Site Management Plan, designed to reduce or eliminate vehicular traffic, as well as to build a world-class visitors' center. For more information, visit the Web site www.english-heritage.org.uk.

In addition to the tours mentioned above, the following companies give special access tours inside the perimeter. The special access fee is £15.

Astral Travels UK Tours   72 New Bond Street, London, W1Y 9DD, England. +44(0)700-0781-016 (tel); +44 (0)705-0073-492 (fax). E-mail: email@astraltravels.co.uk; Web site: www.astral travels. co.uk

Astral Travels, in conjunction with English Heritage Travel, runs minibus tours (maximum fifteen passengers) from London to Stonehenge via Avebury, the Neolithic burial tombs, and Celtic burial mounds. At Stonehenge, you can spend an hour in the inner circle after visitor hours. Guides tell the Stonehenge story then let you wander alone and actually touch the stones. Leaves daily around 1:00 P.M. and returns about 8:30 P.M.; £55.

The Stonehenge Tour Company   10 Midas Estate, Cowley Mill Road, London UB8 2YT, England. +44 (0)870-9020-908 (tel); +44 (0)705-007-3492 (fax). E-mail: email@stonehengetours.com; Web site: www.stonehengetours.com

Runs daily minibus tours from London to Stonehenge and neighborhood, with inner circle access. Special Access tours: £55. Longer tours available.

Journeys of Discovery   E-mail: info@ajourneyofdiscovery. com; Web site: www.ajourneyofdiscovery.com

Gayle Lawrence offers an all-women tour to King Arthur's England and mystical Scotland that includes a ceremony at Stonehenge with Druid priestess Emma "Bobcat" Restall-Orr at sunrise. Tour incorporates evening meditation, lots of free time

The function of these super-straight rows created by this ancient alignment in Cornwall, one of many in the British Isles and Brittany, remains a mystery. (*Courtesy of Merlin Tours,* www.merlintours.co.uk)

to wander around Iona, and a visit to Findhorn. Two weeks: about $3,800, includes airfare from New York.

IRELAND

There are so many standing stones and mysterious megaliths in Ireland that farmers work around them, engineers build roads through them, and housing projects and cemeteries include them in layouts. Local folk give them names as if they were members of the community.

To understand the stones, this is a thumbnail guide to the nomenlature:

- Alignment: A long row of standing stones. Some rows are straight and very long.
- Cairn: A round pile of small stones that marks a burial.
- Cromlech: A stone enclosure, round or oval.
- Dolmen: A small tomb with a large heavy capstone. Large dolmens have standing slabs on the sides; some are called giants' graves.
- Henge: Stone circle, usually with a ditch; many are oriented to the solstices.
- Kerb: A stone around the outside edge of a mound.
- Menhir: A standing stone, often with Ogham script (early Celtic writing dating to the third and fourth centuries); sometimes called healing stones.
- Passage-tomb: A circular tomb reached by a long stone passageway.
- Sheela-na-Gigs: Carved figures of old women, often with exposed genitals, designed to keep away bad spirits.
- Sidh Mounds: Where fairies live, the entrance to the Underworld. Generally, any tomb. Dangerous places.
- Trilithon: Two standing stones with a horizontal stone across the top.
- Beehive Huts: Exactly what the name indicates, except they are made of stone and housed monks.
- High Crosses: Tall crosses covered with the intricate endless knots of Celtic design, some as early as 800 C.E., carved by monks.
- Round Towers: One-hundred-foot tall stone towers of the type from which Rapunzel might have let down her golden hair.

Most spiritual tours to Ireland focus on the spiritual powers of pre-Celtic and Celtic stones and the historic stone remnants of hermetic monks, one of whom, Saint Brendan, is reputed to have crossed the Atlantic Ocean in a leather boat in the sixth century and landed in the vicinity of Nova Scotia. Newgrange, dated between 3000 and 5000 B.C.E., near Drogheda in County

A dolmen. Whoever placed the multiton capstone intended it to last. (*Courtesy of Merlin Tours,* www.merlintours.co.uk)

Meath, is the largest and most beautifully decorated tomb oriented to the midwinter sunrise. Most of these sites were probably places where ancient rituals were practiced, and impart "a deeply spiritual environment and experience," says Antony Lorraine, tour manager of Ancient Ireland Tours. Fairy tales and Celtic myths are in the air in Ireland; your guides weave the stories, and your dreams will fill in the rest. Ireland is breathtakingly beautiful.

Gothic Image Tours   P.O. Box 2568 Glastonbury, Somerset, BA6 8XR, England. +44(0)1458-831281 (tel); +44 (0) 1458-833385 (fax). E-mail: tours@gothicimage.co.uk; Web site: www. gothic imagetours.co.uk

This tour crosses the Irish Sea at Galway to the isolated sheer cliffs of the Aran Islands and Inishmore, inhabited in 1000 B.C.E. It visits Newgrange; the Hill of Tara (the womb of the mother of Ireland); the island sanctuary of Skellig Michael with beehive huts; and makes a special stop at Clonegal Castle, the home of Olivia Robertson, the High Priestess of the Fellowship of Isis. She leads a guided meditation on the Goddess. Twelve days, about £1,900. Leaves from London.

Sacred Journeys for Women   P.O. Box 8007, Roseland Station, CA 95407. 888-779-6696 (toll free). E-mail: alaura@sacred journeys.com; Web site: www.sacredjourneys.com

Ireland of Myth and Mystery, a Path to the Goddess follows the trail starting at the ancient stone remnants at Lough Gur, called the Fort of the Fairies, in the village of Adare, to the island of Skellig Michael, then to the Ring of Kerry and the Dingle Peninsula, with its wealth of sacred prehistoric and historic sites. Tours have a private entrance at Newgrange on the summer solstice, then go to Dublin and a presentation by scholar Mary Condren, author of *The Serpent and the Goddess.* Twelve days, about $2,700; airfare not included.

Celtic Wheel Tours   Michael Walsh, "Solashee," Ballysumaghan, Ballintogher, County Sligo, Ireland. +353 (0)71-65029 (tel). E-mail: goddess@netaccess.ie; or cromcrua@yahoo.com

Michael Walsh was so caught up in the spiritual values of Native Americans that—in his twenties, he said—he actually lived in a tepee in County Clare. No stranger to the rich myth, archetypal meaning, and spiritual significance of hidden places and the stones, caves, and cairns throughout Ireland, he offers a five-day tour "around the eight Celtic solar festival times," (the turning of the Celtic wheel). His ideal group size is three, which is invited to stay at his B and B cottage in County Sligo, with at least one night of traditional music and storytelling by his open fireside. Five days: 762 Euros, includes bed, breakfast, transport, and workshops.

Merlin Tours Cross Keys Motors, Lydford on Fosse, Somerset TA11 7EZ, England. +44 (0)1963-240613 (tel). E-mail: merlin@ merlintours.co.uk; Web site: www.merlintours.co.uk
Enchanted Ireland: Visit the Children of Tuatha De Danann is hosted by the Archdruid of Avondale and Wicklow. You will have special access to Newgrange; visit with Anne Marie, the lightkeeper at Tara; go to Kilkenny and Clonegal Castles, and the famous stone at Blarney. Learn about the Tuatha De Danann, the people of the goddess Danu and a race of divine warriors, now purportedly living in the Underworld. Nine days, £1,299; B and B, minibus, ten passengers maximum.

Earth Mysteries & Sacred Site Tours & Well Within P.O. Box 1563, Nevada City, CA 95959. 530-740-0561 (tel). Or: P.O. Box 31, Brecon, Powys LD38 WA, Wales, UK. +44 (0)1874-624-

Ireland is full of magnificent horses like these. (*Roger Archibald*)

936 (from U.S.); 01874-624-936 (from U.K.). E-mail: wwithin@
nccn. net; Web site: www.nccn.net

The Mythology, Ancient Sites, & Mysteries of Ireland tour visits 5,000 year-old "cathedrals of Neolithic times," Dingle Peninsula, and Funghi the resident bay dolphin, as well as mountainous
County Kerry. Take a horse-drawn jaunting cart trip through the
Gap of Dunloe to the lakes of Killarney for a boat ride. Visit the
lunar landscape of Burren and Brigit's magic well. Trip includes
visits with local healers and workshops in homeopathy, Celtic
and pre-Celtic practices, and historic Ireland. Eleven nights
about $1,800 (airfare not included), includes one medieval cas-
tle banquet. Tours run March to October.

Ancient Ireland Tours   +353 (0)86-8348055 (tel). E-mail:
ancientirelandtours@eircom.net; Web Site: http://homepage.eir
com.net/~ancientrelandtours/

Antony Lorraine (M.A., Stanford), a member of archaeological and historical societies of southeastern Ireland, gives tours
with extensive background information that tell you not only
the archaeological, architectural, and historical facts, but also
the subtler spiritual aspects of the sites. Some of his tours are
arranged around the spring and autumn equinoxes and the
summer solstice; March to November. Lorraine lives in Inistioge,
County Kilkenny, seventy-five miles from Dublin. Will arrange
tours with B and B accommodations in country houses and
farms, and teach you dowsing at the Hill of Tara. Daily tours IR
£30.

MindBody Travel P.O. Box 1535 Nevada City, CA 95959. 888-
888-0717 (toll free). Web site: www.mindbodytravel.com

If your sense of Ireland is so strong that you would like to do
a past-life regression there, accompany Mary Lee LaBay on a
tour to celebrate the autumn equinox in a private ceremony at
Newgrange. Then spend twelve days and nights touring ancient stones, Celtic myths and heroes, druids, fairies, and the
Book of Kells. Expect group meditations and energy work.

Twelve days, about $2,600; airfare not included. Optional four-day tour to Stonehenge and Glastonbury, about $1,300.

SCOTLAND

The Quest for the Holy Grail

The quest for the Holy Grail is by no means dead. Volumes of literature fuel modern-day searches with as much passion as the original quest. Is the Grail under Glastonbury Tor? In France? In Italy? Buried somewhere in Canada or New England? Or is it in Rosslyn Castle in Scotland, built by the Knights Templar when they fled France?

Findhorn Sacred Journeys   Fuaim-Na-Mara Fyrish Road, Findhorn, Forres IV36 3YT, Scotland. E-mail: pilgrims@findhorn sacredjourneys.com; Web site: www.findhornsacredjourneys.com
A Mythical Journey to the Gods and Goddesses starts with a visit to Saint Brigid's Holy Well and perpetual fire, near the marriage bed of Irish lovers Diarmid and Grainne and the entrance to the land of eternal youth. Storyteller and dance teacher Peter Vallance recites the myths of the stones at sites in Dingle, Fore, Newgrange at the Spring Equinox, and in Dublin. Ten days, £1,390, includes bed and all meals from Dublin. Airfare not included.
Vallance also gives a ten-day tour of mystical Scotland, The Spirit of Caledonia, visiting the Orkney Islands, the Outer Hebrides, and Iona, "with song, dance, story, and meditation." Breakfast, picnic lunches, and most dinners included, £1,190 (land only).

GREECE

Greece has clarity: glorious sun and blue sky and a sea that changes color from pale green to deep purple. No matter where you are, climbing the hill to the Parthenon in Athens or listening to the distant bells of goats in the craggy hills of Crete, the air is charged with spiritual energy, not only of the pantheon of ancient Greek deities, but also of Bronze Age gods and goddesses, whose names we may not even know. On Crete, early texts refer to a mother goddess simply as Potnia, mother goddess.

The Myth of Ariadne

Crete is also the home of great Bronze Age myths, many of which concern the bull-headed son of King Minos' wife and a bull. Placed in a labyrinth built by the talented architect Daedalus, the Minotaur annually consumed seven youths and seven maidens from Athens, until a brave Athenian son, Theseus, who was aided by the Minoan king's daughter, Ariadne, killed the Minotaur.

The focus of many rituals in Crete is Ariadne, often pictured with wool or thread spinning out of her head or breast, who gave Theseus the cord to lay behind him so he could find his way out of the labyrinth after his mission was complete. Because she was in love with Theseus, she agreed to become his bride and return with him to Athens. But, less than a day away from Crete, ambivalence overtook him. Without remorse, Theseus abandoned her on the tiny island of Naxos (probably off the Cretan coast), where she spent a night trembling on the beach listening to the distant howls of hungry wolves. Dionysos heard her cries, rescued her, fell in love and married her, and carried her off to Sicily. There, they had many children and lived happily ever after, since Dionysos bestowed upon her his divine gifts of agelessness and immortality.

The Ariadne Institute for the Study of Myth and Ritual, Ltd. 1306 Crestview Drive, Blacksburg, VA 24060. 540-951-3070 (tel); Web site: www.goddessariadne.org

Carol Christ, a former college professor and the author of four books on the divine feminine, including *Rebirth of the*

Goddess, leads a Goddess Pilgrimage to Crete, a tour designed for women, "mothers and grandmothers, single, married, lesbian, bisexual, and heterosexual." In Crete, you will pour libations of milk and honey at former Minoan altars, visit museums, climb the mountains, stay in small villages, and meet and dance with local people. Available to the first seventeen women who apply. Fifteen days, about $2,300, (airfare not included); academic credit through the California Institute of Integral Studies for extra fee. The Ariadne Institute offers a limited number of partial scholarships and loans.

Ariadne Institute also runs a Sacred Journey to Greece on the island of Lesvos which includes yoga movement, ancient Greek song and dance, modern Greek dancing, writing, channeling healing energies, and swimming. About $2,300 (airfare not included). Contact: Kathryn Richer Harris, Ariadne Institute, 2325 NE 12th Avenue, Portland, OR 97212. 503-788-3132 (tel). E-mail: kathmark@uswest.net.

Power Place Tours & Conferences, Inc. 116 King Street, Fredericksted, VI 00840; 800-234-8687 (toll free); 340-772-2030 (tel). E-mail: powerplaces@worldnet.att.net; Web site: www. powerplacetours.com

Healer and author Caroline Myss accompanies the tour, A Healing Pilgrimage to Crete, which includes a spa, entrance to Knossos, plus time in Athens and Delphi. Seven days about $3,000 including airfare from New York City.

Purple Mountain Tours 34 Purple Mountain Road, Putney, VT 05346. 802-387-4753 (tel/fax). E-mail: hshik@sover.net; Web site: www.sover.net/~hshik

Birthing Aphrodite—The Goddess of Love, a journey of healing and celebration of life is an eleven-day tour to Crete and Cyprus. After stopping at Eleusis, site of the Mysteries of Demeter, follow the path of Ariadne in Crete; then participate in a ritual of death and rebirth at Petra tou Romion on Cyprus, the birthplace of Aphrodite and where the Greek goddess of beauty and love rose from the golden foam. About $3,200, including airfare from New York City.

Spirit Journeys   P.O. Box 3046, Asheville, NC 28802. 828-258-8880 (tel); 828-281-0334 (fax). E-mail: info@spiritjourneys.com; Web site: www.spiritjourneys.com

Rebirthing in Greece is a special tour to Santorini, located in the center of the Cyclades Islands in the Aegean Sea. Designed especially for gay and bisexual men, this tour offers the opportunity to practice the transformative technique of conscious breathing which, done with teachers for an hour or more each day, cleanses the body of toxins, renews the cells, and creates a cradle in the psyche for rebirth. The teachers, David Frechter and Christian de la Huerta, share twenty-five years of experience as certified rebirthers. Santorini, possibly the kernal of the myth of Atlantis, was once the site of rites of passage for young men. It exerts its own powerful beauty. Eleven days: about $2,000, airfare not included.

Earth Mysteries & Sacred Site Tours & Well Within   P.O. Box 1563, Nevada City, CA 95959. 530-740-0561 (tel); or: P.O. Box 31, Brecon, Powys, LD3 8 WA, Wales, UK. +44 (0)1874-624-936 E-mail: wwithin@nccn. net; Web site: www.nccn. net

This Goddess tour visits and learns about some of the spots in ancient Crete where goddesses were sacred: Phaistos, Agios Nikolaos, Psycho Cave (where Zeus might have been born; and where Rhea, his mother, and a group of women known as the Kuretes kept up a noisy din to cover the baby's cries, so that Kronos, the baby-eating father, would be deceived). Eleven days rich in mythology, about $1,600, airfare not included.

Sacred Journeys for Women   P.O. Box 8007, Roseland Station, CA 95407. 888-779-6696 (toll free). E-mail: alaura@sacredjourneys.com; Web site: www.sacredjourneys.com

A Pilgrimage to the Goddesses and Sacred Island of Crete gives you twelve days to visit sites in the South and North; hold ceremonies at the Cave of Ilythia (or Eileithyia), goddess of childbirth; do yoga at the temple of Artemis and her mother Leto; take the long walk up Mount Ida; visit a nunnery; hike Samaria Gorge, then stay in small stone houses in a village in western Crete. Those electing not to hike can swim or shop. Twelve days, about $2,500, airfare not included.

Rites of Passage Retreats   Barbara Lange, P.O. Box 1312, Burnsville, NC 28714. 828-682-4684 (tel); 559-751-2163 (fax). E-mail: laughinghearts@yahoo.com;Web Site: http://yancey.main. nc.us/ ~blange/retreats/greeceindex.html or www.ritesofpassage retreats. com

The Path of the Oracle in Greece and Its Islands starts in Athens, then visits Delphi and the site of the Oracle, before taking a ship to islands Mykonos, Kusadasi, on the Turkish coast, Patmos, and Rhodes. Fifteen days about $3,000, includes airfare from New York City.

Add a week and go to Crete; spend a relaxed time doing creativity workshops, taking nature hikes, or swimming in the pool of your villa. Seven days about $800, includes airfare from Athens.

RELIGIOUS SITES

From the fourteenth or thirteenth century B.C.E. to the seventh century C.E., the dry, sunbaked hills and burnt-orange sands—interspersed with occasional palm groves that dot the Middle East—were the sacred places of divine visitations. Centuries of wars, political disputes, and land mines have left some sites, such as the caves and plains where early Christian hermits, like Saint Anthony, gave their lives to contemplation, untouched by archaeologists.

Several early monastic communities built tiny churches, whose dusty mosaic floors are all that remain. Members of one Jewish monastic community, the Essenes, hid their records in hard-to-reach caves above the desert in Qumran, on the border between Israel and Jordan. In 1947, goatherds broke almost two millennia of silence when they accidentally found what came to be called the Dead Sea Scrolls, translated as Biblical texts. The Shrine of the Book in the Israel Museum in west Jerusalem contains many of the original scrolls; fewer but equally fascinating are the scrolls in the Citadel Museum in Amman, Jordan, where active archaeological research continues.

Ancient Artifacts

The Middle East vibrates with a deeply spiritual past. Before the historical events that shaped the world's three major religions—Judaism, Christianity, and Islam—farmers, tradespeople, fishermen, and traders lived in small cities and villages, dating to 10,000 B.C.E., in what is today Jordan, Israel, and the Palestinian Occupied Territories. They had their own deities, temples, visions, and illuminations. The moon and the sun, forgotten as deities, still figure in the calendars of these religions: Judaism determines its annual festivals by a solar-lunar calendar; Christian Easter falls on the Sunday following the full moon of the spring equinox; and Islam counts time by a lunar progression of months.

The following are in chronological order:

Judaism: The Sacred Sites of Moses

Somewhere in Egypt around 1300 B.C.E., the baby Moses appeared in a basket in the bullrushes. From a combination of oral history and Bible interpretation, the sacred sites of Moses begin in Egypt, east of the Nile, at the Monastery of Saint Catherine. When Moses was forty, he saw a "burning bush," from which issued a light and the voice of God. This began a life of rapturous visions of God. In 337 C.E., Saint Helena, mother of the Roman emperor Constantine, built a chapel on the site of the burning bush, now a monastery founded in 527 by Greek Orthodox monks. Within its walled enclosure is the Chapel of the Burning Bush, and an evergreen that is said to spring from the same roots as the original bush.

Visions led Moses to the summit of nearby Mount Sinai, a 7,500-foot peak, where he lived in a cave for forty days. Here God gave Moses the Ten Commandments from a fiery cloud, which Moses recorded on stone tablets. Monks in the early centuries carved 3,700 steps out of sandstone, called the Path of Repentance; the climb takes about three hours on foot. At the summit, a chapel contains paintings commemorating Moses. Some travel companies do the trek in moonlight, which eerily illuminates the desert as far as the Red Sea.

God also gave Moses the rabbinical text, the Torah, and the criminal code, called the Mosaic Law, which some believe were stored in the Ark of the Covenant. The Hebrews remained exiled and enslaved in Egypt, until God instructed Moses to lead them to safety from the cruel pharoahs, to the Land of Milk and Honey, north to the Promised Land.

By then eighty years old, Moses nevertheless led 600,000 Israelites across the Red Sea, which parted for them to cross. Then they walked across the desert (in the Sinai and present-day Jordan) to Jerusalem, and established with King David a temple on the Dome of the Rock in the Land of Moab (present-day Israel). (The Western [or Wailing] Wall is all that remains of the Roman rout of the second temple.)

Still seeking the Promised Land, Moses led the Hebrews across the Jordan River to the east and climbed present-day Mount Nebo in Jordan, where God showed him the Promised Land. Here he died, at the age of 120. His tomb has never been found. A Franciscan monastery houses remnants of early monastic settlements on top; and a recent monument remembers Moses at the site, declared holy by Pope John Paul II in 2000.

Petra Moon Tourism Services P.O. Box 129, Wadi Musa-Petra, Jordan. 962-3-215-6665 (tel); 962-3-215-6666 (fax). E-mail: info@ petramoon.com; Web site: www.petramoon.com

This tour begins in Egypt at the Monastery of Saint Catherine. Then it continues north by ferry across the Red Sea and by jeep through the Jordanian desert near Wadi Rhum (where the movie *Lawrence of Arabia* was filmed), to the carved stone city of Petra, home of fourth-century B.C.E. Nabatean traders. The tour visits Aaron's tomb, crosses to the "land of Moab," then culminates in a visit to Mount Nebo, with its spectacular view of Jordan and Israel.

Keshet: The Center for Educational Tourism in Israel
7 Rabbi Binyamin Street, Jerusalem 96306 Israel. +972 (0)2-6510488 (tel); +972 (0)2-6540365 (fax). E-mail: keshet@ keshet-israel.co.il; Web site: www.keshetisrael.co.il

Discovery seminars offer a chance to combine field work—visits with families, public figures, archaeological digs, and tours—with minicourses in all aspects of Jewish and Middle Eastern history. They also offer "instruction in Hebrew language—so that you can order a cab as Moses would have." E-mail for details.

IN BERLIN

Unterwegs 4-53-53-04 (tel). E-mail: Iris@hagalil.com; Web site: www.hagalil.com/enter.htm

A home that you have been forced to leave or gave you a start on a new life is always sacred to you. Berlin was this to many Jews, many of whom fled there to escape pogroms in eastern Europe and later migrated to the United States or to Israel, before or after World War II. Iris Hagalil gives private motorcoach tours for English-speakers who want to find their roots. Hagalil is a highly respected scholar of Berlin Jewish history. Unterwegs gives tours in English and German, which vary in length depending on your interest.

TAL Tours 800-825-9399 (toll free). E-mail: info@taltours.com; Web site: www.visits-to-germany.com

TAL Tours gives tours of Jewish Berlin and several other German cities. Various times and prices.

IN MOROCCO

Imperial Tours, Inc.   7843 Gum Springs Village Drive, Alexandria, VA 22306-2854. 888-259-9062 (toll free); 703-360-9544 (tel); 703-360-9574 (fax). E-mail: info@imperialtours.com; Web site: www.imperialtours.com

One of the oldest Jewish settlements outside of Israel was in Morocco at the Roman city of Volubilis, and in Marrakesh, as early as 70 C.E. This Jewish Heritage tour takes you from Casablanca to Ouazzane to Fez, across the Atlas Mountains to Sefrou, a caravan stop in the Sahara, which was predominately Jewish until the 1950s. Nine days, about $2,000, includes airfare from New York City.

Christianity: The Sacred Sites of Jesus

As recorded by Christ's apostles in the New Testament, the story of Jesus begins in the manger of a crowded inn in Bethlehem, where his mother suddenly felt the pangs of birth, as she was accompanying her husband Joseph home to conform to the Roman census. Today the sacred site of Christ's birth is marked by a star set in the floor of the central grotto in the Church of the Nativity, built originally by the newly Christian Roman Emperor Constantine in 326.

Jesus spent his childhood in Nazareth, then disappeared from the record until 30 or 33 C.E., when he was baptized by John the Baptist who was living in the wilderness at Bethany Beyond the Jordan. A recently discovered site, consecrated by the Catholic Church in 2000, is in Jordan at a site called Al Maghtas in Wadi Kharrar. Here among the tall reeds and shallow waters of what remains of the Jordan River is where it is believed John baptized Jesus. Numerous monastic churches proliferated in the area around that time.

After his baptism, Jesus went into the wilderness not far from Bethany beyond the Jordan. Here he fasted and prayed for forty days and forty nights. During that time the Devil appeared, tempting him with food, power, esteem. Reachable by cable car, the Greek Orthodox Monastery of the Temptation, built on a sheer cliff around the twelfth century, commemorates Jesus' test of faith.

Jesus then began preaching beliefs that were contrary to Judaism and threatened Roman rule. Around the Sea of Galilee, north of the Dead Sea, he found a group of fishermen whom he exhorted to become "fishers of men." Capernaum on the north shore contains many remnants of first-century houses, including one thought to have been Simon Peter's, one of Jesus' disciples. A recently excavated fishing boat, a good example of those used by fishermen in the first century, is on exhibit in the Kibbutz Ginosar on the Sea of Galilee.

An archaeologist gestures toward the reeds that once were covered by the Jordan River at Al Maghtas, Jordan, where John the Baptist might have lived in the wilderness at "Bethany Beyond the Jordan" and baptized many, including Jesus. (*Roger Archibald*)

A mile or so southwest of Capernaum at Tabkha, Jesus is said to have miraculously fed five thousand people with two loaves and two fishes, today remembered at the Church of the Multiplication of the Loaves and Fishes. Nearby is the Mount of the Beatitudes, the site of the Sermon on the Mount, where Jesus preached to the poor and oppressed, explaining the Kingdom of God and teaching the Lord's Prayer.

Jesus then entered Jerusalem in a triumphal march accompanied by his followers. On the stairs of the Temple on the Dome of the Rock, he routed out a group of money changers. Under intense scrutiny by Romans and Jews, he nevertheless preached to followers on the eastern side of the Mount of Olives. Jesus shared a Last Supper with his disciples on Mount Zion, today marked by a Crusader chapel, which contains the Hall of the Last Supper. Later that night, in the Garden of Gethsamene on the Mount of Olives, Jesus prayed. The Church of All Nations stands on the site of a fourth-century church built to protect the rock on which he sat. Here Judas, his deceiving apostle, gave him a brotherly kiss, which identified Jesus to the arresting authorities.

Brought to trial the next day, Jesus was condemned by the temple rabbis and sentenced to death by the Romans. Forced to carry the cross on which he would die to a place called Golgotha, he stopped along the path now called the Via Dolorosa, which is marked by stations of the cross. The rock outcrop where Jesus was crucified is behind a glass in the Church of the Holy Sepulchre; the tomb in which his body was laid is covered by a marble slab. Other sites in the church remember events that preceded and succeeded the Holy Resurrection, the miraculous disappearance of his body after he was entombed.

After his earthly death, Jesus ate fish with his apostles in Tabkha, marked by the Church of the Primacy of Peter; and spoke to strangers on the road to Emmaeus, in Abu Ghosh, about eight miles west of Jerusalem, today commemorated by a twelfth century crusader church.

The apostles of Jesus took his teachings west along the

Mediterranean to Greece, Italy, and France, from which his message spread through Europe. Christianized Romans carried the religion throughout the remnants of the Roman Empire. In the eleventh century, the church split into eastern and western factions, at Istanbul and Rome; and in the sixteenth century, into Protestantism and Catholicism.

Sunlight Travel 884 North First Street, San Jose, CA 95112. 408-971-6114 (tel); 408-971-3774 (fax). Web site: www.sunlighttravel.com

The Israel and Jordan tour begins on Israel's Mediterranean coast with visits to major biblical sites and a boat ride on the Sea of Galilee, drives to Amman and Petra in Jordan before going to the Red Sea coastal cities of Aqaba in Jordan and Eilat in Israel, then drives back via the Dead Sea to Jerusalem, and ends in Tel Aviv. Fourteen days includes international airfare, about $2,500 to $3,000 (depending on the season).

ITS International Tours, LLC 3945 North 1-10 Service Road, Suite 200, Metairie, LA 70002. 800-892-7729 (toll free); 504-831-0843 (tel); 504-837-2920 (fax). E-mail: itstours@itstours.com; Web site: www.itstours.com

The Holy Land tour begins in Tel Aviv and Mount Carmel, then travels to Galilee, Nazareth, Bethlehem, Jerusalem, and Masada and the Dead Sea, covering major sacred sites of the Bible. This thirty-five-year old company allows Catholics to attend daily mass in holy shrines. Ten days of "inner peace" is about $1,700, including airfare from New York City.

MEDIEVAL PILGRIMAGE

Santiago de Compostela

Medieval pilgrims with a spirit of adventure but not enough money to go to the Middle East walked across Europe, annually, to cathedrals near home, such as Canterbury in England or Mont-Saint-Michel in France; and maybe, once in a lifetime, to more distant sites, such as Santiago de Compostela in Spain.

Santiago, Saint James, was symbolized by the scallop shell, which pilgrims wore proudly around their necks to signify that they had made the trip.

Pilgrims still wear the scallop shell on the trek to Santiago de Compostela, starting at Roncesvalles in the Spanish Pyrenees and ending 500 miles away. Some walk parts of the trail, some walk the entire trail over several months and some do it on bicycle. The pilgrimage is open to members of all religions. In the summer it can be crowded.

Certain formalities do accompany it: Before you begin, you must register and get a pilgrim's passport, at the Augustinian Monastery at Roncevalles, to prove that you are a genuine pilgrim. This gives you entrance to the various hostels, inns, and eating places along the way, where you can expect reduced fare. Your passport is stamped at each place, so that when you arrive at the cathedral in Compostela (after you visit the statue of Saint James and give thanks), you can present it to the abbey. The monks congratulate you and give you a sheet in Latin, stating that you completed the pilgrimage to Santiago. Total cost: usually under $500. Time: your own pace.

It took David G.P. R. Duffy about three and a half weeks, as he recounts his experience in the *New York Times*. "For those who wish to complete the entire route," he said, "while the Camino is not Everest, neither is it a walk in the park." Half the route crosses through mountain passes, one of which is more than 5,000 feet high. The original path has evolved into everything from narrow muddy roads to super highways. The casual cameraderie of fellow pilgrims is a little like hikers on any long trail, but each pilgrim usually goes as a result of private pain—in Duffy's case, to recover from the recent senseless deaths of two close friends.

To read Duffy's article, visit the Web site www.nytimes.com/library/travel/europe/990530sant.html.

For a good list of routes and other information, consult the Web site www.pilgrimsprogress.org.uk/europe.htm.

Bike Riders Tours P.O. Box 130254, Boston, MA 02113. 800-473-7040 (toll free). E-mail: info@bikeriderstours.com; Web site: www.bikeriderstours.com

Minho & Galicia, The Pilgrim's Trail is a luxury tour that allows you to bike through little-used back roads in Portugal and Spain, and spend the nights in manor houses or luxury hotels. The tour convenes in Porto, Portugal, and travels north to Santiago de Compostela via an ancient pilgrimage route. Bike twenty to forty-five miles a day. Eight days, about $2,500.

MODERN PILGRIMAGE

Fatima

In 1917, when Europe was in the throes of World War I, three children saw apparitions of the Virgin Mary, the mother of Jesus,

The three children who saw a brilliant light illuminating a vision of the Virgin Mary at Fatima, in 1917. Two died a couple of years later in a flu epidemic; the third became a nun. (*tourist photo*)

in a tiny village in mountainous central Portugal. Since then, millions of pilgrims have visited the sacred site of Fatima for healing and spiritual connection. A large basilica was built there in 1928.

Glory Tours 1730 K Street, NW, Suite 1000, Washington, D.C. 20006. 877-424-5679 (toll free); 205-530-8899 (tel); 202-530-5818 (fax). E-mail: info@glory-tours.com; Web site: www.glory-tours.com

Glory Tours runs trips to Fatima and related sites. Seven days: about $800 (double) and $1,200 (single); airfare from New York City included.

Pilgrimage International 35 South Thirteenth Street, Allentown, PA 18102. 800-455-5514 (toll free); 610-434-3201 (tel); 610-435-3874 (fax). Web site: www.catholicpilgrimagetour.com

This company runs tours to Lourdes, Fatima, Santiago de Compostela, and other sites throughout Europe. Its tour guides are international scholars.

Islam: The Sacred Sites of Muhammad

Have they not traveled in the land so that they should have hearts with which to understand, or ears with which to hear?
—The Koran 22:46

Between the time of Moses and Jesus, Saudi Arabia was a desert crossed by numerous camel caravan routes, taken by traders carrying goods from the Orient and India to the Middle East. Tribal kingdoms lived in oasis villages and small towns. Mecca, at a crossroads of the caravan routes, was a holy city from time immemorial; and the Kaaba, a small building that contained a sacred black cubic stone with a meteoric relic, was the focus of worship of a group of gods and goddesses. Today the central point of Islam, the Kaaba is believed to have been built by Adam and rebuilt by Abraham.

In 570 C.E. Muhammad was born in Mecca, and orphaned at the age of six. He became a shepherd, at twenty-five a servant, and later the husband of Khadija, an older and wealthy woman. She enabled him to become a prosperous trader in Mecca, where Muhammad chose moments in which to be contemplative. Both Judaism and Christianity were represented in Mecca, as was a new movement against the old deities.

When he was forty, Muhammad climbed Mount Hira near Mecca, and received a vision of the Archangel Gabriel who commanded him to preach. Among a small band of followers, Muhammad encouraged belief in one almighty and merciful god, and taught the power of prayer, fasting, and charity for the poor, as methods to escape hell and inherit everlasting life. Visions accompanied Muhammad for the rest of his life; his teachings are contained in the holy book, the Koran.

As Muhammad preached and collected believers, the ruling powers of Mecca revolted against him, and he fled north to Medina, in what is known as the Hegira, the migration. There, with one hundred families, he entered the city on camelback, after the arduous journey over rough and unfriendly terrain. Where the camel stopped, he would build his first mosque. The date was 622, the beginning of the Muhammad era and the subsequent Islamic calendar.

For the next six years, Muhammad ruled as the judge of two powerful tribes during which time he waged a holy war with Mecca. Finally, in 628 he marched into Mecca with ten thousand men, took political control of the city, and was declared Prophet. Islam took hold and spread quickly to the rest of Arabia; by the end of the century, it spread into the Middle East, then east to China and west to Spain.

Muhammad went back home to Medina. His final visit to Mecca established the pilgrimage, or hajj. He died in 632 and is buried in Medina.

Aside from Mecca and Medina, the site most sacred to

Muhammad is the Dome of the Rock in Jerusalem. Built in 691 by a caliph of the Omayyad era and considered a superb example of Islamic art, the Dome covers the sacred rock where Prophet Muhammad experienced his Night Journey. According to legend, one night he was carried by angels from Mecca to the "most distant mosque," or El Aqsa, which contained the rock from which he ascended into the heavens to talk to God, before returning to Mecca by morning.

See Web sites www.ismaili.net and www.islamicsites.20m.com for lists of Islamic mosques.

Travel Resources

The following companies offer tours that cover sites of all three major religions:

Sun Tours Travel and Tourism P.O. Box 1305, Aqaba, Jordan. +962 (0)3-2018700 (tel); +962 (0)3-2018701 (fax). E-mail: suntours@go. com.jo; Web site: www.suntours.com

Caravan-Serai Tours, Inc. 3806 Whitman Avenue North, Seattle, WA 98103-8724. 206-545-1735 (Tel). E-mail: info@caravan-serai.com; Web site: www.caravan-serai.com

Petra Moon Tourism Services P.O. Box 129, Wadi Musa-Petra, Jordan. 962-2-215-6665 (tel); 962-3-215-6666 (fax). E-mail: info@ petramoon.com; Web site: www.petramoon.com

Nebo Tourism Services P.O. Box 910043, Amman 11191, Jordan. +962 (0)6-464-7116/8 (tel); +962 (0)6-464-7117 (fax). E-mail: Hanna@nebo.com.jo; Web site: www.nebo.com

You need a passport, visa, and a roundtrip ticket for travel to Egypt and Jordan. Israel requires a passport and roundtrip ticket for Americans. If conditions allow travel between Israel and Jordan across the Allenby/King Hussein Bridge, you will need a special visa in Jordan. (Contact the United States Embassy in Amman.) Expect to pay an exit tax from each country.

Saudi Arabia does not issue tourist visas, only transit visas (no fee) lasting seventy-two hours if you are not on official business. You will need a passport, roundtrip ticket, and a visa to your next destination. A woman traveling alone must be met at the airport by her "sponsor"; dress is conservative for westerners; the holy sites at Medina and Mecca are closed to non-Muslims. The Museum at Riyadh is rich in treasures, and will issue permits to visit archaeological sites, including a Stonehenge-type artifact of unknown origin. For information, see Web site: www.saudiembassy.net.

INDIA AND THE EAST

> *India will bend your mind, assault your body, flood your senses . . . from the moment you step off the plane into its smoky, unforgettable perfume of burning cow dung, diesel fumes, and a few thousand years of accumulated human sweat. And ultimately, if you're lucky, your old identity will break down, and you'll have to walk on without it. . . . It's this breakdown and the attendant possibilities for transformation . . . that's the real blessing India has to offer.*
>
> —Anne Cushman and Jerry Jones, *From Here to Nirvana.*

Buddhism: The Sacred Sites of Buddha

Siddhartha Gautama was born sometime between 568 and 563 B.C.E., the son of a wealthy rajah, about a hundred miles north of the sacred Indian city of Benares at Kapilavastu, or Lumbini (in present-day Nepal). Neither Jesus nor Muhammad had been born; and the Greeks were almost a century away from building the Parthenon.

In the lush world of tribal India, Siddhartha was raised and educated within the court and continued the same privileged life after he married a beautiful woman. Much of the story of the man who was to become Buddha was collected from oral histories passed on in villages and not recorded until the first century B.C.E. His birth was miraculous: His mother Maya dreamed an elephant with a red face entered her right side; he was born already walking. On the soles of his feet were marks of thousand-spoked wheels.

But at the age of thirty, something happened to change him from an idle court prince into a spiritual leader, the Buddha or Enlightened One. On a tour of the world outside his protected one, he saw four sights: old age, disease, death, and love of the wrong thing. The impact was so profound, he left his wife, the court, life as he had known it, and went into a contemplative fast for six years. During this time he was tempted by Mara, the King of Passions, and attacked by horrific visions of anthropomorphic creatures carrying weapons.

Realizing from his self-imposed exile that extremes, either of earthly pleasures or severe denial, led to imbalance, Buddha, in his enlightenment, embraced the Perfect, or Middle Way. Because of their evils, Buddha said, men were forced to transmigrate when they died and return to the miserable existence they had left. His four sights became the four noble truths: existence is suffering; suffering is caused by desire; desire leads to death; nirvana is the release of death. He realized that nirvana—non-existence or non-clinging—was possible by following the eightfold path: right opinions, right intentions, right speech, right conduct, right livelihood, right effort, right mindfulness, and right concentration.

Returning to normal life, Buddha Sakyamuni (the Sage of the Sakyas) collected followers to whom he taught the Middle Way for forty years. He died in Kusinagara in 430 B.C.E., when he was about eighty years old; his ashes were distributed among six shrines.

Buddhism Travels and Evolves

For two centuries both the philosophy and art of Buddhism spread north to Tibet and Burma (Myanmar), south to Sri Lanka, and east to China and Japan by monks who built spare monasteries. In the third century B.C.E., Emperor Ashoka Maurya erected monuments commemorating Buddha's sacred sites. Some still stand, but many were destroyed in the eighth and ninth centuries by Muslims who invaded India.

Over time, many monks gave up the continuous practice of self-denial. Buddhism evolved into Hinayana, a stricter form practiced mostly in monasteries and still followed in Sri Lanka and Thailand, and Mahayana, a more accessible form that spread the Buddha teaching of compassion. This form has become popular in the West. Today, Bhutan is the only country whose dominant religion is Buddhism, the practice of which remains unchanged from the seventh century. In Tibet, Mahayana Buddhism has blended with indigenous beliefs.

In the early centuries of this era, Hinduism, the religion of the Brahmins—not exported, for fear of losing caste—declared Vishnu an incarnation of Buddha, and incorporated his worship into the Hindu pantheon of personal deities, Krishna, Shiva, and Shakti.

Many tours today visit not only Buddha's sacred sites in India, but also magnificent Hindu temples and stupas, conical and hemispherical buildings that serve as funeral monuments as well as metaphorical models of the universe. In the tiny Himalayan countries of Nepal, Bhutan, and Tibet, Buddhists celebrate in a devout and robustly colorful way. Extraordinary examples of Dravidian religious art exist in temples in south India, the most untouched of the cosmopolitan mixture of Buddhism, Hinduism, Jainism, Sikhism, Islam, and Christianity practiced in the rest of India.

For a list of Jain, Hindu, Sikh, and Buddhist temples and reli-

Monks receiving teachings at Kopan monastery, Nepal. (*Thomas Warrior,* www.findhornsacredjourneys.com)

gious communities in the United States, go to Web site: www.pluralism.org. The Pluralism Project at Harvard University aims to map the "religious demography" of the United States, which is unique in its concentration of world religions. The project also studies the changes experienced by the religions as they settle into American communities, and explores the impact of religious diversity on the nation. (See *A New Religious America* by Diana Eck.)

Insight Travel Pilgrimages 800-688-9851 (toll free); 937-767-1102 (tel). E-mail: info@insight-travel.com; Web site: www.insight-travel.com

India and Nepal: The Way of the Buddha is a three-week pilgrimage that begins in Delhi, visits Bodh Gaya, where Siddhartha Gautama received enlightenment; then Varanasi (formerly Benares), where Hindus bathe in the Ganges; Sarnath, the Deer Park in which Buddha preached the Four Noble Truths (1. Death, disease, old age; 2. Hatred, wrong love; 3. Clinging to life or death; 4. Destroying sorrow by uprooting desire). Then you continue to Kushinagar, where Buddha died, and Lumini, where he was born, before going to Kathmandu in Nepal. This company is composed of scholars who have been leading groups since 1979. To get into "balance with the rhythms of India," you travel by train and bus. Three weeks, about $3,900, plus airfare.

Pilgrims at Annapurna Sanctuary, at 4,000 meters, one of the most breathtaking peaks in the Himalayas, shortly after sunrise. (*Thomas Warrior,* www.findhornsacredjourneys.com)

Spirit Travel P.O. Box 218, Eugene, OR 97440-0218. 888-883-9304 (toll free); 541-461-3659 (tel); 541-689-5284 (fax). E-mail: info@spirittravel.com; Web site: www.spirittravel.com

The Buddhist India and Bhutan Pilgrimage tour meets with local scholars before and after tours to original Buddha sites, as well as the Missionaries of Charity (Mother Teresa's Home for the Poor), and the Root Institute (a healthcare facility and school funded by fees collected from Western Buddhist visitors). The tour also provides a sunrise boat ride on the Ganges River in Varanasi. In Thimpu, Bhutan, your guide will take you to the National Library and School of Arts and Crafts, and a private monastery to meet old lamas who have completed meditation for three years and three months. At Wangdi Phrodang, you can attend the annual religious dance festival, with masks, music, and rituals. A monk from Changangka Lhakhang will raise a prayer flag for the group. Then you can hike up a path over a 2,000-foot cliff on which is perched the temple, Tiger's Lair, where Guru Rinpoche, the Second Buddha, flew to a cave riding a tiger. Fifteen days, about $4,900.

Myths and Mountains 976 Tee Court, Incline Village, NV 89451. 800-670-6984 (toll free); 775-832-5454 (tel); 775-832-4454 (fax). E-mail: travel@mythsandmountains.com; Web site: www.mythsandmountains.com

Rhythms of the Villages of Muktinath is a tour to Nepal that allows you not only to visit an important Buddhist and Hindu pilgrimage center, but also to become more deeply involved with the people who live there now. Myths and Mountains' Rural Education and Development (READ) project contributes to the creation of libraries in Nepal, and already has financed a furniture factory that helped to rebuild a nunnery in Muktinath. (For details, see Web site: www.educationinnepal. org.)

This tour begins in Kathmandu before breakfast (and before the arrival of tourists) with a walk up the 365 steps leading to the Swayambunath lotus stupa, then around its perimeter, a holy walk for locals. Traveling by van you then visit other Hindu and Buddhist shrines before flying to Pokhara, a tropical city at the base of Annapurna. Several long walks in the area wind among peach trees, often with views of flocks of cranes. These walks allow you to visit local industries, as well as sacred sites, including the holy city of Muktinath, whose boiling springs are sacred purification waters for Hindus and Buddhists. You stay overnight at the nunnery rebuilt by READ. The following day you walk or ride ponies to Jomosom, where you spend the night with a Nepalese family. Sixteen days, about $1,800 for two to three people; about $1,400 for eleven to fifteen people. International airfare not included.

Findhorn Sacred Journeys Fuaim-Na-Mara, Fyrish Road, Findhorn, Forres IV36 3YT, Moray, Scotland. +44 (0) 1309-691444 (tel); +44 (0) 1309-690699 (fax). E-mail: pilgrims@find hornsacredjourneys.com; Web site: www.findhornsacredjourneys. com

The Art of Pilgrimage, which is intended to deepen your understanding of holy sites in Nepal and Tibet, begins with a full week at Findhorn in Scotland, where you are introduced to the ancient art of pilgrimage as a transformative experience, and to the basics of Tibetan Buddhism. You study and practice meditation, recite mantras, and learn how to make offerings and prostrations and how to circumambulate sacred sites.

Thus prepared and focused, you fly from Scotland to Nepal, stopping in Kathmandu at the Kopan Monastery, organized in 1970 specifically to teach Westerners Eastern spiritual guidance. Here you meet with the holy lamas for blessings for a safe trip. After crossing the Himalayas to Tibet (by air), you visit monasteries and temples in Lhasa before driving into the hinterland of Tibet's high plateau (15,000 feet) to Gyantse and Shigatse and the monastery of the seventy-five foot-high Maitreya Buddha. The trip ends by driving back (and down) to

Buddhism spread to Japan about 2,000 years ago. This Buddha, *Daibutsu*, at Kamakura, is one of the largest in the world. (*Roger Archibald*)

Kathmandu. Fourteen days: £2,500. Because this trip demands high altitude endurance, Findhorn provides health and medical advice before you go. They also give a 5 percent discount if you prepay at least five months before the trip, or if you are a repeat traveler.

Sacred Sites International 1442A Walnut Street, #330, Berkeley, CA 94709. 510-525-1304 (tel/fax). E-mail: sacredsites@aol.com; Web site: www.sitesaver.org

Exploring Sacred Bhutan allows you to visit some of Buddhism's most ancient sites, some of them built on the sides of cliffs. Traveling by vehicle to the peaceful Bumthang Valley, you are able to take walks and hikes, and visit with local religious officials and village elders who inform you of the local culture. In addition to a Bhutanese guide, your Sacred Sites guide is a knowledgeable veteran who introduces you to lamas and takes you to little-known sites. Seventeen days about $6,500, including airfare from the East Coast. It also includes a $250 tax deductible contribution to Sacred Sites International, a nonprofit enterprise working to protect and repair sacred sites.

Cross Cultural Journeys One East Pier, Kappas Marina, Sausalito, CA 94965; or: P.O. Box 1369, Sausalito, CA 94966-1369. 800-353-2276 (toll free); 415-332-0682 (tel). E-mail: info@crossculturaljourneys.com; Web site: www.crossculturaljourneys.com

Cross Cultural Journey's stated intention is "to honor the inner journey as well as the outer adventure." In the Footsteps of Buddha takes you to sacred sites with the guidance of Robert Thurman, the founder and director of Tibet House in New York City. Other pilgrims visit major Buddhist centers in Tibet. In addition to providing informed tour leaders, Cross Cultural Journeys contributes a portion of each traveler's fee to the Cross Cultural Journeys Foundation that funds grass roots projects in the countries they visit. (Footsteps of Buddha: eighteen days, $5,500, includes everything except airfare.)

Shambhala Conference and Seminars 310-446-4660 (tel); 310-446-4670 (fax). E-mail: conference@shambhala.com; Web site: www.shambhala.com

Mount Kailash in Tibet, considered the embodiment of the

Buddhahood for Buddhists, and the source of all rivers and purification for Hindus, is the once-in-a-lifetime pilgrimage destination for all Buddhists and Hindus. A spectacular 22,000-foot mountain, the sacred peak will confer enlightenment on the pilgrim who circumambulates the base 108 times. The thirty-two-mile outer path is marked by cairns, flags, temples, caves, and places where Buddhists attained enlightenment and became Boddhisattvas. To do the trip three times is considered powerful. Most pilgrims do it once.

This trip, guided by Tibetan historians Erik and Marcia Hein Schmidt, circumambulates the mountain once in three days, then joins the annual Saga Dawa festival, which celebrates the enlightenment of Sakyamuni Buddha. The tour begins and ends in Nepal, traveling by Toyota Land Cruiser. You camp or lodge in Tibetan guesthouses. This is a serious pilgrimage, and you must be in fairly good physical shape as well as prepared for the altitude, which averages about 14,000 feet. Roads can be unpaved and bumpy. A Tibetan guide, a group of Sherpas, and a local cook look after you. Twenty-five days, about $5,700, including international airfare from Los Angeles or San Francisco.

Spirit of India   P.O. Box 446, Mill Valley, CA 94941. 888-367-6147 (toll free); 415-381-5861 (tel). Web site: www.spirit-of-india.com

Spirit of India runs many types of trips to the Himalayas and India, including Walking with the Buddha. This two-week pilgrimage traces the path of Buddha's sacred sites, and ends with a visit to the Taj Mahal at sunrise. Your guide is Arun Acharya, a Sanskrit scholar. Fourteen days, about $3,700 (six to nine people); about $3,200 (ten to twelve); airfare not included.

Buddha Treks & Expedition P., Ltd.   P.O. Box 10813, Thamel, Kathmandu, Nepal. +977 (0)1-431812 (tel); +977 (0)1-226959 (fax). E-mail: info@buddhatreks.com; Web site: www.buddha treks.com

Way of Buddha begins in Kathmandu, Nepal, visits Buddhist and Hindu temples, as well as the Tibetan Refugee Camp. Then it goes to Lumbini, birthplace of Buddha, before a rare visit to the Chitwan National Park (a World Heritage site), with its spectacular collection of African and East Asian animals, including Royal Bengal tigers. Eight days, between $400 and $500, international airfare not included.

You need a passport and visa for travel to Nepal, India, and Bhutan. Your tour company will facilitate getting your visa in Bhutan; you pick it up at the point of entry for $20. For travel to India, the fee for a sixty-day tourist visa is $30. For more information see Web site: www.travel.state.gov.

The Anasazi populated most of the present-day southwestern United States until about 1200 C.E. Many lived in precarious rock shelters like this one in Canyon de Chelly, Arizona, and held religious ceremonies in huge round kivas, some of which could hold hundreds of people. (*Stephanie Ocko*)

UNITED STATES

Chaco Canyon

The people known as the Anasazi populated the American Southwest in the early years of the first millennium, well before visits by Europeans to this country. Acoma Pueblo, the tiny village on a mesa west of Albuquerque, New Mexico, is the oldest continuously occupied city in North America, dating from about 1150.

Anasazi artifacts—their villages, city and sacred complexes known as kivas, and a few archeoastronomical carvings—are widespread. But mysteries remain. They left no written history and disappeared over the course of a few generations. Spread across high, spare desert with rolling and empty hills, the area of the vanished Anasazi is magical, a fact attested to by the archaeologists who work there.

Far Horizons Archaeological and Cultural Trips, Inc. P.O. Box 91900, Albuquerque, NM 87199-1900. 800-552-4575 (toll free); 505-343-9400 (tel); 505-343-8976 (fax). E-mail: journey@farhori zon. com; Web site: www.farhorizon.com

Southwestern Archaeology and Things Chaco is the name of a trip that takes you to a corn dance in Acoma, the mesa home to Pueblo Indians since the twelfth century; and to even more ancient sites in Chaco Canyon. Here, between 1150 and 1300, Anasazi created a vigorous culture, with trade and roads that stretch from the foot of the Rocky Mountains to Mexico, huge towers to guard the scarce water supplies, and great kivas, where elaborate religious ceremonies were held for the entire population.

This trip is led by Dr. Bruce Bradley, distinguished archaeologist whose seminal work in the Southwest has brought the Anasazi alive. He is an informed, enthusiastic, and accessible speaker; he also takes you to see Kokopelli, carved in the rock bluffs above the San Juan River. Eleven days, about $3,000.

The Effigy Mounds

Hopewellian Mounds, including the Little Bear Mound, are located in a National Park, on Iowa State Highway 76, three miles north of Marquette, Iowa. Scattered through the American Midwest, these mounds remain an enigma.

Native Americans, in what is today Wisconsin, built more than 14,000 earth mounds in the shapes of animals and ovals from about 1000 B.C.E. to about 1200 C.E. Often placed around lakes, the mounds are constructed in the shapes of rabbits, panthers, eagles, deer, bears, and snakes. Always subject to highways and subdivisions, an amazing number survive, including the better part of a bird, once more than 600 feet across.

The melting ice from the last glacier 10,000 years ago simply missed northern and eastern Wisconsin. Writers John-Brian Paprock and Teresa Peneguy Paprock believe this is a reason that so many different people experience a deepened spiritual sense there.

The mounds are open to the public, and free unless they are in a state park. Whatever they were intended for, consider them sacred sites today. The Paprocks suggest approaching the mounds in silence and sprinkling tobacco as an offering to Great Spirit.

The Paprocks' *Sacred Sites of Wisconsin* is an excellent guide; it is available from Trails Books by calling 800-236-8088, or going to Web site www.trailsbooks.com.

Serpent Mound

Serpent Mound 3850 State Route 73, Peebles, OH 45660. 800-752-2757 (toll free); 937-587-2796 (tel). E-mail: serpent@bright. net

A quarter of a mile long, the Serpent Mound was built on a plateau in Ohio sometime between 800 B.C.E. and 100 C.E. Part of a series of mounds of the Adena People, its meaning eludes archaeologists who speculate that it was part of religious rituals. Some mounds nearby are conical or huge platforms; some contain burials.

Part of the Ohio Historical Society, the Serpent Mound is open daily from 10:00 A.M.

Web Sites and Organizations

Sacred Sites International Foundation 1442A Walnut Street, #330, Berkeley, CA 94709. 510-525-1304 (tel/fax). E-mail: sacred sites@aol.com; Web site: www.sitesaver.org

Sacred Sites International is a nonprofit organization that works with local governments to preserve sacred sites, both natural and man-made.

At many sacred sites, the future is imperiled, not only from tourism, but also from local mining, farming, neglect, and abuse. For example, Silbury Hill in Avebury, not far from Stonehenge, is a mysterious mound thought to have been sacred to the mother goddess. It is now riddled with holes, possibly from water seeping in from below, and is closed to visitors.

To join Sacred Sites International's mailing list, send a blank E-mail to: newsletter1234-subscribe@sacred-sites.org

World Heritage Organization, a division of United Nations Educational, Scientific and Cultural Organization (UNESCO), is dedicated to "protecting natural and cultural properties of outstanding universal value against the threat of damage in a rapidly developing world." The list of World Heritage Sites is long and surprising. Take a look at: Web site: www.unesco.org/whc/heritage.htm.

How can you help? Start by observing and being aware of potential dangers at any heritage site you visit.

To subscribe to their free print or electronic newsletter, contact: WHNews@unesco.org. The *WHNews* says your "money, poems, artwork all welcome."

The snow leopard, rare, elusive, sacred to many Himalayans. (*Roger Archibald*)

Travel Web Sites

www.infohub.com is an excellent compilation.

www.sacredtravel.com has a link to metaphysical tour companies.

www.travel.state.gov has visa, passport, and country information.

www.sacredsites.com is one Martin Gray's personal list of sacred sites with photographs.

www.mysteriousplaces.com is Robert Donald Matthew's personal sacred site choices with spectacular photographs.

Chapter 4
Dolphins

*In myth, there is a contract between men and animals,
either hunters or keepers of the ritual, that the animal—
no matter, the mastodon, the bear, or the deer—agrees to
participate in the ritual.*

—Joseph Campbell

No less mysterious than aliens from other planets are some of
the zillion other species with whom we share the earth. How
can we know what it's like for them? How can we communicate? Philosopher Ludwig Wittgenstein, commenting on the in-
adequacy of our language as a communication tool, said, "If a
lion could talk, we would not understand him."

Some insects might as well live in another universe, with
their waving antennae, hairy legs, and opalescent eyes. Even our
fellow mammals challenge our understanding: Fascinated, we
take our kids to the zoo and our cameras to game parks. At
home, we negotiate boundaries with neighborhood raccoons,
Canada geese, coyotes, squirrels, and a host of other formerly
"wild" creatures that nibble our lawns and are nourished by our
garbage. Usually, our communication centers around feeding—
it's our bottom-line technique for other-species diplomacy.

But on another level, animals, wild and domestic, touch us
deeply without words. The image of the rescue dogs scrambling
for sure footing in the rubble of the World Trade Center after the
September 11 attack, or catching a moment of rest at the feet of
their trainers, telescoped the horror of the incident into our

Park squirrels tolerate us as much as we tolerate them. (*Roger Archibald*)

hearts. The *Wall Street Journal* reported that a woman who had never had pets dealt with her emotional loss of the twin towers by going to the animal rescue league and adopting two cats.

If domestic animals are our resident therapists, with whom we safely feel our crazy and chaotic feelings without the noise of apology or explanation, wild animals invite us to spiritual connection with the divine. In ancient Greece, mythmakers gave animals to the gods to understand. Dionysos changed pirates into dolphins, as a way of curing them of their wayward lifestyles. Poseidon threw a dolphin among the stars to become a constellation as a reward for finding his wife and rescuing a poet. Healing snakes, whose sinuous rapture evokes ecstatic states; rabbits, mixing the elixir of immortality on the moon; clever coyotes, sacred wolves; and eternal snow leopards throughout history and throughout the world are central to the myths that glue cultures together and open holy doors to the soul.

DOLPHINS

If the New Spirituality has an animal icon, it is the dolphin. Whether they came to us first, or we went to them is not clear; we have a long history of interaction. However, what is happening now is more intense: They seem to heal our broken spirits without asking; in turn, we fall in love with them.

Unfortunately, swimming with dolphins has become a highly profitable business. Modern day pirates steal them and put them in tanks, where they face further abuse and raise moral issues: Do we enslave them and use them selfishly? Do dolphins really heal? Or do we co-create a healing atmosphere? Do they heighten our global consciousness and encourage compassion for all living things, as some say?

Have they come to *us* in an act of diplomacy?

Critics say this is nonsense. But enough people report life-changing psychological experiences to suggest at least investigating the possibility of a spiritual link with dolphins. Many who swim often with them report that dolphins appear to be trying to communicate with us.

You decide.

Structured Swims

Dolphins have a charming ability to become our spontaneous, no-strings-attached buddies, without a hidden agenda. But how we relate to them requires the same strategies that we might use relating to a species from another planet. We have major differences in our bodies and our environments, but we share an empathy that suggests we can communicate telepathically.

For a fee, you can swim with dolphins at about fifteen facilities in the United States in what is called a structured swim. This takes place with resident dolphins, many of which have been born or sent there after aquariums lost funding for them. Facilities range from fairly pricey hotel/resort pools to research labs.

Sailors from Odysseus to present-day ship captains depend on dolphins to bring them good luck and hope after stormy nights at sea. These lead a research ship. (*NOAA:* Personnel of the *Pierce,* 1985)

The best have natural sea water lagoons that are deep and big enough for dolphins to take off when they feel the need for speed. Most have buffer zones that are dolphin off-limit areas of the lagoon to which they can swim to rest or be away from people and other dolphins.

In Florida, where hurricanes are a threat for half the year, the best facilities let their dolphins go into deep water to ride out the storm, being confident the dolphins will return when the storm is over. And they do.

In pre-swim briefings, sometimes as long as an hour, guides educate you about dolphins and their environmental problems, and instruct you on how to behave during the choreographed moves that you will make with the dolphins in the water.

It's safe. Obviously, dolphin-swim guides are not about to put anyone in a tank with an aggressive dolphin. But it pays to follow whatever rules you are given: You have no way of knowing if dolphins are having a bad day.

At the Dolphin Research Center (DRC) in Grassy Key, Florida, the dolphins decide whether or not they feel like "working." "It makes it more interesting for them," said a trainer. Of the seventeen resident dolphins at DRC—many of them orphans from aquariums that could no longer afford to keep them, a few native-born, and one retired from its underwater work with the navy in California—only three females, two of them pregnant, have chosen to swim with humans today.

Being with dolphins in a pool for the first time can be terrifying. "I feel nervous. Anticipating. Scared. Excited," said a swimmer as she joined her small group on the floating dock at DRC. Clad in wetsuits, six men and women groped for balance on the trembling dock as three large dolphins cruised nearby, checking them out, and setting off a rolling swell under the dock. Sitting on the edge, the trainer called the dolphins by name and gave them fish from a bucket, talking to them in a low voice, but loud enough to compete with the screaming seagulls that competed for the fish.

PRE-SWIM BRIEFING

Each group is briefed for forty-five minutes on environmental issues of tourist abuse, the anatomy of dolphins, where never to touch one (on the belly, the genitals, the blowhole, the mouth), what the skin feels like ("a hot dog," "waterproof velvet"), and what to expect in the pool. They sign a paper agreeing to the rules of the swim for which they reserved a place a month or more in advance: They must be competent swimmers, older than five years old, follow the trainer's commands at all times, and understand that the dolphins have a buffer zone in the pool which is off-limits to humans.

THE REALITY OF THE WATER

One by one, each swimmer slips off the dock at the trainer's command and waits, hand flat on the water, for a dolphin to swim under the hand. The water is not really cold, but it feels cold, and, oddly, *wet*. This is the dolphins' domain.

"I couldn't remember where we were supposed not to touch!" said a swimmer afterwards. "But the dolphin rubbed my hand. It left grit, like sand, that the trainer said was skin cells." Dolphins regenerate their skin every two to three hours, a speedy healing process.

Next, one by one, each swimmer tread water, arms in front. Suddenly, one of the dolphins rose up in front of the swimmer, presenting its flippers, which the swimmer stroked ("The Introduction") until the dolphin swam away, circling back to get a fish and praise offered by the trainer.

Gaining confidence, the swimmers relaxed farther away from the dock as they thought up an act to do for the dolphin to imitate. One man held an inordinate amount of water in his cheeks which he spurted at the dolphin, which returned with twice the amount of squirted water. A woman twirled in the water, which the dolphin imitated by twirling faster and longer than the swimmer ever could. One dolphin refused to imitate a swimmer splashing the water, and instead, bobbed up and down in the water, making up its own trick.

"Now comes the tour," said the trainer, feeding the dolphins and motioning them to swim away from the dock. A swimmer lay on her back, feet up, head facing her feet. Out of nowhere came two dolphins, and pushed the bottoms of her feet, swirling the squealing swimmer around the pool.

Then each swimmer was told to swim on his stomach toward the mangroves on the opposite side of the lagoon. Gracefully, two dolphins positioned their dorsal fins at each hand of the swimmer and took the swimmer for a ride. Gentle swimmers received slow and measured rides. More athletic swimmers got the "turbo ride." One young woman clung tenuously to her dolphins as they cut white-water swathes through the tranquil pool and deposited her in a breaking wave at the dock.

The final connection was the kiss. Back at the dock, each swimmer put out a hand, into which a dolphin placed its rostum (beak) and "kissed" the swimmer on the cheek. The dolphin that had given the young woman a super turbo ride presented her with a long mangrove seed, carried in its mouth like a cigar.

"What's that?" asked the woman.

"She's giving you something," said the surprised trainer.

"Thank you," said the swimmer to the dolphin, who then planted a kiss on the swimmer's cheek.

AFTER THE SWIM

Usually, after a session of diving or snorkeling, swimmers gather on the boat or the dock to trade stories and discuss what they saw. But after the dolphin swim, people prefer solitude; some,

The Greek god of the sea Poseidon threw a dolphin into the stars to form a new constellation, Delphinus, as a reward for having saved a friend.

sitting on the dock, gazed into the far distance, with smiles on their faces; others made their way to the lockers, with solemn looks of private contentment. "It might be the ocean," said one participant, leaning against a post and staring at nothing. "I'm a diver, and I always have a different—spiritual—feeling in the ocean. But I was really impressed by the intelligence of these dolphins," he said. "I liked the way they were willing to play with me."

His partner said, "I have an extreme feeling of fear of both deep water and large animals. I went from being totally terrified up to being at a level of comfort. It's sort of love and fear," she said, adding, "with a healthy respect for the dolphins."

Who are the dolphins?

Dolphins have an enormous capacity for play, behavior that has no purpose other than what we would call the expression of sheer joy. They love to jump and spin out of the water, toss balls, bodysurf on waves at the shore, and push things, like small boats or maybe you. Like cats, they sometimes tease their fish prey. Boaters report seeing them tweak the tail feathers of pelicans or give resting seagulls a sudden, surprising ride. Dolphins are dazzlingly beautiful, slipping through the sea effortlessly, one with the ocean.

When they need to communicate with us, they do. Recently, for example, near Key West, Florida, a fisherman felt a tug on his anchor line. He ignored it, felt it again, then looked and saw two dolphins playing around his boat. When they had his attention, they led him through the straits between two small mangrove islands, where the fisherman saw a young dolphin caught in a net in the tangled mangrove roots. He jumped in, cut the net, freed the dolphin; and the three dolphins spent the rest of the day with him, playing around his boat.

Telepathic?

But many who swim with dolphins believe there is another dimension in dolphin/human communication: telepathy. "They send thoughts, which to me sound like my own thoughts, except they have a more forceful energy," says Ilona Selke, whose book *Journey to the Center of Creation*, is based on her experiences swimming with wild dolphins. Swimmers who sense messages from dolphins report little things: One man was uneasy being in deep water, until he heard a dolphin tell him that he was safe. A woman who had traveled several thousand miles to swim with them in the wild off the Bahamas for a week wished that a dolphin would come back at a certain time, and lo, the dolphin did.

Dr. Dolphin?

Seldes and others believe dolphins have the ability to diagnose physical and emotional problems, and to untie the knots of illness with focused echolocation. Some swimmers report that they feel that dolphins are "scanning" them when they enter the water, which might be the effect of the combination of their acute vision, hearing, and sonar which behaves in a way similar to Magnetic Resonance Imaging. One swimmer in the wild reported that a couple of dolphins kept poking him in the ribs. When he later went to a doctor to see if any ribs had been broken, the doctor found no broken ribs, but a previously undetected tumor in his chest.

Seldes and others believe that dolphins see the world, and us, holographically, three-dimensionally. Most researchers agree that their amazing eyesight, coupled with their precise echolocation, allows them to see the object and its context with alarming detail and accuracy. "You keep no secrets from dolphins," said a research assistant at Dolphin Research Lab.

Ancient fossils of skulls thought to have belonged to dolphin ancestors indicate the same hollow jawbone and rise in the forehead for the "melon" which houses their echolocation abilities. This means that dolphins have been listening and translating sounds into meaning for tens of thousands of years. What they "hear" when encountering a human form must far outweigh any human "physical exam."

Dolphins and Healing

Dolphin-Assisted Therapy, which was started a few decades ago, engages therapists and psychologists who work with ill patients and dolphins in pools. Many dolphins in the United States and Russia, retired from searching for underwater mines in the service of the navy, adapted beautifully to pool therapy, sensing and helping physically challenged children. At a handful of facilities in the United States, documented results with all kinds of severe problems are impressive.

After swimming with dolphins, deeply depressed teenagers actually and genuinely smile; stroke victims feel atrophied muscles working again. A man who had been a paraplegic from a fall reported feeling his legs for the first time in ten years; cancer victims see their tumors vanish. Critics say it is a placebo effect, but those who have been touched by the "healing" attest to its longevity.

Recently, at the Dolphin Research Center in Grassy Key, Florida, an autistic nine-year-old, who had never spoken, spent a few days working with therapists and a dolphin from a dock until the final day when the boy gained enough confidence to get in the water. At the end of the week, he spoke his first word: the dolphin's name.

Exactly how dolphins heal is not known, but the healing process seems authentic. Some theorize that the vibrating ultrasound itself activates the human immune system, especially if the sonar is directed at a specific area. Marine researcher David

Cole of the Aqua Thought Foundation believes that the pulses create cavitation—alternating areas of compression and expansion—that changes cells and stimulates neurons. Cole speculates that dolphins adjust their ultrasound to levels appropriate to augment the weaknesses in the electromagnetic fields that they perceive in humans. Some healing groups, such as the Dolphin Energy Club of the Monroe Institute in Faber, Virginia, meditate and simply imagine dolphins scanning or being inside the ill body to diagnose and heal.

The ocean might be a player, as well. Emotional changes in the psyche of the swimmer, just from being in the ocean with dolphins, might stimulate a hormone release which, in turn, augments the immune system.

In studies of swimmers given electroencephalograms (EEGs) directly after interaction with dolphins, researchers at the Aqua Thought Foundation found that eighty percent of the subjects experienced a synchronization of the hemispheres of the brain that engendered a change in consciousness from the beta (awake) state to the theta (meditative) state. This might explain the feelings of euphoria that so many report afterwards, or what some dolphin center assistants call "perma-grins." Many swimmers find that old psychological problems suddenly seem simple; obstacles dissolve; new attitudes and aspects are created as soon as they pull themselves out of the water.

Wild Swims

The ocean is definitely a player in "natural" swims with wild dolphins. Ask yourself how comfortable you are in deep water with snorkeling equipment, wearing a wetsuit if necessary. Many people who have done one or two structured swims feel the need to swim with dolphins in the wild. You can join a group on a boat or, if you are a strong swimmer, swim out from the beach.

Swim From the Beach

This is what Ilona Selke did the first time she and her husband, Don Paris, brought a camera to record their swim with spinner dolphins in deep water off Hawaii.

Wild swims can be thrilling, because you meet the dolphin in the wild ocean, which is as unknown as outer space and has the same alien-encounter feeling to it. Intelligent and curious, the pod of spinner dolphins surrounded Selke and Paris, making eye contact and adjusting their speed to the swimmers' speed. Selke carried a big orange leaf which she tried to give to one of the dolphins, but the dolphin turned away. Only when the leaf slipped out of her hand did the dolphin capture it under its flipper. Then the game was on. The leaf again slipped free and became stuck to the chest of Paris's wetsuit. The dolphin examined the situation and stared into the camera, but would not take the leaf. Not until it was floating free again did the dolphin swoop to secure it, then playfully raced away with it under its flipper.

The danger of swimming without a boat is that you can swim too far from shore. On another swim, Selke said, she and her companions had to swim far into the deep ocean to find the dolphins. Swimming and playing with the pod, they lost all sense of time. Suddenly, she realized the palm trees on the beach were just specks on the horizon. Simultaneously (they discovered later) she and her companions heard the telepathic message: *Get back now!*

The swim back was hard and long; her leg cramped up, Selke said, and she was already exhausted far from the beach. When they finally reached the beach, breathless and grateful to be alive, she and her companions thanked the dolphins for having saved their lives: They had just enough energy to get back. If they had stayed a moment longer, they might have drowned.

Swimming From a Live-aboard Boat

In natural swims, you travel by boat to places dolphins are known to inhabit. Then you drop anchor and wait patiently. Dolphins will swim with you, or not.

"I have been out on a boat in a group, anchored, minding our own business, then looked up to see dolphins swimming straight for the boat like greyhounds, then hanging around until we got in to swim with them," said Katryn Lavanature, director of Spirit of Dolphin Journeys in *Spirit of Change*. "What's so wondrous about wild dolphin swims is that they make a clear and conscious choice to be with us."

You can choose a company that houses your small group at a hotel at night, after full days spent with dolphins, or you can spend the better part of a week on a "live-aboard," where you eat, drink, and sleep dolphins.

On a week-long dolphin swim from a catamaran in the Bahamas with animal communicator Penelope Smith, who talks to animals telepathically, Peggy Kornegger describes the experience:

"When someone would yell 'Dolphins!', a chill would always run through me. We would rush to get on our snorkel equipment, and one by one, jump into the water to join the amazing water ballet that the dolphins initiated," Kornegger wrote in *Spirit of Change*. Empowered by being with the dolphins, she said she learned how to dive deep to meet them well below the surface. She imitated their movements, doing things like spiraling slowly up. "Best of all," she wrote, "I swam right next to them, looking into their eyes, experiencing a oneness that is almost indescribable."

The final day of their trip was the summer solstice. Sunburned and feeling as liberated as castaways, the group excitedly waited for the dolphins. The pod had not come the day before. The bond that they had established was deep, and the group was fearful that they wouldn't come. All day they waited, delaying their return to port.

"Suddenly around 5:30 P.M., there they were. There were forty of them, more than on any of the other swims!" said Kornegger. While the boat headed back to port, as lightning played on the horizon, Penelope Smith spoke individually with each swimmer, translating the messages of the dolphins.

But, Kornegger said, on that and on subsequent swims, *all* members of her groups experienced easy telepathic communication with the dolphins as they swam together, the dolphins often allaying swimmers' fears and instilling in everyone a tremendous sense of joy. "We are here on earth to learn," Kornegger wrote, "and to learn how to love above all else. That is dolphin spirit, pure and simple."

What You Should Know

"Dolphins are not little people in wetsuits," says mammal researcher Randy Wells, of the Sarasota Dolphin Research Center in Florida. The Atlantic bottlenose dolphins are big, bulky, fast, slippery, and have seductive smiles—"a result of anatomy, not attitude," says Wells. Warm-blooded, they have gestation periods of a year, give live birth to fully formed babies that stay with the mother, nursing, for three to six years. Dolphins engage in recreational sex "three-hundred-and-sixty-five, seven-twenty-four," one researcher observed. Females are fertile well into their forties; healthy dolphins live to be between fifty and sixty years old.

Dolphins usually travel in pods of several males, females, and young, but sailors have lots of stories of lone dolphins that lead ocean-stranded humans to islands. Wells reports that some males buddy up for life with another male, probably for protection against sharks, their mortal enemies. Dolphins spend most of their time hunting fish, which they swallow whole, and consume thirty pounds a day. Dolphins don't chew; their surgically sharp teeth are used to cut off things like catfish heads, which they don't like to eat.

Dolphins catch cat naps, sleeping near the surface for a few minutes at a time. This one is enjoying warm shallow water. (*Roger
Archibald*)

The Amazing Parts of Dolphins

Dolphin brains are significantly larger and have more complex
divisions than humans,' which means that we really don't know
the capabilities of dolphin intelligence. Ditto their senses: Their
vision is enormously acute, both in and out of the water. Some

dolphins are "people-watchers," turning on their side to allow one eye to focus on people on docks and boats. Their sense of hearing is so refined, they are able to hear frequencies as high as 150 kHz (human hearing falls off at 17–20 kHz).

SONAR AND OTHER CLICKS AND WHISTLES

Often, you can hear dolphins forcefully blow air out of their blowhole, which is also a communication signal among the pod. If you walk on a beach at night where dolphins are known to swim and imitate their blowhole expulsion, you may get a response from the dark distance offshore.

Underwater, you hear all kinds of noises coming from the dolphins, from piercing whistles to Bronx cheers to what some researchers think are imitated human words. With their echolocation, they are able to reach frequencies that are both well below and above the range of human hearing, which means that you don't consciously hear all their sounds. If you feel their ultrasound (which is sixty times more efficient in water, four times stronger than that used in hospitals), you will feel it vibrate in your bones. Oceanographer Jacques-Yves Cousteau clocked their sonar clicks as high as twelve hundred per second—higher, he believed, than any known vibrating muscle or membrane in nature. The pulse is sent out from the melon in their forehead, and the returned vibration travels through their hollow lower jaw and a fat-filled cavity to their skullbones and brain.

UNDERWATER STRESS

In the wild, dolphins also are subject to stress, the sources of which we do not fully understand. Researchers in the United States and the United Kingdom have reported separate incidents in which wild dolphins have hurled their bodies at porpoises while traveling at high speeds and killed them without eating them. Worse, there are incidents of dolphins killing their young, also without eating them. Why? We don't understand enough about them or their environment.

THE DARK SIDE

Unfortunately, the rumor of the "quick fix" draws a lot of people to dolphins: The traffic in captured wild dolphins—taken from their pods, often from their nursing mothers—rises as tourist interest swells. Worth between $40,000 and $70,000, each, on the international market, Atlantic bottlenose dolphins are regularly exported from Cuba around the world, shipped in iced containers in the bellies of transport planes. The worst offenders are profiteers who pen them in four cement walls, teach them tricks for tourists, and neglect them after the tourists have left. Once in the facilities, the dolphins become trained prisoners for life.

Uncontested in many parts of the world, the trade flourishes, despite protests by individuals such as Ric O'Barry. Formerly the trainer of dolphins, including some of the five dolphins that portrayed famed dolphin Flipper, O'Barry now advocates keeping dolphins in the wild. For more information, consult his Web site: www.dolphinproject.org.

Abuse is kept in check by watchdog groups, like the International Dolphin Watch, www.idw.org, as well as the many visitors to dolphin facilities who have been briefed on how to spot dolphin abuse. The worst facilities with starving, sick, and untended dolphins, have been closed.

EVERYDAY ABUSE

But other kinds of tourist abuse happen every day. Researchers warn that there is a fine line between the education that comes with dolphin facilities and the circus qualities that surround an animal being used for profit-making purposes.

More numerous are careless tour guides on day trips who encourage tourists to feed and touch dolphins from boats, and to expect some kind of spiritual miracle. Feeding wild dolphins creates atypical dependent behavior; they may take on the worst of beggar traits and become what Australian researcher Jim Curtis calls, "career moochers." Mothers no longer bother to teach their young how to hunt. In Florida, one excited dolphin mistakenly bit off half a tourist's face to get the fish the tourist was holding in his mouth while leaning over the railing of the boat.

Our history with animals is not good: A hundred years ago we shot wild animals and had them stuffed for trophies. We risk imposing the same imperialist attitude on dolphins, making them do magic for us.

What do they think of us?

The jury is out on what dolphins think of us. Are they reaching out to us? Maybe some are. Selke's telepathic messages from dolphins have concerned abuse of their environment—the ocean. Dolphins "told" her about the nuclear test in the Pacific executed by the French in the 1990s, an event she had no knowledge of until she researched it.

If dolphins are as smart as we think they are, there are probably as many individual differences among dolphins as there are among us. Swimmers report that not all dolphins are interested in humans, and some seem to have no desire to be with us, let alone bring us to new states of consciousness. And a lot of people just enjoy being around dolphins, without healing, without telepathic messages, without consciousness-raising.

But if a dolphin speaks to you, listen.

BASIC RULES:

- Never feed dolphins anything. Human food can make them sick as well as dependent.
- Don't touch wild dolphins. In a structured swim, touch dolphins only where guides tell you: They have extremely sensitive skin and are naturally shy. Wait until they ask to be petted.
- Don't chase or grab dolphins.
- Don't swim with them if you have an infectious disease.

Dolphins are highly susceptible to human viruses, like flu and hepatitis.

- Don't expect to ride on the back of a dolphin. This trick is reserved for dolphin performers in shows and films, as well as the children in Greek myth whose playmates were dolphins.
- Don't make sudden jerky movements. Dolphins are easily frightened and confused. They learn quickly how to read body language, but you have to be crystal clear and consistent about what your body language says.
- If you are scuba diving, don't release a lot of air bubbles at once. This can be interpreted by dolphins as aggression.
- Make sure your guide knows when dolphins are feeding or resting, and stay away from them during those times.
- Be aware of the Marine Mammal Act which prohibits harassment of dolphins and whales, and requires your boat to stay at least fifty feet away from dolphins, and one hundred feet away from whales in the wild.

SIGNS DOLPHINS ARE ANNOYED OR AGGRESSIVE:

- slapping the water with their tails
- chattering jaws
- head nodding
- swimming with an open mouth in the wild

HOW TO TELL THE FOLKS BACK HOME

It won't be easy.

The slides you show and the anecdotes you recount may not completely describe your experience. As one swimmer said, "What happens in the slides—'Here we are on the boat. You can see the dolphins in the water'—is different from what's happening on the inside—'And the dolphins are telling me that life is all joy, and that I'm okay, and that they will follow me wherever I will go, and I'm about to burst into tears I feel so great!'"

Please note: Most companies have restrictions on swimming with dolphins. Ask first. In structured swims, you must understand English and not be pregnant.

You need a passport and return ticket to travel to Israel, New Zealand, or Honduras. To Costa Rica, you need a passport and photo ID. To Egypt, you need a passport and three-month tourist visa ($15).

Theater of the Sea 84721 Overseas Highway, Islamorada, FL 33036. 305-664-2031 (tel); 305-664-8162 (fax). E-mail: info@the aterofthesea.com; Web site: www.theaterofthesea.com

A dolphin facility since 1946, it offers structured swims with dolphins as well as sea lions in an ocean lagoon. Thirty minutes of swim is preceded by thirty minutes of class instruction. Cats are as much a part of this dolphin center as dolphins. The community cats, which visitors are prohibited from touching, daily visit the dolphins who rise out of the water for a kiss and a feline nose rub. Dolphins: one hour, about $135; sea lions, one hour: $90.

Dolphins Plus P.O. Box 2728, Key Largo, FL 33037. 305-451-1993 (tel). E-mail: info@dolphinsplus.com; Web site: www.pennekamp.com/dolphins.plus

In Key Largo, Dolphins Plus sponsors two-hour structured swims in an ocean pool. Children under thirteen must be accompanied by an adult; thirteen- to seventeen-year-olds are allowed in the water alone, but an accompanying adult must observe them.

Wild swims (with snorkels provided) last thirty minutes, and are preceded by a one-hour briefing. Minimum age is eight.

All participants must be confident swimmers, comfortable in deep water, understand English, and not be pregnant.

Island Dolphin Care, Inc. P.O. Box 2728, Key Largo, FL 33037. 305-451-5884 (tel). E-mail: fonzie@islanddolphincare.org; Web site: www.islanddolphincare.org

Island Dolphin Care, Inc. is a nonprofit dolphin-assisted therapy center associated with Dolphins Plus. Programs run throughout the year.

The Human Dolphin Institute   118 Treasure Palms Drive, Panama City Beach, FL 32408. 850-234-7019 (tel); 850-234-6748 (fax). E-mail: info@human-dolphin.org; Web site: www.human-dolphin.org

"Dolphins will share with you what you expect of them," is the institute's slogan, which expresses the belief that respect is primary in any interaction with wild dolphins. Encounter wild bottlenose dolphins off Shell Island, Florida, after observing to see if they are "hunting, courting, nursing, or teaching their young"; and be relaxed enough to swim with them. One- and three-day programs; internships offered for serious students of dolphins.

The Human Dolphin Institute sponsors Advanced Dolphin Seminars, an in-depth intensive two-day program for those who have already swum with dolphins. This is a combination lecture/meditation/tai chi/energy work program with lots of time spent swimming with dolphins. Two days: about $600, includes lodging, all meals, and tuition.

In conjunction with the Med-Medicine Research Institute, they invite you to join a five-day marine biology course, Biology of the Sea, studying marine organisms off Panama City Beach.

The Child Empowerment Program enables children to find themselves with dolphins: 231-237-9360 (tel/fax).

Dolphin Research Center   58901 Overseas Highway, Grassy Key, FL 33050-6019. 305-289-1121 (tel). E-mail: DRC@dolphins.org.; Web site: www.dolphins.org

Since 1988, the Dolphin Research Center has been a not-for-profit research organization dedicated to enhancing understanding between marine mammals and humans. The center sponsors structured swims, Dolphin Encounter, with a forty-five minute preparatory workshop followed by twenty minutes in the Gulf of Mexico ocean lagoon with dolphins. A week-long, college-accredited Dolphin Lab with daily seminars and hands-on activities also is offered. Dolphin-assisted therapy is available, as well as sea lions and programs for children. Dolphin Encounter: $135, includes daylong admission.

Spirit of the Dolphin Journeys 133 East Gorgas Lane, Philadelphia, PA 19119. 800-414-7763 (toll free). E-mail: dolfun@dolphin-spirit.com; Web site: www.dolphin-spirit.com

Katryn Lavanture sponsors sensitive wild dolphin swims from a live-aboard boat forty miles off the Bahamas. Snorkel or dive. Lavanture emphasizes being informed and respectful of the dolphins at all times and open to learning whatever they have to teach, which includes, she says, "bliss." She welcomes people who have felt "the call" to swim with dolphins. An all-women summer solstice trip with a shiatsu practitioner is offered, along with Bodywork Bliss Week for men and women, with aquatic massage and acupuncture. Live-aboard, seven days: about $1,400–$1,600.

Living From Vision P.O. Box 1530, Stanwood, WA 98292. 800-758-7836 (toll free); 360-387-5713 (tel); 360-387-9846 (fax). E-mail: dolphinlove@sos.net; Web Site: www.livingfromvision.com

Ilona Selke and her husband Don Paris share their passion for dolphins on wild swims from a catamaran on a shallow sand bank off Key West, Florida. Half-day swims; on land, explore Key West. Snorkeling equipment provided. Four days, including lodging, meals, about $1,600.

Anima Mundi, Inc. P.O. Box 1060, Point Reyes, CA 94956. 415-663-1247 (tel); 415-663-8260 (fax). E-mail: penelope@animaltalk.net; Web site: www.animaltalk.net

Animal communicator Penelope Smith helps you understand what dolphins are saying as she connects telepathically with a pod of wild dolphins off the Bahamas. Swim daily, then rest for

Mother dolphins stay with their young for about three years. This juvenile accompanies his mother in a dive to deeper waters. (*M. Herko,* OAR/National Undersea Research Program, NOAA)

journalling or chatting with clinical psychologist Deborah Taj Anapol.

Trips are on a live-aboard ninety foot triple-deck motor catamaran. Seven days and nights, about $1,600.

Natural Habitat Adventures 2945 Center Green Court, Boulder, CO 80301. 800-543-8917 (toll free). E-mail: nathab@world net. att.net; Web site: www.nathab.com

Follow the pods—if the dolphins choose to check out your boat. Natural Habitats sponsors seven- and eight-day live-aboard cruises on a catamaran or a seventy-foot sailing schooner to spotted dolphin territory and natural swims off the Bahamas. Small groups are assisted by a team of research scientists. Swimming ability not required, but you must be comfortable in deep water.

Dolphinswim P.O. Box 8653, Santa Fe, NM 87504. 504-466-0579 (tel/fax). E-mail: Seaswim@bellsouth.net; Web site: www. seaswim.com

Fly the Air Bridge Flying Boat from Miami Harbor to Bimini Harbor in the Bahamas for five-day swims with wild dolphins. Daily trips return to beachfront lodging at the hotel where Ernest Hemingway wrote *Islands in the Stream*. Run by psychologist Rebecca Fitzgerald, each trip is preceded by a pre-breakfast meditation. Fitzgerald emphasizes the sensitivity of the wild swim. Five days: about $1,700. Dolphinswim also offers family programs.

Wildquest 800-326-1618 (toll free in U.S.); 561-731-1909 (outside U.S.). E-mail for reservations and information: wildquestre serv@mindspring.com, for administration: wildquest@sprynet. com;Web site: www.wildquest.com

For a metaphysical flavor to wild swims from a catamaran off the Bahamas, Wildquest sponsors Human-Dolphin Connection, six-day land-based swims. Some groups are accompanied by musicians or a storyteller; Quantum Light Breath teaches you new breathing techniques; Sacred Journey seeks out new energy levels and travels to a site thought to be the sunken Atlantis. The Goddess-Dolphin trip is for women only. Accommodations: shared house, two-to-a-room with private bath, common cooking/eating facilities. Swim with dolphins from catamaran day trips. Six days: $1,300–$1,400. Family and kids' trips offered, too.

OneLoveOneSpirit.com 877-677-1166 (toll free, Hawaii time: minus six hours from East Coast). E-mail: info@oneloveonespirit. com; Web site: www.oneloveonespirit.com

Off the Big Island of Hawaii, One Love One Spirit offers swims with wild spinner dolphins, Pacific spotted dolphins, and Pacific bottlenose dolphins. A variety of programs allows you to choose half- or full-day wild dolphin swims; week-long land-based wild swims; and week-long retreats, land-based shore swims with spiritual retreat. Swims with pilot whales, false killer whales, and, on rare occasions, orcas, also are offered. Seven-day retreats range from $1,700 to $2,500.

The Divine Dolphin Interlink 827, P.O. Box 02-5635, Miami, FL 33102. 305-443-0222 (tel); Or: Delfin Amor Eco Lodge, Apartado 92-Lodge 8150, Palmar Nortes, Osa Puntarenas, Costa Rica. +506 394-2632 (tel); +506 786-7636 (fax). E-mail: dolphins@ costarica.net; Web site: www.divinedolphin.com

At the Delfin Amor Eco Lodge, located in the rainforest and on the beaches of Drake Bay, Costa Rica, you can alternate days with dolphins with trips to the Corcovado National Park and Cano Island Marine Biological Reserve. "Ecoswims" are with wild dolphins. Call for details.

Anthony's Key Resort Roatan, Honduras. For reservations call 504-445-1327; for information call Bahia Tours 800-227-3483 (toll free). E-mail: Akr@anthonyskey.com; Web site: www. anthonyskey.com

On Roatan Island in Honduras, Anthony's Key Resort, a collection of bungalows and a restaurant on the beach next door to the Roatan Institute of Marine Services, offers weeklong dolphin-centered vacations. You can dive on forty-five-minute natural swims with dolphins and a dolphin behaviorist; snorkel with them on thirty-minute swims; or observe dolphins, while listening to lectures, and interact with them at the Institute. Dolphin dive: about $112.

Special programs for youths thirteen and up are available, along with a weeklong dolphin summer camp for children five to fourteen. About $600. Passport and dive certification required.

Dolphin Camp   1654 Hamlet Chapel Road, Pittsboro, NC 27312. 800-451-2562 (toll free); 919-542-1332 (tel); 919-542-2148 (fax). Web site: www.dolphin.com

Mayan Dolphin Expedition is a week in the Yucatan spending part of each day in the water, snorkeling or swimming with wild dolphins; the rest, hiking, exploring ruins, and doing meditation or Tai Chi. Eight days: about $2,300.

Dolphin Camp offers programs for teens fourteen to eighteen; and adults over eighteen at the Cheeca Resort Lodge in the middle Keys, Florida. Six-day programs include mind-body reconnection, awareness skills, and communication with dolphins on land, with daily dolphin swims in a lagoon or from a catamaran in the blue ocean. About $2,200.

Delphines Centre   P.O. Box 87, Russell 0255, New Zealand. +64 (0) 9-403-81-63-025-759-733 (tel/fax). E-mail: Mhdelphines@compuserve.com; Web site: www.dolphinswim.com

Share chores and keep watch from the decks of a fifty-foot sailing trimaran until dolphins come to check you out. Meanwhile, listen to lectures, watch dolphin videos from a fish-eye camera that takes film during the day, meditate; eat delicious vegetarian food. Live-aboard. Four days NZ $900; five days NZ $1,125.

Polperro Dolphin Swims   P.O. Box 11, Blairgowrie VIC 3942, Australia. +64 (0)3-5988-8437 (tel); +64 (0)3-5988-8734 (fax). E-mail: crew@polperro.com.au; Web site: www.polperro.com.au

If you are in Australia and want a professional, safe day-swim with wild bottlenose dolphins, try this company. Three- to four-hour trips leave twice a day; snorkeling gear provided. Polperro is a two-decades-old company devoted to protecting marine environment and dolphins.

Wild and Free P.O. Box 5872, Forres, IV36 1WA, Scotland, UK. +44(0)207-691-9447 (tel/fax).

In the warm, clear waters of the Red Sea, on the east Egyptian side of the Sinai Peninsula, Wild and Free oversees natural swims with a dolphin mother and babe that live off the coast of a small Bedouin village. Stay in a five-star Hilton or in beach huts; scuba, camel trek, or do yoga when you're not swimming with the dolphins.

Dolphin Reef Eilat Southern Beach, P.O. Box 104, Eilat 88.100, Israel. +972(0)8-637-1846 E-mail: info@dolphinreef.co.il

"We do not always touch them," is the slogan of this dolphin center located on the clear Red Sea. Sensitive dives with wild dolphins are one-hour long; snorkel trips are thirty minutes, preceded by a thirty-minute briefing. You must be in good health and respect the dolphins.

Snorkel trips go in groups of four, require experienced snorkelers, and swimmers comfortable in forty-five-foot-deep water. Equipment can be rented.

Passport and dive certification required.

Earthwatch Institute 3 Clocktower Place, Suite 100, P.O. Box 75, Maynard, MA 01754. 800-776-0188 (toll free). E-mail: info@earthwatch.org; Web site: www.earthwatch.org

If structured or wild dolphin swims are not enough for you, and you would like to put your compassion to work, join Dr. Randy Wells in Sarasota, Florida, as a volunteer fieldworker. At the Mote Marine Laboratory there, you can work on the only study in the world that is collecting detailed data on a free-ranging dolphin population. Work in the water off Sarasota, netting wild dolphins to be weighed, measured, and recorded.

In Hawaii, join Dr. Louis Herman and Dr. Adam Pack at the

Seeing dolphins arrive willing to play is a lovely sight. (*NOAA*)

Dolphin Institute in their studies to understand dolphin intelligence and the mysteries of their echolocation. During the two-week program, you get to know individual mammals very well from boats and the lab. Some participants cry when their expedition is over; many return every year.

In Kaikoura Peninsula, New Zealand, marine mammal biologist Dr. Bernd Wursig is conducting a long-term study that examines the effects of tourism on dolphins. From boats, volunteers photograph dolphins and record their sounds with a hydrophone. From a steep limestone cliff, they record dolphin interactions with tour boats.

Lodging for all programs is in shared houses; you help cook. Two weeks about $2,000, plus airfare.

MANATEES

Manatees not only look like children's cuddly stuffed animals, they act like them. Slow and big, with tiny eyes and poor hearing, manatees are often the victims of motor boaters in shallow fresh waters near mangrove swamps—accidents that frequently orphan manatee babies and leave the majority of adult manatees with terrible scars. A large number die each year from boat accidents, or from being cold or lost.

At the Dolphin Research Center at Grassy Key, Florida, a manatee appeared one day, completely dehydrated from a long swim in salt water. For twenty-four hours, lab assistants pumped fresh water into its body through a hose inserted in its throat. Despite their massive presence, manatees evoke feelings of protectiveness in adults and children alike.

Earthwatch Institute 3 Clocktower Place, Suite 100, P.O. Box 75, Maynard, MA 01754. 800-776-0188 (toll free). E-mail: info@ earthwatch. org; Web site: www.earthwatch.org

In Florida, Marine mammal biologists Dr. John Reynolds and Teresa Kessenich are addressing the problem of manatees and boats in Pansy Bayou, near Sarasota. From a boat, you can help the scientists scan waters for manatees, record their identifying scars, and track individual manatees to find out what adaptations—if any—they have developed to avoid boats or to change their habitat.

In Belize in the Drowned Cayes, marine scientists Kathryn LaCommare and Caryn Self Sullivan are tracking manatees to understand how they live. You can help video, photograph, and record data, as well as use a GPS to map the Cayes.

Both projects will produce information to help governments make policies to help manatees. Lodging is homestyle; two weeks, about $2,000.

WHALES

Swimming with whales is a lot different from watching them from a boat. Whales, like dolphins, leave those who experience them in their natural habitat with a deep sense of respect and reverence. Humpback whales gather north of the Dominican Republic to mate each year. Underwater, whale song is beautiful and eerie; some have described it as the voice of angels. Because of whales' vast size, humans are advised to wear scuba gear and to be comfortable in the water.

The Divine Dolphin Interlink 827, P.O. Box 02-5635, Miami, FL 33102. 305-443-0222 (tel). E-mail: dolphins@costarica.net; Web site: www.divinedolphin.com

On a live-aboard catamaran trip off Silver Banks in the Dominican Republic, Divine Dolphin offers an experience with humpback whales. In this breeding ground, you can observe them, listen to them sing, and, if they permit, go on brief swims with them.

Divine Awakenings 10788 North 104th Place, Scottsdale, AZ 85259. 602-234-6111 (tel).Web site: www.divineawakenings. com

For seven days off the Silver Banks of Dominican Republic, live aboard a boat and immerse yourself in humpback whales, including swims when possible. Your guide is a certified hynotherapist and intuitive healer. Seven days, about $2,500.

Anima Mundi, Inc. P.O.Box 1060, Point Reyes, CA 94956. 415-663-1247 (tel); 415-663-8260 (fax). E-mail: Penelope@animal talk.net;Web site: www.animaltalk.net

Swim with whales and join Penelope Smith as she communicates with whales (whales are the leaders; dolphins, the messengers, she believes) on the live-aboard ninety-foot catamaran, *Bottom Line II*, off the coast of the Dominican Republic. One week, about $2,400.

A mountain lion considers his options, Tucson, Arizona.
(*Roger Archibald*)

WEB SITES

www.nmfs.noaa.gov is the Web site of the National Marine
Fisheries Service of NOAA, which publishes information about
marine mammals around the world. Also contains rules for approaching mammals in the wild.

www.idw.org is the Web site of the International Dolphin Watch, a nonprofit membership organization, and its director, Dr. Horace Dobbs, of Cambridge University.

www.wspa-americas.org The Web site of the World Society for the Protection of Animals, an international federation of animal welfare organizations, which rescues individual animals at risk around the world.

www.livingfromvision.com Ilona Selke's Web site.

www.aquathought.com The site of the Aquathought Foundation.

www.dolphinear.com has a lot of information on dolphins.

www.tursi.yiffco.com/dolphins is another dolphin Web site.

Chapter 5
Vision Quests

The real vision has to come out of your own juices. It's not a dream; it's very real. It hits you sharp and clear like an electric shock.

—John Lame Deer

In the Native American tradition, vision quests are a calling received by youths in their early teens to spend time alone, fasting, in the wilderness, until they meet with the spirit who will be their guide for life. Sometimes the quester, weakened by hunger, must wait a very long time before the spirit vision appears; sometimes the quester falls seriously ill and is called to be a shaman.

That's a pure vision quest, a bedrock part of the culture of several Native American tribes. New Spirituality vision quests are different, modified to "adapt to contemporary life styles." Never grounded in traditional religion, they developed about thirty years ago out of a union between transpersonal psychology (losing the ego) and wilderness trekking.

In the early 1970s, before the environmental movement was organized, a handful of Americans who had had their own significant and deeply spiritual experiences alone in the wilderness decided to share them with others. About the same time, therapists who identified in their patients the telltale signs of *missing* rites of passage—a prevailing sense of being a ghost in their own lives, lacking authenticity, not knowing where to go

125

next—saw the value of the combination of wilderness isolation, as practiced in many primitive rites of passage, and the support of the safety network of group therapy.

ENTER THE VISION QUEST

Today the two are combined in what is known as the vision quest, vision fast, or other names; but the structure remains uniform: preparatory guidance, the solo wilderness experience for a few days and nights, then the guided return to a group of fellow questers and the sharing of experiences. Uniting with the stars, rivers, the ocean, rocks, animals, insects, birds, thunder and lightning exposes the quester to his own vulnerability as well as to his genuine power. Add fasting, solitude, and gentle therapy, and profound changes in the human psyche occur.

More and more people are turning to vision quests from what seems to be a universal fulcrum of change, rather than a personal one. Many people do more than one quest a year; and some companies offer longer quests and the opportunity to become a trainer.

Change Is Certain

In *The Spiritual Quest*, Robert M. Torrance points out that rites of passage and the vision quest are two separate ceremonies in Native America. The vision quest is far more dangerous because the outcome is unknown. Participants in a rite of passage ceremony know exactly what will happen when they go back to the tribe: they will be an adult or a bride or a groom or a warrior or a parent. But in the vision quest, the arrival of the vision is a wily and unpredictable thing; in fasting, the ego dissolves; and the quester can return significantly changed.

It is the same for the contemporary quester. Exposed to the weather, challenged by monotony, ridding him—or herself of the useless aspects of the daily ego, the vision quester often meets himself for the first time. Returning to the community, questers may find themselves so changed that they quit their jobs, leave their lovers, change their diet, reorganize their whole selves in a completely different way. And the change continues.

"People definitely noticed a change in me," said Steve Armstrong, who did an ocean quest in Newfoundland. "There's an awful lot to this process. It's dynamic. I go back to my vision again and again, and there's always a new aspect of it I didn't see before, a new meaning that becomes evident. As I grow, it grows."

ACT ONE: PREPARATION

Your preparation begins the moment you decide to go, because that's when you focus seriously on what aspects of your life experience you want to change. Once you've paid the fee to hold your place, your guide sends you advice on how to prepare yourself for what is really an enormous internal journey. He or she also sends information on the nuts and bolts of the quest.

You spend three or four days at the retreat center where you meet your guides and the other members of your group. Groups are always small; some have a maximum of ten.

Your fellow participants will come from different places—psychologically, spiritually, geographically. "I had divorced after an eighteen-year marriage," said one. "Just shaking loose from the habits that my wife and I had developed was the hardest thing for me. I had to face in another direction, but I did not know where."

Vision quests are excellent for people who are in a life transition: before getting married or after the death of someone close; or before changing careers or simply moving to a new locale. One woman who was being treated for cancer went on a vision quest, because, she said, "I couldn't stand being a *sick* person

If you take a vision quest in the Southwest, big-horned sheep may come to check you out. (*Roger Archibald*)

anymore. Doctors, nurses, even my own family looked on me just as someone who was sick. Inside, my spirit felt well. I didn't get rid of the cancer," she said. "But I came back a warrior."

Because they provide distance on problems, quests attract CEOs eager to reconnect to what's really important. Parents who need to get away from the combat zone of life with teenagers, and teenagers eager to test their own mettle benefit equally from vision quests. Some go to cure addictions or sort out early childhood problems. "My family endured a devastating series of tragedies in my childhood, and my goal was to reclaim what I had lost," said one quester. "I didn't expect a resolution at that time," he said of his quest. "I was looking for instructions on how to embark on a healing path. I got exactly what I needed."

More and more, people are going on quests because they suf-

Saying goodbye before the solo is a critical moment. (*Awen Journeys,* www.andsoitbegan.com)

fer from a spiritual pain that is non-local and all-pervasive. They feel the need to reconnect with the spirit.

"Ask yourself: What parts of your life do you want to bury? Who are you? Who are your allies? What are the demons in your life?" asks Jy Chiperzak of Awen Journeys. Guides help you establish a myth or a story that exemplifies you, and often encourage you to bring your own spiritual objects, which you take on the solo part of your quest. Some teach you how to build a gate to go through, a fence to protect you, and a path by which to go back.

In addition to psychological counseling, mental focusing, and spiritual preparation, guides instruct you in the pleasures and perils of the outdoor terrain; and the nuts and bolts of how to camp, if necessary; how to fast; and how to be in nature. Many teach low-impact camping and the ethics of the wilderness.

Some companies call the fast optional, and certainly waive it if you have dietary restrictions or health problems. Others recommend a light fast, with a few nuts and fruits.

But a total fast packs a powerful punch. The biochemical

changes created by complete fasting facilitate your own "vision." Denying the body food and comfort speeds up access to the *theta* state, a level of meditation in which dreams and memories blend. Food is everywhere in our culture and binds us together socially. Armstrong said, "I particularly use food and drink to distract myself, and not having it—or any other distractions—is what made the quest work."

Providers also address your fears. Questers' biggest pre-solo fears are wild animals. One woman said she was too embarrassed to ask about her fear of mountain lions. "I mean, it sounded like such a naive question when you're supposed to be focusing on the big things, like spirit," she said. When she finally did ask, the guide laughed, and said. "Don't worry, the place you're going is too high for mountain lions."

"'Too *high*?'" I said. "*Then* all I worried about was mountain sickness!"

Safety on the solo is almost *the* prime concern of providers, and no provider is going to flex a macho muscle and send you to the lions' den. Oddly, many questers report that fear of wild beasts is the first fear to go—alone in the wild, animals begin to look like friends.

Just being alone outdoors can be a big challenge for some. Guides give advice about sleeping outdoors or setting up tents, as well as instruction on how to handle emergencies. Often they pass out whistles that can be heard at base camp. They also arrange buddy systems, in which questers leave some sign (a stone, for example) at an agreed-upon place, to indicate that all is well. Finally, guides station themselves around the solo sites to ensure safety.

The help and attention in the process of affecting specific change within your own private drama distinguishes the vision quest from a solo backpacking wilderness trek. Unlike a backpacker, you have psychological guidance from the beginning. You stay in one place, called your sacred place or power place. And, unlike most backpackers, who spend an inordinate amount of time thinking about, preparing, and relishing food, you fast. Solo backpackers might report unusual experiences, but they don't have the luxury of therapists and fellow questers with whom to discuss them.

When it's time for the solo, wilderness guides take you to the place where you choose your solo site. You visit the site and decide where to construct your sacred space.

Then you go.

ACT TWO: THE SOLO

Being ferried out shortly after dawn to an island off Newfoundland, quester Steve Armstrong said he felt "a hundred percent fear, with the absolute knowledge that there's no turning back. The only thing I could do was to put my trust in the process and let go. Believe me, heading out to a place of discomfort with only water and something to keep the mosquitoes off you at night keeps you very focused on the physical realities!"

What you do on your solo is your secret. Some report that they sing or shout or recite poetry or perform rituals or dance or go naked or hide in some shelter. As the biochemical effects of the fast begin, your focus becomes more internal and intense. The relationship to nature changes. Trees seem to talk, insects observe, birds bring messages, the wind speaks. You become a part of the landscape. "Many people report that they feel the earth is breathing *through* them, that each of their senses is one with the earth," says John Milton. "It's not just an *intellectual* ecological interconnectedness," he says. "It's the true experience."

The Magic Night

Many companies schedule the solo as close as possible to the full moon. Your guide may suggest staying awake all night on the final night to listen to whatever spiritual message might be around you. Something usually happens on this night. "I went someplace," said a woman who said she considered herself

The solo is an excellent time for contemplation, self-examination, and simple revelation.

(*School of Lost Borders*, www.schooloflostborders.com)

grounded in reality. "I entered a zone I did *not* operate in on a daily basis."

Some questers have visions of the dead. "Was it real or was it Memorex?" asked Lorna Tychostop, recalling a vision quest in New York. "I was lying there in my sacred circle, dozing, when suddenly there's my grandmother. My grandmother had been the family scourge. She lived with us, and we never got along. But there she was. She didn't actually speak, but I heard her say, 'I forgive you.' I just broke into tears and said, 'I forgive you, too!'"

Visions of the supernatural occur. One quester, trying to

Things happen on the final night of the solo if you are willing to let them. (*Roger Archibald*)

sleep on impossibly sharp rocks, dozed, he said, four times one night. On one of his dozes, a huge man appeared, lifted him up, and carried him into a cave where he laid him on a bed of sweet-smelling sage and told him he would be all right. The quester slept like a babe.

Make Sure It's the Right Time for Your Quest

If you are well-prepared, focused, and feeling well, your solo territory becomes your place in the universe. But it's not a walk in the park. It takes a lot of concentration. "My period came on the second day of my solo," a woman remembered of her quest in New England. "It was cold, it started to rain, I didn't feel well, and I just didn't want to be there."

On a quest in the southwestern high desert, a participant who had never been out of New York City panicked and ditched the solo. The provider, who had gone into town to buy provisions for the final feast, was surprised to bump into him at the shopping mall. The ex-quester apologized and said he simply couldn't do the solo. "I gave him a lift back to the center where we talked. The solo failed, but the therapy worked," said the provider. "He called later to say he had changed his life to reduce his unreal level of stress."

ACT THREE: INCORPORATION

> *You do not have to be good.*
> *You do not have to walk on your knees*
> *for a hundred miles through the desert, repenting.*
> *You have only to let the soft animal of your body*
> *love what it loves.*
>
> —Mary Oliver, *Dream Work*

Coming down from a solo can take a few days. This is considered the incorporation, and is probably the most important aspect of the quest, when you integrate your experience in such a way that you can bring it back to your communities. "You have to have witnesses to manifest your vision in the real world," said quester Steve Armstrong. "Otherwise it stays locked up in you and goes nowhere."

When questers regroup, either at base camp or at the retreat center, they tell their stories and listen to others' stories; and guides help them bring their new realities into focus. "Very often they have undergone an incredible experience that they won't recognize because it was too deep to be immediately assimilated," says John Milton. "One man reported that a mountain lion had stared into his eyes, then walked away. He came out without immediately realizing what an extraordinary transformation came with that experience."

Coming face-to-face with the wilderness can be a beautiful thing, as on this island of Bloody Gulch in Newfoundland. (*Awen Journeys*, www.andsoitbegan.com)

Some providers end the experience in a group sweat lodge or a dip in hot springs; others celebrate the return with a big feast (at which you might not be able to eat much); or hold a Council of Elders before which you summarize your experience. Understanding what happened to you is tremendously important; that's why it's imperative to stick around for Act Three.

The Return to Reality

> *To complete the heroic journey, the returning hero must survive the impact of the world.*
>
> —Steven Foster with Meredith Little, *The Book of the Vision Quest: Personal Transformation in the Wilderness*

Back home, reintegration takes a little while. Some companies (in California) hold monthly meetings for former questers to reinforce the benefits. *You* may have changed, but your life is probably the same. One woman said she thought her whole DNA was changed. "I actually dragged a mattress out into the backyard to sleep under the stars," said a woman after her first vision quest. "My kids woke me up the next morning, leaning out the window, yelling, *'Mom*, what are you *doing?'*"

"If they have gone deep," says Milton, "Spirit and Mother Earth will give them guidance."

You Should Know

Safety is a prime consideration, and guides spend a lot of time talking about it. Beyond a few scrapes and cuts, the record is good for solos. To minimize problems, one provider limits solo questers to their own 108-pace perimeter.

- You will be asked to sign a disclaimer and encouraged to carry your own insurance.
- You can take water with you on the solo.
- Diabetics and those with hyperglycemia or other dietary restrictions are not expected to fast.
- Backpacking equipment can be rented, if not supplied by the provider. You need it if you camp out at base camp; and if the weather is bad, for your solo; but this load is very light if you fast. Nearly all companies stress that you do not need any prior backpacking experience. In fact, some take the time to teach ecological camping practices.
- You do not have to be in great physical shape. Some companies hike from the retreat center to the base camp, about four or five miles. You can probably bum a ride, or join a group that drives to base camp, if needed.
- Preparatory information—some of it found in manuals specially prepared for that company—includes practical

advice on what to bring, such as insect repellant, sun lotion, and water.

- Generally, the advice is to travel light, physically, psychologically, emotionally. Have no expectations. Go from the heart. Go from your own need.

School of Lost Borders   P.O. Box 55, Big Pine, CA 93513. 760-938-3027 (fax). E-mail: lostbrdrs@telis.org; Web site: www.school oflostborders.com

Steven Foster and Meredith Little wrote the book on vision quests, both literally (*The Book of Vision Quests*) and figuratively: roughly eighty-five percent of the companies currently in the vision quest business had their start at the School of Lost Borders in Big Pine, California.

Begun in 1975 to train people in "initiatory and field therapy," it is now considered to be the "oldest wilderness initiation school in the U.S."

Coming out of the cultural revolution in the 1960s, Foster and Little supported the belief that "true revolution will never come about until the children find a way to get to true adulthood, and the adults have a way to attain true elderhood and death. And none of this can ever come to pass until we learn the ancient art of birthing people via rites of passage in wild nature, our true home."

Situated on the eastern slope of the 14,000-foot Sierra Nevadas, the School of Lost Borders has helped thousands "cross borders into new lives": the borders of limitations, civilization, psyche, mind, and spirit. The school teaches "the simple truth that it is supremely good for us humans to find our way down to the thundering sacred river and then to jump as high as we can."

Foster and Little retired as emeriti in 2002 and passed the key to Joseph Lazenka and Emerald North.

School of Lost Border's Vision Fasts are eleven days with a four-night solo reached from base camps near Big Pine, and in

Death Valley. The importance of "an empty belly and a bare minimum of equipment" is emphasized to evoke a deeper introspection. $650.

The Vision Fast Training Program is graduated from two days (with a twenty-four-hour solo fast) to four weeks (with a four-day solo fast and the prerequisite of a two-week vision fast). Two days: $350; ten days: $700; fourteen days: $850; twenty-eight days: $1,700.

The School of Lost Borders also has trained guides in Europe: In North Wales, Pippa Bondy gives vision fasts in the mountains, twice a year. Eleven days £500. E-mail: pippa.bondy@virgin.net.

In Austria, Tuscany, Crete, as well as Granada and Namibia, Franz P. Redl and his assistants give vision fasts. Ten days: between 550 and 700 Euros, plus room and board. E-mail: franz.redl@net way.at

Sacred Passage & The Way of Nature Fellowship Drawer CZ, Bisbee, AZ 85603. 877-818-1881 (toll free); 520-432-7353 (tel/fax). E-mail: sacred@primenet.com; Web site: www.sacred way.com

"The vision quest is the oldest spiritual path on earth, as much as fifty thousand years," says John P. Milton of Sacred Passages. If the vision quest has a direct legatee, it is Milton, who made his first solo quest at the age of seven, has two degrees in ecology, has been an adviser to presidents on the environment and a Woodrow Wilson scholar, and who prefers to give vision quests to genuine seekers.

Probably the only vision quest trainer *not* trained by the School of Lost Borders, Milton developed his own Way of Nature Awareness Training, "opening the sacred view," based on his personal wilderness experiences and teachings from "Taoism, Native American Way, Shamanism, Buddhism, Tibetan Dzogchen, Tantra, Hindu Vedanta, and Christ Consciousness."

He actually owns twelve thousand of the acres on which he gives quests. These tracts and others are part of the Sacred Land

The surreal landscape in Death Valley, California, resembles ancient ruins or, in the moonlight, giant figures. (*Roger Archibald*)

Trust that Milton has established to protect land that otherwise would be subject to exploitation. His connection with the rest of the earth stretches around the world: his current programs are held in Baja California, Bali, Hawaii, the southern Colorado mountains, the Himalayas, the Appalachians, and Utah's Canyonlands.

Milton's programs have "an emphasis on communion with nature as a path toward liberation." At a deep level, Milton says, "we are all pure Source awareness by simply being." After his quests, he says, questers have the freedom to continue with "all the tools they need for true liberation."

Sacred Passages offers a wide variety of programs from Qi Gong and Gaia Flow weekend seminars to a forty-nine day "pure" vision quest, which he describes as a "stringent, severe process" modeled after Native American rites of passage and intended only for experienced questers. The quester spends twenty-eight days on a wilderness solo in southern Colorado, part of which is a five-night solo within an eight-foot mandala, naked, without food, water, shelter, movement, or sleep.

Five- to seven-day Nature-Quests are intended to help participants cultivate "internal energy" through Gaia Flow™, which uses Tai Chi, plus a variety of other skills, including tracking, shamanic invocation, and sacred sound immersion designed to "transform blocked emotions." It also includes a wilderness solo.

Twelve-day Sacred Passages is a traditional vision quest with a seven-day solo. Milton does not enforce fasting, but encourages a short fast. Bring your own simple foods, he advises, as well as your own sleeping bag and tent. Depending on location, the cost is between $990 and $1,260.

Milton also offers two intensive guide trainings: Intermediate (forty-nine days with a twenty-eight-day wilderness solo); and Advanced (108 days, with a forty-four-day wilderness solo). His international pilgrimages at places around the world, last three to four months, with four to five hours a day training, eight hours practice, and long and extreme solos. This is for the experienced and hardy only.

Circles of Air, Circles of Stones   P.O. Box 48, Putney, VT 05346. 802-387-6624 (tel). E-mail: Sparrow@together.net; Web site: www.circles-of-air.com

Sparrow Hart, a trained counselor and wilderness expert, began giving guided vision quests in Vermont in 1988 after he was certified at the School of Lost Borders. His gift, he says, "is the extent to which I can help you find your own voice, your own truth, your authenticity. There is no greater tragedy than a life unlived."

Hart offers ten-day vision quests in New Mexico, Vermont, and Death Valley, California, with four days preparation, four days solo fast, and two days incorporation, with emphasis on "owning the lessons learned" in the solo. Cost: $650 if you register a month or more in advance; $700 thereafter.

Hart created the unique Mythic Warrior program for men who feel they were "underfathered and overmothered." Offered on serial weekends over nine months at a retreat center in the Berkshires in Massachusetts, this program incorporates sacred rituals, holotropic breathwork, the wilderness with solo quests, and many other interesting techniques.

Awen Journeys Jy and Gail Chiperzak, Burnside, Newfoundland A0G 1KO. 709-677-2331 (tel). Web site: www.andsoitbe gan.com

Jy and Gail Chiperzak live on "the edge of Squid Tickle on Bonavista Bay" in Newfoundland, about as close to nature as you can get. A victim of chronic fatigue syndrome that took the life out of his life for seven years, Jy studied at the School of Lost

Gail and Jy Chiperzak, vision quest guides. (*Awen Journeys*)

Borders and has been giving vision quests, or Troscads (Celtic ritual fasts), since 1996 in the remote Atlantic Gulch and Bloody Islands. Named for battles between the Beothuks and Europeans five hundred years ago, the islands are now home to birds, insects, rocks, and ghosts.

Jy and Gail give a four-day preparation, four-day fast on the island, then a two-day incorporation with "witnessing" to lock in your vision. When possible, the group takes part in a Celtic sweatlodge, whose ceremony, Jy says, came to him in a dream. Ten days: $750. They also offer a quest in Caprock Canyon, Texas. "A place," says Jy, with "amazing power and intimacy," that is "touched by the spirit of the desert sun and wind." Cost: $700; a three-day ocean retreat canoe journey to islands in Bonavista Bay, $300.

Animas Valley Institute   54 Ute Pass Trail, Durango, CO 81301. 800-451-6327 (toll free); 970-259-0589 (tel/fax). E-mail: soulcraft@animas.org; Web site: www.animas.org

Bill Plotkin, an associate of the School of Lost Borders and a depth psychologist, has been offering vision quests, life transition, and rites of passage programs for twenty years.

Animas Valley incorporates deep ecology, depth psychology, and the teachings of Carl Jung, James Hillman, Thomas Moore, Joseph Campbell, Jean Houston, among others; and offers Soulcraft™, a set of forty experiential practices and wilderness-based ceremonies that are designed to uncover the true soul.

Vision quests are eleven days, with five days of preparation at retreat centers in the Four Corners area of Colorado and the Utah Canyonlands; three days solo fast; and three days incorporation which includes an empowering one-on-one session with a professional mentor. Some quests hike from the center to spend five days at base camp, carry a forty-five pound pack two to three miles before the solo. Guide fee $1,125, plus $280 lodging and meals at the center.

Also offers quests for German-speakers.

Wilderness Rites 1257 Siskiyou Boulevard, #1172, Ashland, OR 97520. 541-512-1739 (tel). E-mail: astine@wildernessrites. com; Web site: www.wildernessrites.com

Wilderness Rites teaches, in addition to more ephemeral things before the solo, how to practice minimal-impact camping and wilderness ethics. Their ten-day quest in Death Valley, California, begins with a pre-preparatory meeting one week before leaving, includes a two- to four-night solo fast, and ends with incorporation ceremonies with a council of elders and storytelling. One of their guides is a physician. Ten days, $725.

Wilderness Rites has apprenticeship programs in wilderness rites of passage, applied ecopsychology, and earth-based healing practices, which offer six to thirty-six continuing education credits (CEUs).

If you live near San Rafael or Petaluma, California, you can drop in on their monthly follow-up sessions, offered to all who have taken a vision quest.

Vision Quest Wilderness Passage 201 San Antonio Circle, #212, Mountain View, CA 94040. 650-306-8188 (tel) Web site: www.lifepassage.com

Transpersonal psychologists Brian Winkler and Chayim Barton, who share twenty years' experience as vision quest guides, offer a seven-day vision quest, with a three-day solo fast in Mount Shasta or Joshua Tree National Monument, California. The price includes a one-day pre-preparation meeting a week before and a sixty-five-page manual developed for vision questers. Doctors Winkler and Barton work with individuals and the group as a whole in dreamwork, Eastern meditation, and Jungian symbology. Seven days: $725, includes some meals.

Rites of Passage P.O. Box 2061, Santa Rosa, CA 95405. 707-537-1927 (tel). E-mail: mikeb@ritesofpassagevisionquest.org; Web site: www.ritesofpassagevisionquest.org

"We are not separate from the rest of creation. The loss of nature has meant losing part of our own soul," says Michael Bodkin, executive director of Rites of Passage, as well as a marriage and family therapist and certified vision quest guide from the School of Lost Borders.

Rites of Passage offers quests in the Owlshead Mountains near Death Valley, California, "home of coyote, redtail hawk, and very shy cougar." You hike a mile to base camp for preparation before your three-day solo fast. Then incorporate back at base camp. Seven days: $650.

Rites of Passage also offers all-women quests, as well as ongoing reinforcement meetings held twice a month in Santa Rosa.

Ojai Foundation 9739 Ojai-Santa Paula Road, Ojai, CA 93023. 805-646-8343 (tel); 805-646-2456 (fax). E-mail: contact@ojaifoun dation.org; Web site: www.ojaifoundation.org

The Ojai Foundation, an intentional and educational community, emphasizes family, community, and relationship to each other and the earth. It offers a nine-day vision fast in eastern Arizona, The Land of the First People, located in the high desert. Nine days includes camping, ceremonies, campfire stories; three-day solo fast; and incorporation with a sweatlodge: $600.

Jesse Jessup and Amber McIntyre, who guide a couples' trip to South Africa with Ojai Foundation, also offer a nine-day vision quest in the Cedarburg Mountains in South Africa, with a three-day solo fast under the full moon. Amber is a native South African. The quest includes ceremony, storytelling, and fire circles: South African Rand 2,800 (about $250). 9739 Ojai-Santa Pula Road, Ojai, CA 93023. 805-640-902 (tel). E-mail: contact@ transformativejourneys.com; Web site: www.transformativejour neys. com

Charles Tilt 1150 West 17th Street; Eugene, OR 97402. E-mail: ctilt@govisionquest.com; Web site: www.govisionquest.com

An alumnus of School of Lost Borders, Tilt offers seven-day vision quests at Lava Camp Lake in McKensie Pass, near Bend,

Think twice before entering the spirit world, cautions this living-tree sculpture on Calvert Island, British Columbia. (*Roger Archibald*)

Oregon, with a three-day solo fast at Squaw Creek North, near the Oregon town of Sisters. Bring your own food and camping equipment; cost $375.

Tilt also offers a five-day program for youths fourteen to twenty with a one-night solo; also learn camping skills. Cost $175.

Three Hawks Quests   8 Jefferson Avenue, Takoma Park, MD 20912. 301-270-1022 (tel). E-mail: info@ThreeHawkQuests.com; Web site: www.threehawkquests.com

Three Hawk Quests offers seven-day camping vision quests with "drumming, dreamwork, sweatlodge, dialogues with nature, guided imagery," and other techniques, plus camping skills and a three-night solo fast. Quest sites are near Sperryville, Virginia, and Ithaca, New York. Seven days: $650; the company also offers a sliding scale for the fee based on income.

TO LEARN MORE

Read: *The Book of the Vision Quest: Personal Transformation in the Wilderness* by Steven Foster with Meredith Little (Several editions: Simon & Schuster, 1992.) About $12. Available from: Lost Borders Press, P.O. Box 55, Big Pine, CA 93513. 760-938-3027 (fax); E-mail: lostbrdrs@telis.org

The Sky Above, the Earth Below, a six-tape series recorded by John Milton in the Chiricahua Mountains in Arizona gives vision quest teachings and many "rare meditations." About $60. Available from: Sounds True, 800-333-9185 (toll free); Web sites: www.soundstrue.com. Also available from orders@sacredpassage.com, or 877-818-1881 (tel).

Chapter 6

Shamans

*At the present time the human race is out of touch with
Mother Earth, Father Heaven, and the natural world. . . .
There is great danger of fire, snowstorms, floods, and
earthquakes. For this reason, the shamans of the earth
need to work together to bring cleansing and healing to
the earth. . . . Because this cleansing and healing have not
been done, the present state of the earth is the root cause
of many problems and illnesses. This is the great work
that shamans are now required to do.*

—Manchurian shaman Byambadorj Dondog

Five millennia ago, Mayan priests in Mexico created a bafflingly
accurate calendar based on readings of distant galaxies and the
orbits of the smaller planets. The calendar ends abruptly on
December 21, 2012.

Native American Hopi elders, keepers of the prophecies said
to have been recorded several thousand years ago, warn of the
imminent "great day of purification," when a series of natural
catastrophes—volcanoes and earthquakes—in addition to another world war will bring sudden change to the earth. Violence
will be rampant. The only modification possible is if man "cor-
rects his treatment of nature and fellow man."

"There is an uncanny similarity among the indigenous inter-
preters who are revealing prophecies that have been kept secret until now," says Oscar Miro-Quesada, a Peruvian-born shaman.
He ticks off a few. "Peru and Bolivia have a prophecy of 'the age

of re-encounter'; the Mayan Fourth World, the Hopi Fifth World, the Dogon. It's an extraordinary overlap as we head toward 2012," he says.

Keepers of the secret knowledge now are fully as anxious to teach as members of non-shamanic societies are restless to learn, says Miro-Quesada. "We have a desire to weave together the emerging rainbow tribe or the global shamanic culture—one planet, healing the divisions between people, and between people and the natural world." Such an order is tall even for the United Nations. But it might be just the right size for shamans.

Who are shamans?

Anthropologists who have studied shamans around the world believe that shamans are the weavers of the sociological, psychological, spiritual, and political fabric of each culture, that their tradition is ancient, and that they are everywhere on earth. They move easily between what we call the reality of everyday life, and non-ordinary reality, the spirit world. They are the Tarot Magician, curing things that are hard to explain.

Shamans heal—mystically, herbally, or in combination—not just individual illnesses, but the whole enchilada: fever, family, community, tribe, locus, earth. Because shamans journey to the past, the future, to other places on earth, as well as to the realms of the spirits, they can bring back the spiritual balm appropriate to the needs of injured minds, bodies, and souls.

Shamans—The Ultimate Ombudsmen

They are agents of change. Anthropologist Michael F. Brown, working with Aguaruna shamans in the Peruvian Amazon, observed that the messages brought back from the spirit world were not only practical, but political, as able to settle minor disputes as to marshal the warriors.

Because they are able to access invisible worlds, shamans can find miscreants, evildoers, sorcerers, causes of illness, lost souls, and the thoughts and plans of enemies. In parts of South America, they remove the "darts" of illness by sucking them out of the afflicted body; they cure pain by singing and blowing tobacco smoke in great noisy ejections. Throughout Africa, they dance, shaking their bells and whistles, sometimes masked or feathered like birds, sending up clouds of dust, and reciting the tribe's history, the ancestors' histories, the story of their present evil affliction. Their art creates harmony; their drumming and song reunite the troubled tribe with the rhythms of the natural world.

But can they heal us?

Our current global culture might appear to be connected by the internet, but it is hugely diverse, and we don't yet share a natural commons. Our technology feeds on change; we exhaust natural resources to maintain private pleasures. The speed needed to keep this lifestyle in orbit has given us the same desperate discipline as doctors in triage: save the best, let the hopeless go.

The message delivered by shamans now is that we have gone too far doing terrible things to each other and to the earth, and we need to celebrate our community, not our differences.

The warning lights are flashing red.

Shamans Are Back

Your heart is the thing that has to change,
and it's not going to change overnight.
—Hopi elder

In Peru, the Bolivia, the Brazilian Amazon, Ecuador, Mexico, South Korea, Russia, Siberia, Manchuria, and Tibet, shamans are busier than ever before. Historically, many were forced underground because they were persecuted by ruling religions or political regimes like communism. Soviet police would disguise themselves as sick strangers seeking a cure, travel to villages, ask for the shaman, then take him to the forest and shoot him. Now, slowly, rural shamans are bringing their practice back to the open in villages; around the world, urban or neo-shamans operate often as herbal healers in crowded cities, such as Seoul.

But interest among young members of the shaman community is at an all-time low. Ethnobotanist Mark Plotkin commented that in his first fifteen years of studying shamans in the Amazon, he was surprised to see that shamans were at least twice and sometimes three times as old as he was. "If the medical-savvy missionaries and government-sponsored nurses insisted that shamanism was a sham, why should the young pay

This rock art in remote Utah resembles shamanic art elsewhere in the world: the large hand and strange emanations from the tops of the heads of the figures imply a spiritual event. (*Roger Archibald*)

any attention to some great-grandfather who said otherwise?" Plotkin asks in his book, *Medicine Quest.*

Incentives to become shamans seem to be more alive in North America and the United Kingdom than in the Andes or the Amazon.

How Shamans Become Shamans

Traditionally, shamans are created by:

- inheriting skills from a parent, aunt, uncle, or grandparent;
- receiving a "calling." Typically, around puberty, they experience a life-threatening illness that leaves them changed; or they are struck by lightning; or endure a similar shock to the system that might create a near-death experience;
- being chosen to study with masters.

A traditional shaman, say anthropologists who have studied them for a century, spends his or her life as the medium between the invisible world of spirits, deities, the unseen present, and the future, and the daily realities of life in his community. He commits to a long time of study with a master teacher, and in the process, develops talents that are hard to codify. Constantly on call, he lives in a realm without earthly laws, governed by spiritual wisdom, which is often chaotic and messy.

In the trance, he can project his psyche into other life forms—large or small animals, trees, whatever—and "shape-shift," but only if it is necessary to his well-being. Some anthropologists believe that shape-shifting is simply an extension of the shaman's intense spiritual integration with the natural world.

Barbara Myerhoff witnessed, with another anthropologist, the gymnastic flight of a shaman in a trance, while she was studying the Huichol in Mexico in the 1960s. In the style of the digitalized flights performed by the warriors in the film, *Crouching Tiger, Hidden Dragon,* the shaman "leapt" across a waterfall at a height of several hundred meters, Myerhoff reported.

Do not try this at home. You need a teacher for every step of the shamanic way.

Are there shamans among us?

For twenty years, Constance Grauds was a happily married pharmacist. In her early forties, her life changed. As she writes in her book, *Jungle Medicine,* she found her career was getting stale, her marriage was falling apart, and she was plagued with migraine headaches. "I had no job, no job prospects, no marriage, no peace of mind, no faith," she said. Alone, without an income, and in bad health, she was diagnosed with cancer of the thyroid.

After a successful surgery, but dissatisfied with the coldness of western medicine, she turned to a lifelong interest in natural medicines. She formed the Association of Natural Medicine Pharmacists, and made a trip to the Peruvian Amazon rainforest. There, like many other travelers, she met a shaman. But when she got home, he came to her in a dream and whispered, "You have enough energy to become a shaman yourself."

Grauds went back, of course; and her subsequent ten-year apprenticeship led to a deep understanding of healing and the complexity of the process, which often demands a complete change of lifestyle. The first years of her apprenticeship were hard, she said—"rigorous *dietas* and *disciplinas."* But her master shaman was pleased and found in her—"an ordinary middle-aged Western woman and his only non-indigenous apprentice—someone to carry on his lineage of healing knowledge." Grauds says he calls her "'the blue-eyed White shaman who has become the spirit of the jungle.'" She adds, "Who would have thunk?"

Grauds' becoming a shaman was the result of the meshing of several life events, her own profession, and her willingness to risk everything to answer a call. It also was part of an apparent outreach program among some shamans to continue their knowledge. And their knowledge is complex. Some pharmaceutical companies, eager to collect the healing secrets from aging shamans, find that reducing their vines and herbs to chemical components mysteriously misses the magic ingredient.

Peruvian shaman, Don Agustin Rivas Vasquez, plays the pan-pipe.
(*Puma Shamanic Journeys,* www.spiritjourney.net)

Is everyone a potential shaman?

Not everyone feels the need to apprentice with a shaman, however. Stacy Bell, who has made several trips to study with Ecuadorean shamans with her husband, a sociology professor, says,

"I'm suspicious of North Americans who do [apprentice]. I think we have shamans in our culture here, and we need to figure out who they are and what makes them shamans, and try to cultivate those qualities." Bell believes we might have a lot to learn from Ecuadorean shamans, but asks if the knowledge is really transferable. "It's a gift to be in the presence of a shaman," she says. "Why then do we feel like we have to become one, too?"

New Age Shamanism

Anthropologists have criticized so-called New Age shamanism, as practiced by members of the urban middle class for a couple of decades, because it is not, by definition, shamanism. Although some anthropologists point out that traditional shamans can be culturally flexible enough to borrow from other cultures— whether it is over-the-counter drugstore items for healing or Jesus Christ as the spirit guide among the Huichol—New Age shamanism nevertheless tends to take the symbol, without the responsibility of the meaning, like stealing someone else's child. When a shaman borrows, it is to augment what is already in place.

Anthropologist Michael F. Brown, who lived in Santa Fe, New Mexico, after living with the Aguaruna in Peru, says that the New Age shamanism reduces a shaman's lifelong discipline "to a set of techniques for personal development." Nothing about traditional shamans is superficial; loss of ego precedes everything they do.

Stanley Krippner, a psychiatrist who has studied global shamanism, says shamans can be defined by the common elements of what they do. All shamans:

- take enormous risks;
- self-regulate;
- provide services;

- take dangerous trips to the netherworld; and
- bring back intelligence that services their community.

Core Shamanism Apprenticeships

New Age shamanism may or may not smoke out the real shamans in our society, but opportunities exist for apprenticeships. They are not designed to produce individuals with extraordinary shamanic access to power, as much as to introduce sensitive people and groups to their interconnectedness with each other and the earth—the fundamental shamanic message.

A Shaman prepares for a ceremony, laying out the sacred objects on his table. (*Puma Shamanic Journeys*, www.spiritjourney.net)

In the 1950s, Michael Harner was among the first anthropologists to study the Jivara in the Ecuadorean Andes. His subsequent research with the Conibo in the Peruvian Amazon led him to commit his life to a study of shamans. Several decades later, Harner developed what he calls Core Shamanism, the distillation of the basic properties of shamans around the world.

Harner formed the Foundation for Shamanic Studies, based in Mill Valley, California. Dedicated to preserving tribal shamanic knowledge, the foundation responds to requests from native peoples, such as the Inuit, whose shamans were forced underground and who have lost much of their tradition. Harner sends training teams to work with the tribes to ensure that their knowledge will continue.

The foundation also sponsors a fascinating project called the Mapping of Nonordinary Reality. By creating a database of accounts of visits to the spirit realm, researchers intend to "construct a map of the hidden universe." What people in shamanic trance see and experience—the cosmic tree, crocodilian creatures, crystal cities, flying, rainbows, brilliant colors and forms—are remarkably similar across cultures and time. Can it be mapped?

Shamanic Counseling

Psychotherapists, many of whom have studied with shamans or who are neo-shamans themselves, offer therapy that replicates techniques in shamanic healing: shape-shifting (taking on as-if personalities to induce change); guided imagery hypnosis that encourages the patient to visit the underworld and heaven to access the appropriate healers; and soul retrieval.

Rick Gossett, a Vancouver psychotherapist and shaman, says soul retrieval can apply to a person who is emotionally frozen. Often the result of a trauma, iced-in feelings represent a lost part of the personality, and therapists, like shamans, can retrieve that lost part. After completing the shamanic process, the cured patient then is able to share his talents in the service of his communities.

Hallucinogens

Not always, but often shamanic healing sessions in Central and South America are facilitated by natural hallucinogens, sacred and healing psychoactive herbs that are an integral part of the cultural context of the shaman. Employed by shamans as a reliable means to access other realities—and older shamans often no longer need to use them—the drugs were used and abused by recreational drug experimenters in the 1960s and 1970s as an end in themselves. Users became like travelers who never got off the bus.

That was then, this is now. Some healing rituals assume that participants will use psychoactive herbs, mushrooms, cacti, or vines: the option to say no is always yours. "The five D's," says shamanic researcher Stanley Krippner, "are what characterize shamanic ritual: drumming, dancing, drugs, dreams, and deprivation (food, sex, society)." Fasting usually precedes the ritual, and other things—rattles, drumming, smoke, dust, whistles, dancing—contribute to the trance state. Many believe the power of percussion rhythm is enough to induce trance. Bushmen rely on hours of rhythmic clapping and dance to access the spirit world.

Mexican Mayan and Aztec healers use the sacred mushroom psilocybin or the cactus flower peyote. Mexican shamans believe that the spirit of the deer resides in the peyote cactus and therefore hunt it, shooting an arrow into the cactus. Participants in the healing ceremony chew the peyote buttons, which are covered with little hairs and very bitter.

Among Andean shamans, psychoactive drugs are rarely used; but in the tropical rainforests of Peru and Bolivia, shamans gather and cut the ayahuasca vine, boil it for the better part of a day sometimes with other herbs and water.

An ayahuasquero healer convenes a circle two or three times a week at a village center, when needs arise. Usually beginning about 10:00 P.M., the ceremony involves drinking the ayahuasca vine mixture, the amount adjusted to the taker's size and weight, a judgment made by the shaman.

Despite the daylong fast beforehand, the intense bitterness of the vine induces gut-wrenching vomiting, and sometimes diarrhea, one or more times during the night. Participants report flying or swimming underwater and visiting, receiving messages from, being guided by, consumed by, or terrified by jaguars or anacondas or hideous reptilian creatures. Colors are intense; sounds are amplified. In some villages the dogs are muzzled to keep participants from going insane.

This is where the experienced shaman is the true guide to the other worlds, or "non-ordinary reality." Through the auspices of her master teacher, Grauds came to know a man and a woman spirit healer who taught her their techniques. On one occasion they asked her to sit down while they healed someone else because, they told her, "Your job is to host the vision."

Anthropologists are beginning to ask: Do spirits exist? Is there a separate spirit world? and, How would we know? Huston Smith, a longtime professor of comparative religions and consciousness studies, commented at a recent conference, "I am totally baffled how a small change—microscopically small change—in a certain area of matter, neurons, chemistry, whatever, can open the windows onto ultimate reality."

Timothy White, editor of *Shaman's Drum* magazine, wrote recently that he was seeing more and more articles cross his desk that indicate a burgeoning interest in "exploring entheogenic mystery rites," both in the form of ancient rites and "more loosely structured modern therapeutic sessions."

Cautioning readers to avoid the "disastrous crashes and wipeouts that plagued the 1960s" when "gurus" couldn't get enough recreational psychedelic drugs, White called for an informed cadre of "entheogenic hierophants" properly trained to guide novices through terrifying experiences and bring them back to the "light of holy, life-affirming ecstasy."

How to Know What's Real, What's Not

Aside from hallucinogens, you have to navigate in the shaman's world.

In any situation—anywhere in the world—when members of indigenous cultures meet tourists willing to spend money, decadence blooms. Tourists who are uninformed and locals who see an easy profit do no good to anyone. Do not buy condor feathers, for example, or believe everyone who says he is a shaman. Anthropologist and psychotherapist Marlene Dobkin de Rios says some street shamans are "common drug dealers dressed for deception." They are clever enough to see a market, says de Rios, in which they can "make money, seduce women, obtain personal power and control over others from activities with drugs." De Rios personally treated a woman near psychosis from reckless drug and romantic experiences with a "shaman."

Good guides, who understand the area they represent, are sympathetic to your expectations, and who will introduce you not only to the local people but also to authentic shamans, are priceless.

Alan Leon, who has been leading pilgrimages to the Andes since 1992, says you should ask yourself honestly before you go if learning a whole new culture for your soul path is what you really want. If you are serious, then go for it, he advises. "But if it is not deeply you, why further complicate your perhaps already full life with more words and practices to work out?"

Leon warns against tour companies that sell you a superficial or phony bill of goods, with visits to villagers who *say* they are shamans. He likens them to making you put out "big money to buy honorary Mickey Mouse ears." Oscar Miro Quesada warns, "Watch out for the companies that are run like corporations."

How can you relate?

The banquet of choices for your spiritual pilgrimage to shaman country, in this case, Central and South America—requires some research on your part.

- You can go as a passive tourist, interested in art, architecture, and archaeology. Cusco, Macchu Picchu, and Lake Titikaka will not disappoint.
- You can go as an adventure traveler, and join hikes up to peaks as high as 15,000 feet. Or you can canoe on the Amazon River, over caimans and pink dolphins; go on deep jungle treks to see rare species of birds, mammals, and insects, and spend the nights in jungle huts.
- You can stay in small villages in the Andes or the Amazon and have cultural exchanges with people who share with you a simple, sincere lifestyle, which might include a village healing ceremony that you can observe. "The quality that draws me back to Ecuador," says Stacy Bell, "has to do with the people, the Quechua. They make me feel very humble."
- You can get involved with organizations working to preserve traditions as well as pre-Inca buildings. Bell says experiencing the local culture is a privilege and makes her and her husband "able then to come back here and speak intelligently—and with real feeling—about why we need to protect indigenous cultures and the environment."
- You can visit a *curandero,* someone who assesses your physical pain and prescribes the appropriate herbs. If your pain is what you believe to be spiritual or psychological, you can participate in a ceremony with an *ayabuascuro.*
- Or you can stay home and do workshops in shamanic apprenticeship.

All you have to decide is how much and in what way you want to connect. This requires self-knowledge.

Ask yourself:

- Where am I coming from?
- Where am I going with this?
- How much of my mental and spiritual health, as well as safety, am I willing to risk?
- Am I doing this for good and positive reasons?
- Will this adventure increase my understanding of the world and my place in it?
- Will going on this trip help me to help others?

All roads do lead to Rome: any of the pilgrimages described below will nourish your own private spiritual quest, as long as *you* know what that is (even if it is still nonverbal). And if you think you may be being called to be a shaman, expect to invest the rest of your life.

Passport information—Ecuador and Peru: You need only a passport. No pre-trip visa is required if you stay fewer than ninety days. Russia: You need a passport and visa, a return ticket, and proof of a hotel in Russia. Visa cost: $70 for a two-week stay; $80 for one week; $110 for fewer than three days.

The Foundation for Shamanic Studies   P.O. Box 1939, Mill Valley, CA 94942. 415-380-8282 (tel). E-mail: info@shamanic studies.org; Web site: www.shamanicstudies.org

This organization was founded by Michael Harner, who was one of the first to recognize the importance of shamans in the twentieth century. The foundation gives basic workshops in Core Shamanism—"without specific cultural perspective"—at places around the world. This is the prerequisite for subsequent courses. The Core introduces you to your spiritual and animal guides who further guide you on your spiritual quest.

The foundation also offers advanced training in soul retrieval, shamanic healing, and a three-year advanced shamanic healing training.

Mesa Works: Oscar Miro-Quesada 525 Flagler Drive, #27C, West Palm Beach, FL 33401. 561-265-1446 (tel); 561-471-7378 (fax). Heart of the Healer Foundation: 757-223-6282 (tel for information on Peru trips). Web site: www.mesaworks.com

Oscar Miro-Quesada is an American-educated, Peruvian-born and shamanically-indoctrinated master curandero, or healer of the highest order. Those who travel with him are introduced to his "mesa," which is a physical map of the spiritual world in which he operates. His traditions are based on his teachers from coastal Peru; his mesa begins at Cusco, considered the center of the universe. To the south is the home of Pachamama, the earth mother who heals the physical body. To the west is the Pacific Ocean, aligned with the Moon and the emotional body. In the north lives the supreme creator, Wiracocha, the spiritual body. And in the east is the Sun and mental body.

Cusco, symbolized at the center of the mesa, is the refined energy body, represented by the llama and the rainbow.

Using the mesa as a map of the world you will enter, you can travel with Oscar and other shamans on a two-week Trekking Pilgrimage to the Ancestral Origins of Heart Island Curanderismo. Camp and hike in the Cordillera Blanca Range, visit rarely seen ancient monuments, and visit Machu Picchu. Fourteen days, includes airfare from Miami to Lima, about $3,800.

Sacred Heritage Travel P.O. Box 1070, Sedona, AZ 86339. 888-971-8815 (toll free). E-mail: info@sacredheritage.com; Web Site: www.sacredheritage.com

Alan Leon (see above) lives most of the year among the people to whom he will introduce you on a variety of trips he offers that include participation in sacred sites ceremonies and visits with healers. His Sacred Ausengate Camp takes place at the base of, and up to 14,000 feet of, a sacred peak near Cusco. You travel with two shamans who conduct ceremonies of "cleansing, supplication and strengthening." Ascent is slow and assisted by llamas and horses. Two weeks: about $2,400. Thirty percent of Sacred Heritage proceeds go directly to the healers and villagers who assist.

Poqen Kanchay Foundation   Casilla 220 Cusco, Peru. +51(0)84-277243 (tel/fax in Peru); 561-658-8136 (tel/fax in USA). E-mail: info@poqenkanchay.com; Web site: www.poqen kanchay.com

Named for a Quechuan phrase that means *where light germinates*, the Poqen Kanchay Foundation is a group of archaeologists and anthropologists whose mandate is to "rescue, research, and teach ancient knowledge of the societies which culminated with the Incas." To this end, they support projects that augment local village cultures, such as Quillarumiyoz, designed to preserve and to teach locals the skills necessary to preserve the archaeological Temple of the Moon; and Patacancha, to record the stories of village women weavers who pass on their skill and knowledge to their daughters. Ten days: about $2,600.

Apprenticeship Program: Poqen Kanchay offers seminars for serious students of shamanism. Their Journey to the Sacred Apus is a trek to four of the seven sacred mountains around Cusco, called Apus, powerful spirits that manifest in shamans. Traveling as high as 16,000 feet on foot and horseback, participants become immersed in the human-divine culture between villagers and the mountain spirits, with the guidance and ceremonies of shaman teachers. Limited to fifteen. Seven days.

Innervision, P.C.   Gail Danto or Art Roffey. 248-865-9416 (tel). E-mail: info@innervisionpc.org; Web site: www.innervisionpc. org

Theo Paredes, anthropologist, and founding director of Poqen Kanchay (see above) and Ruben Orellana, shaman, formerly Head of Archaeology at Machu Picchu and now consultant to the National Institute of Culture in Cusco, join Innervision in an unusual trip that includes visits to pre-Columbian and Inka sites, numerous healing ceremonies at the sites, and an opportunity to climb Huayna Picchu, the conical mountain next to the "crystal city" of Machu Picchu. At each point, Drs. Paredes and Orellana give you in-depth understanding of the meaning of the sacred sites. The journey is assisted by Gail Danto and Art Roffey, shamanic trainers. Nine days: about $2,500.

Dr. Roffey is a psychologist who founded Innervision with his wife, Gail Danto, to provide shamanic counseling, host visiting shamans, and sponsor expeditions to shamans. Innervision also hosts Drs. Paredes and Rubellana as shamanic trainers for four three-day sessions over a period of two years in the United States, in a program called, The Art of Living: Exploring the Andean Cosmic Vision. Contact Innervision for current dates.

Magical Journey 888-737-8070 (toll free in North America); +27-82-478 (tel). E-mail: info@magicaljourney.org Web site: www. travelperu. com

Carol Cumes went on a shamanic trip to the Peruvian Andes in 1984, and since then has been dedicated to providing accurate information about the Quechuan families with whom she fell in love. Now a respected pilgrimage leader, she invites participants to begin and end their journey with her at Willka T'ika, her home and luxury Garden Guest Lodge in Peru.

Cumes offers several in-depth journeys, including specialty yoga and artists' spiritual tours. Her Journey to Machu Picchu begins with exploring the ruins and the people who live around Willka T'ika, and enjoying the place itself, with its outdoor solar baths, massage room, and yoga facilities. Take the train to Machu Picchu for a complete tour and lots of time for meditation and private exploration. Her Amazon extension include three days at a new lodge in the rainforest, visits to a parrot salt lick, flora and fauna guides, and a sacred ayahuasca healing ceremony with a shaman. Two weeks Machu Picchu only: about $2,800; Amazon extension: $550.

The Spirit of La Selva Constance Grauds, The Center for Spirited Medicine, P.O. Box 150727, San Rafael, CA 94915. 415-

453-4937 (tel); 415-453-4963 (fax). E-mail: spiritedmedicine@aol. com; Web site: junglemedicine.net

Constance Grauds offers to share her understanding of shamanism to help "infuse our lives with the sacredness of nature by connecting with the deep shamanic medicine of la selva . . ." Her Amazon Journey "outward and inward bound" expedition takes you up the Yarapa River in Peru to live in an indigenous rainforest village. As your guide, Grauds introduces you to living plant medicines and spirits. Two weeks: about $4,000, including airfare from Miami, Florida. Grauds also gives healing cruises in jungle medicine out of Hawaii.

Puma Shamanic Journeys P.O. Box 1950, El Prado, NM 87529. 505-758-1491 (tel/fax). E-mail: jayabear@taosnet.com; Web site: www.spiritjourney.net

Leave your cell phone at home and travel three hours by boat up the Amazon River from Iquitos, Peru, then hoist your backpack for a one and one half-hour walk deep into the jungle. Here at Yushintaita, a retreat community of open-air thatched-roof huts on stilts, you can work with shaman and *ayahuascero* Don Agustin Rivas Vasquez. Free from technological pollution, Don Agustin conducts healing and purification ceremonies that introduce you to the pure spirituality of the jungle. In his earlier years, Don Agustin was a musician and one of Peru's most notable sculptors. Seventeen days: about $2,000, including airfare from Lima to Iquitos, hotel and meals in Peru; international airfare not included.

For an introduction to shamans and the jungle, listen to one of Jaya Bear's excellent CDs, including Don Agustin's music, and Songs of the Plant Spirits, with shaman Don Pedro Guerra Gonzales. Available from www.spiritjourney.net.

Refugio Altiplano Calle Napo 145, Iquitos, Peru. +51(0)94-224020 (tel/fax). E-mail: Scottpetersen@refugioaltiplano.com; Web site: www.refugioaltiplano.com

Refugio Altiplano, located in the Amazon rainforest, is a herbal healing center which holds shamanic ceremonies three times a week with two Shipibo Indian shamans who live at the Refugio with their families. The ceremonies are held for local villagers, as well as for visitors. Scott Petersen, whose home it is, brings in other shamans from both the Andes and the Amazon from time to time. Beautiful jungle cats, called *tigrios*, or Peruvian ocelots, are permanent residents, as well. The flat fee of $100 a day covers everything; Petersen can customize your tours to include a seven-day camping adventure trek into the deep jungle to fish, swim, explore, and appreciate the rhythm of the earth. Also offers onsite counseling, and courses in natural and shamanic medicine accredited by San Marcos University.

Far Horizons Archaeological and Cultural Trips, Inc. P.O. Box 91900, Albuquerque, NM 87199-1900. 800-552-4575 (toll free); 505-343-9400 (tel); 505-343-8076 (fax). E-mail: journey@ farhorizon.com; Web site: www.farhorizon.com

If your interests lie in understanding what happens to people's belief systems over time, Far Horizons, which sponsors trips with archaeologists and anthropologists, offers treks to study the archaeology of ancient pre-Columbian cultures in Peru and Bolivia; the rock art of northern Chile; and in Guatemala, On the Trail of the Shaman, an opportunity to explore ancient shamanic sacred sites, still used, well after the Spanish conquest and the introduction of Christianity. Nine days: about $4,000, including airfare from Houston, Texas.

Myths and Mountains 976 Tee Court, Incline Village, NV 89451. 800-670-6984 (toll free); 775-832-5454 (tel); 775-832-4454 (fax). E-mail: travel@mythsandmountains.com; Web site: www.mythsandmountains.com

The Shamans of Ecuador is an excellent opportunity not only to get to know villagers but also to meet and experience ceremonies with shamans from three different ecological zones in Ecuador: the rainforest, the Andes, and the middle hills, or cloud forest. Their significant differences give you insights into the true meaning of shamanism to the community. You also explore the jungle on foot and along the Napo River in dugout canoes. Your guide, an ecologist and a shaman, explains some of the luxuriant flora and fauna. Ten days, about $2,100, airfare not included.

Luminati, Inc. P.O. Box 2162, Carefree, AZ 85377. 888-488-1151 (toll free). E-mail: luminatiaz@aol.com; Web site: www.lumi nati.net

Luminati's Mayan Adventure for women is a spiritual pilgrimage that begins in Mexico City and visits sacred sites in Mexico, Guatemala, and Honduras. You have time to explore the sites, which includes swimming in pools and waterfalls at Teepee Village, a 4,000 year-old Mayan place of pilgrimage; and, at

Central America is covered with Mayan temples like this one in Belize. Some of them are still buried in dense jungles. (*Stephanie Ocko*)

night, participating in a drumming fire circle and dancing. In addition to visiting and staying overnight at missions and convents, you participate in healing ceremonies with shamans in Zinacantan, and experience the Temple of the Cross in Palenque in a lighted night ceremony. Thirteen days: about $2,300, not including airfare. *Luminati encourages participants to take part in their travel savings plan: If you commit with a $500 deposit, and pay the balance in full before departure (seven installments), Luminati will give you a $450 discount.*

Cross Cultural Journeys P.O. Box 1369, Sausalito, CA 94966-1369. 800-353-2276 (toll free); 415-332-0682 (tel); 415-332-0683 (fax). E-mail: info@CrossCulturalJourneys.com; Web site: www.CrossCulturalJourneys.com

Sponored by the Institute of Noetic Sciences travel program, Cross Cultural Journeys offers trips with informed guides who introduce you not only to the indigenous cultures you visit, but also go deeper into their spiritual aspects. The Sacred Sites and Ceremonies pilgrimage to Peru is led by Jose Luis Herrera, a native Peruvian, who is trained as an engineer, but also fully indoctrinated in the knowledge of the natural world and medicine traditions. Plus, he is an experienced mountain guide. This "learning odyssey" begins with ceremonies with Q'ero elders in Cusco, travels to the Sacred Valley and Inca ruins before going to Machu Picchu, then to Lake Titikaka. Two weeks: about $4,000, including international airfare.

Dance of the Deer Foundation Center for Shamanic Studies, P.O. Box 699, Soquel, CA 95073. 831-475-9560 (tel); 831-475-1860 (fax). E-mail: shaman@shamanism.com; Web site: www.shamanism.com

Brant Secunda apprenticed with famous Huichol shaman Don Jose Matsuwa. Since 1979, Secunda, through his Dance of the Deer Foundation, has dedicated himself to integrating shamanic healing into modern Western medicine. In addition to shamanic tours around the world, he offers a pilgrimage to Mount Shasta, California. One of the most beautiful natural sacred sites in the world, Mount Shasta provides the place for sacred ceremonies of purification, drumming, dreamwork, and the Dance of the Deer. Option of a one-day vision quest, as well. Four days: about $500.

Dream Change Coalition P.O. Box 31357, Palm Beach Gardens, FL 33420. 561-622-6064 (tel). E-mail for details about the following trip: maryten@jps.net; Web site: www.dreamchange.org

John Perkins formed the Dream Change Coalition about a decade ago to work to preserve the rainforest and to promote environmental sustainability using indigenous wisdom. From time to time, he stages a Gathering of Shamans at the Omega Institute in Rhinebeck, New York (see: www.eomega.org). Dream Change Coalition also organizes expeditions to shamans not only in South America but also in South Africa and Siberia. The Dream Change expedition, Arutam Journey to Shapeshifters and Shamans, takes place in the Ecuadorean rainforest among Shuar, Quechua, and Inka shamans and elders who teach the transformation of shape-shifting. It includes workshops in John Perkins's Dream Change, Psychonavigation, and Shamanic Healing techniques, and experiences of the rainforest. Ten days: about $3,000, international airfare not included. Dream Change Coalition contributes to rainforest conservation.

The Circle of the Sacred Earth Roy Bauer, 21 Aaron Street, Melrose, MA 02176. E-mail: info@circleofthesacredearth.org; Web site: www.circleofthesacredearth.org

This unusual organization offers shamanic services for spiritual healing, "direct spiritual revelation through shamanic journey," rites for weddings, births, deaths, and a host of other life changes, and gives training courses in shamanism. Roy Bauer, a Michael Harner-trained neo shaman, has established centers around the United States and in six countries abroad. For a list, visit the Web site.

Russia

Russian shamanism went underground a long time ago, suppressed first by organized religion, then by Communism. Yet it was once one of the strongest holds of shamanism, and, some believe, the generator of ancient Native American rites. In fact, the word *shaman,* trickster or healer, is from the Tungus tribe in eastern Siberia.

Siberian Shaman Sarangerel c/o Lydia Kulesov, 2634 West River Parkway, Minneapolis, Minnesota 55406. 888-645-0542 (toll free). E-mail: lydis@siberianshaman.com; Web site: www. siberianshaman.com

Sarangerel is an American-born Buryat shaman, descended from a Buryat Mongol family, who now serves as foreign outreach representative of the Golomt Center for Shamanist Studies in Ulan Bator, Mongolia. In early summer, you can catch her two-day workshops in Minneapolis on Siberian and Mongolian divination and healing, and on working with earth spirits to heal the earth. Two days: $200–250.

Baikaler.Com +7 (8)3952-511979 (tel in Irkutsk). E-mail: baikaler@ omen.ru; Web site: www.baikaler.com

Jack Sheremetoff, an English-speaking guide who runs a tour company in Irkutsk, on the shores of Lake Baikal, offers many interesting trips around Lake Baikal, in what was once shaman country. His four-day stay with fisherman families on Olkhon, Lake Baikal's largest island, introduces you to the people who depend on the lake for their livelihood and their spirituality. The fishermen live simply, with electricity, but no running water or indoor toilet. Sheremetoff takes you to the island's Burkhan stone and cave with ancient inscriptions on the walls, which are believed to be remnants from ancient shamans. If you add an extra day, he guides you to the Tazeran Steppes and a visit with a shaman. He requires you to be truly serious in order to avoid commercialization of shamanism.

Russian shaman, Valentin Khagdayev, enters a trance. A Buryat, he was born with a split thumb, a sign that he was to be a shaman. (*Jack Sheremetoff,* www.baikaler.com)

Web Sites and Other Resources

www.ausbcomp.com is a Hopi Web site

www.iprimus.ca is an exhaustive list of gurus, shamans, and others

www.shamansmarket.com contains workshop listings and shamanic items

www.animalspirits.com contains lists of animals with their respective qualities

www.crystalinks.com/dogon.html links you to Dogon sacred geometry and origin legends

www.earthwatch.org has numerous projects helping scientists in Central and South America

www.urep.ucdavis.edu also sponsors scientist-helping anthropological and archaeological trips to South America

Shaman's Drum magazine covers all aspects of shamanism and spiritual healing.

DRUMMING

To understand shamans and sacred drums, you have to know that the *axis mundi* is the central post around which Earth spins, and which connects it to the cosmos, above and below. Also known as the cosmic pillar, or the world tree, it is the sacred path which the shaman travels when he visits the spirit worlds. Among the Buryats in Siberia, and in North American and Arctic tribes, the structure of the drum is made from a branch of the cosmic tree, so they say; so drumming is what connects the shaman to the universe.

Ask any drummer you may see outside the subway beating on upturned buckets, or any lawyer after work beating out the rhythm with his or her buddies in the park: they will agree. You don't need herbs, you don't need drugs, just let the percussion put you on the road to cosmic happiness. "We become one spirit through rhythm," says Babatunde Olatunji, master Yoruban musician.

Various studies indicate that drumming has at least as much benefit as meditation. It increases natural "killer cells" to fight

Valentin Khagdayev begins to drum. Russian shamanism is ancient, with roots in Paleolithic cave dwellers. (*Jack Sheremetoff,* www.baikaler.com)

disease, it lowers blood pressure, reduces stress levels, and it even, some say, rewires your neural circuits. Rumor has it that fifteen minutes of steady drumming shifts your brainwaves from the alpha (relaxed) state to theta (deeply relaxed) state, and one hour of sustained drumming provides access to non-ordinary reality. Psychologists suggest that it's the camaraderie of your group and your freed self-expression that also contribute to your well-being.

WEB SITES WITH LISTS OF DRUMMING CIRCLES:

www.DrumsontheWeb.com
www.drummingcircle.com
www.allonetribe.org

Drum Making Workshops

How you acquire your drum is a very special thing; most approach it as if they were adopting a child. You can take a drum-making workshop and start from scratch. At one workshop, participants wrap themselves in their deer hides and go swimming (to soften the deer hide and to get closer to the elements of the drum). One man described it as "spiritual lovemaking."

As the wood is put together and the hide is stretched across, makers are encouraged to imagine and project into the spirit of the drum their divine intentions. The shape is important, since drums are beaten on only certain areas of the surface. Some prefer an ovoid shape to achieve certain sounds.

If you buy a drum in a store, or acquire a used drum, it is important to make it your own first, by smudging it and conducting some kind of cleansing ceremony around it.

Wind Spirit Teachings P.O. Box 1183, Arizona City, AZ 85223. 520-466-5163 (tel). E-mail: muse@primenet.com; Web site: www. windspiritteachings.com

Lench Archuleta teaches your group how to make a drum "the old way, with singing, ceremony, prayer, and meditation"; then how to bless it with sage and sweetgrass and offer it to Grandfather Sun.

Spirit Dance Healing Center P.O. Box 542, Westminster, MD 21158. 410-596-3022 (Cathy); 410-404-9382 (Jim). Web site: www. nativeamericandrums.homestead.com

Holds workshops Spring through Fall. They help you make a

fifteen-inch hand drum and drumstick. Dry them by the bonfire, then have a drumming circle. $165.

Jalbun Lodge   890 Monck Road, RR1, Sebright, ON, Canada. E-mail: jakbun@bconnex.net; Web site: www.miditrax.com

Long-weekend workshops throughout the year. Arrive Friday night, make the drum on Saturday, have a sweat lodge ceremony on Sunday, and a drumming circle on Monday. Four days and the drum: $445. Also gives five-day drumming retreats, $995. Live in a tepee.

Talking rocks communicate in private, in interior Alaska. (*Roger Archibald*)

A carved wood totem in the forests of Shumak, Russia. (*Jack Sheremetoff,* www.baikaler.com)

Drum Making.net Margate, Florida. 954-471-6685 (tel). E-mail: Paivi@drummaking.net; Web site: www.drummaking.net
Paivi Kivela was born in Finland and studied with a shaman. She offers single-day workshops; uses hickory for drumsticks, as well as elk or deer skin when in season. Once a month, limited to ten, $170, plus $20 for the drumstick.

Drum Travel

If you want to take your drumming act around the world, that, too, is possible.

Global Alliance for Intelligent Arts 140 Pine Studio, #13, Northampton, MA 01062. 413-584-3022 (tel/fax). E-mail: info@ global-alliance.com; Web site: www.global-alliance.com
   Global Alliance is an international network of artists and producers. Their Drums Around the World is an annual drumming day observed around the world. You can also travel with them to places such as Mali, Gambia, Cuba, Jamaica, Morocco, Mexico, and Brazil for drumming and meeting musicians and artists in a global community. Call for updates; one-week trips: about $1,500; two weeks: $2,500–$3,000. International airfare included.

Chapter 7
Science and Spirituality

The Lord is subtle, but malicious he is not.

—Albert Einstein

As former Apollo-14 astronaut Edgar Mitchell was returning to Earth from the Moon in 1971, he experienced an epiphany in which he understood the interconnectedness of Earth and the universe in ways, he said, that were "like getting kicked in the head by a mule." So great was his enlightenment, Mitchell teamed up with Willis Harman to found the Institute of Noetic Sciences, to investigate that mysterious place where science and spirituality meet.

But the story begins earlier.

THE QUANTUM BEGINS: OCTOBER 19, 1900

What has to be the most intriguing series of revelations about the universe began on October 19, 1900, when German theoretical physicist Max Planck presented his finding that matter was composed of little packets of energy he called *quanta*. For centuries before what we believed had been safely inert was suddenly a bundle of energy. That means that at the atomic level, even so-called inanimate things that we rely on for every-day "reality"—tables, tools, billiard balls—are *vibrating*.

Classical physicist Planck worried about a quantum theory because of its radical implications that Isaac Newton (what goes up must come down) and René Descartes (I think, therefore I am) might be seriously challenged. Newton and Descartes had presented immutable laws of the universe that firmly anchored Earth in a perpetual security. In the spirit of the new century, however, Einstein found the quantum theory inspiring as he developed his special theory of relativity in 1905.

Unfolding slowly like a science-fiction plot, the atom story grew more baffling. Quantum physicists found in the mid-1920s that electrons sometimes acted like waves and sometimes acted like particles. At the same time, physicist Werner Heisenberg realized (in what was to become Heisenberg's Uncertainty Principle), that it was possible to measure a particle's speed or its position, but impossible to measure both at the same time. Even stranger, when isolated, an electron spins clockwise and counterclockwise simultaneously (you have to believe) until it is looked at or measured or otherwise "interrupted," when it immediately commits to one direction or another.

By the 1950s the quantum theory had introduced a completely flaky view of the atomic universe composed of elements that, left to their own devices, vibrated in formerly inanimate things, changed shape, were subject to a dizzying flux, and played games. Physicists went after atoms (after smashing them into bombs), and sought to break them into ever-smaller units, for which they built accelerators, seeking the answer in quarks. Thirty-five years and thirty-six "quarks" later, the smallest unit is still a mystery.

Then physicists discovered that when photons (light electrons) hit, for example, a mirror, 95 percent are absorbed or reflected. But what happens to the other 5 percent? Therein lies the terrifying thing about the quantum theory: The other 5 percent don't do either. Nobody knows which photons are part of the 5 percent, nor when or what they will do. In other words, there is always a 5 percent probability at the quantum level that anything can happen.

Out of all of this came the realization that everything is composed of vibrating packets of energy that are unpredictable and filled with infinite probabilities. The smaller you go, the more it appears that there is nothing holding anything together. Deepak Chopra, who has built an industry on ever-renewing, possibly never-aging body cells, identified this as a "field of infinite potentialities," because, he said beautifully, "at the level of the atom, we don't exist."

Entanglement

Einstein's now famous phrase, *"Spooky action at a distance,"* referred to what he saw as a real possibility with photons: being in two places at the same time. For twenty years, physicists did lab work in which they "entangled" photons, on which measurements on one packet of photons had a contemporaneous effect on the other. In 2000, physicists entangled two atoms, one spinning clockwise, the other counterclockwise, separated them through a fiber optic wire, and found that, even at a seven-mile distance, the separated twin reacted in a way relative to the other—and at the same time. In 2001, Danish physicists entangled two clouds of *trillions* of cesium atoms, and *they* behaved in the same way.

Teleportation

If trillions of entangled atoms can be in different places at the same time, can other, larger matter—say, *us*—be both here and there? Stay tuned; researchers in the United States and abroad are working on that. But at the moment, teleportation has been confined to transmitting information between quantum computers, being developed for speed to solve complex problems as well as to break unbreakable codes.

Biology

In 1979, British physicist James Lovelock developed the Gaia theory, in which he saw the earth as a species in itself, a self-regulating, breathing organism in a larger ecological system of the universe. Lovelock came face-to-face with the same inter-connectedness that Mitchell had experienced in space.

Nevertheless, the Gaia theory met with resistance, Lovelock said, "by reductionist scientists" who rejected "anything that smells of holism, anything that implies that the whole may be more than the sum of its parts."

Lovelock said recently in *The Skeptical Inquirer*, that "the

Transformation in action: A beautiful butterfly emerges from its ugly chrysalis case. (*Roger Archibald*)

deepest error of modern biology is the entrenched belief that organisms interact only with other organisms and merely adapt to their material environment. In real life both organisms and people *change* their environment as well as adapting to it." What matters, he continued, are the consequences of the changes. "We reject her care at our peril," Lovelock warned.

In the 1980s Stephen Jay Gould observed that evolution could make quantum leaps in ways that challenged traditional thinking. The Law of Natural Selection states that, over long periods of time, only the fittest of the species are selected to reproduce, evolving into better adapted species. But Gould found (in a theory called Punctuated Equilibrium) that evolution can take great random leaps forward quickly if species are isolated in favorable ecological pockets.

Astronomy

Biology and physics are not the only scientific fields undergoing major changes. The development of super sharp telescopes launched into space threw us into contact with the "edge" of space and the beginning of time. The grand panorama of the magnificent entity of space is as beautiful as it is mysterious. In 2001, astronomers in Australia found that the speed of light in a collection of gases 12 billion light years away changes wave lengths and actually appears to slow down. Once believed to be a staple of the immutable rules of the universe, the speed of light unites us with time and distance.

Now what?

Symphony in the Blue

Stephen Hawking said, "We are on the verge of reading the mind of God." Astrophysicist Michio Kaku, one of the young physicists for whom imagination is all, postulates that there is not one universe, but multi-verses constantly being created, and a holistic hyperspace with ten dimensions. His aim is to develop a "theory of everything" (TOE), one-inch long, that will explain the four forces of the universe—electromagnetism, weak nuclear force, strong nuclear force, and gravity.

Working with the controversial theory that the universe is composed of long cosmic strings that vibrate, he said recently that he believes music—the music of the spheres that Pythagoras believed comprised the universe in the sixth century C.E.—will explain the mind of God. Strings, densely composed of subatomic particles, create vibrating notes that cause melodies in matter (planets, stars, galaxies), and a symphony in the universe. Kaku, professor of astrophysics at the City University of New York, theorizes that the string theory unites Einstein's special theory of relativity, (strings warp space and time), with the quantum theory of universal instability.

Time Travel

In the movie, *Contact*, Jodie Foster slipped through a wormhole and entered a whole new dimension of time and space that she was reluctant to leave. Astrophysicist Kip Thorne at California Institute of Technol-ogy got her there and back in one of those beautiful marriages of scientific possibilities and Hollywood that can bring the quantum theory into everybody's home.

But problems surround time travel. Assuming you are able to swim through a black hole (what Michio Kaku said used to be known as "the ultimate roach motel"); or a wormhole, the skinny tube between two blackholes that, at the moment, is not at all friendly to matter; or between two cosmic strings, the basic question is: What should you pack for? You may as well ask *this* question as get into discussions of what would happen if you went back in time and killed your grandfather or married your great-grandmother; or go forward in time and alter the lives of your great grandchildren. If you go back in time, you might need either diapers or a toga, depending on the strength

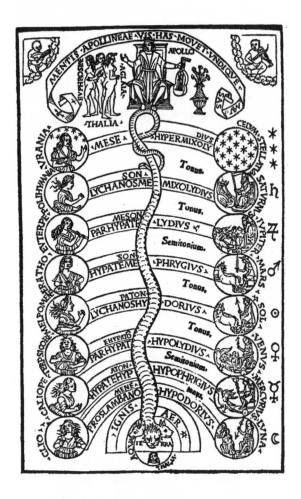

Sixth century B.C.E. Greek philosopher and mathematician Pythagoras was able to hear "the universal music of the spheres" and believed that the universe was a vast symphony, composed of the harmony created by the constant movement of the "seven planets" and the fixed stars. In this engraving done in Italy about 1500, the Muses are on the left, the planets and starry sky on the right, with Apollo, Greek god of harmony and order, at the pinnacle. (Gafurius, *Practica Musice,* 1496)

of the thrust; if you go forward, think *Star Trek*, shiny suits, and defense against possibly hostile inhabitants.

But for your spiritual journey through space and time, do you really *need* a body?

Quantum Consciousness

Ask a remote viewer.

In a pitch-black chamber at the Monroe Institute in the Blue Ridge Mountains in Virginia, Joseph McMoneagle lay on a bed, his vital signs monitored, while an interviewer gave him map coordinates from a nearby control room. McMoneagle was part

Birthplace of stars farther than the eye can see. The Hubble cameras caught this stellar formation, NGC 3603. (*NASA*)

of an experiment conducted by the CIA in 1983. He was a good remote viewer (and the only one to be kept through the entire twenty-year project), and this task was difficult. In his 1997 book, *Mind Trek*, McMoneagle described the event. He was somewhere strange, he said, surrounded by very tall people whom he later described as "gargantuan." They were wearing what he described as silk suits shaped to fit the body.

With prompting directions ("Move in now, this time to eighty degrees south, sixty-four degrees east."), McMoneagle followed the mental map and came upon a group of huge pyramids. "These are like shelters from storms," he said. The interviewer directed: "All right, go inside one of these and find some activity to tell me about. . . ."

Joe: "Different chambers . . . but they're all stripped of furnishings . . . it's like it is a strictly functional place . . . for . . . hibernation. . . . I get real raw inputs . . . storms . . . savage storms . . . and sleeping through storms."

He talked to some of the tall people (who thought he was an "hallucination") who told him they were looking for a way to survive, holed up in their vast pyramids, waiting for some who had left to find help. Elsewhere were volcanoes, electrical storms, and isolated pockets of vegetation, and an overall sense of catastrophe. McMoneagle had the impression, he said, that he was looking at "the aftereffects of a major geological trauma." When the interviewer told him to go back in time in the same place to identify the source of the trauma, he saw a globe passing through what he described as the tail of a comet.

Only after the session was over was he told the coordinates were for Mars.

Psi

One of the best-funded investigations into psychic abilities— telepathy, remote viewing, precognition, psychokinesis, and clairvoyance—was conducted under the auspices of the CIA from the early 1970s to 1995. At its close, CIA Director Robert

Gates, Jr. described the project as having grown out of a need to counteract research that had been going on in the Soviet Union for several decades (see Ostrander and Schroeder: *Psychic Discoveries*, for a description of Russian psi experiments.); but he also said the research had found nothing to substantiate belief in psychic abilities.

Whatever the official ruling, Star Gate, one of the project's code names, produced a lot of data and several articulate spokespeople, in addition to McMoneagle (see Targ and Katra, *Miracles of Mind*; and Graff, *Tracks in the Psychic Wilderness*).

Remote viewers see "shapes, forms, feelings," says Russell Targ, a physicist who was part of Star Gate for twenty-three years. In keeping with the idea of quantum non-locality, Targ believes we are all part of the same reality. "Eyes are the recipient of illumination," he says. "Our mind is not the source of the experience. We align with awareness in the universe."

Psi may also be something generic to humans: Bushmen, for example, travel out of the body to find the best game necessary to survival; Tibetan monks travel in spirit across Himalayan peaks to pay important visits; travel to other planets with hostile environments would be much cheaper without the burden of body and craft. "Regardless of theories about psi, or how it can manifest, the pursuit of psi applications will continue, as it always has," wrote Dale Graff. "If it works, then use it. There are no useless phenomena in the universe."

Distance Healing

The scientific jury is out on intercessory prayer as a reliable healing tool. In 1999, a major study at Saint Luke's Hospital in Kansas City, Missouri, was conducted with nine hundred cardiac patients, and a group of people who prayed daily for some of them for four weeks. The patients did not know the people who were praying, nor did they know prayers were being said for them; nor did the people who were praying know the patients.

Results showed a statistically measurable improvement in the prayed-for patients, enough to recommend that prayer was an "effective adjunct to standard medical care."

In 2001, however, a two-and-a-half year study on 799 cardiac patients released from the Mayo Clinic in Rochester, Minnesota, found that intercessory prayer had no effect on the "medical outcomes" of discharged patients.

Talk to any healer, and he or she will tell you about miracles. Healers say they send an image of the person, healed, to the patient; and it is up to the patient to take the healing from there. Curing is easier, because it involves attacking the superficial symptom, such as a headache or a tumor; but healing addresses the root cause, which might be a complex mixture of mind/body interaction, that may also be difficult to express in words.

Higher Consciousness

It is only with the heart that one can see rightly;
what is essential is invisible to the eye.
—Antoine de Saint Exupery, *The Little Prince*

The revelations from the quantum world have had deep resonance in consciousness explorers. "The missing link between science and religion," said Edgar Mitchell at a recent conference, "is: *What is the nature of consciousness?*"

If we can induce that we are interconnected to such an extent that twinned photons behave in identical ways even though separated (non-locality), this implies that we might live in a holographic universe, where any part equals the whole. That we share a world that is unpredictable, unstable, in a constant state of flux, and subject to all possibilities is a definite new reality, one that requires a paradigm shift in our thinking about just about everything. Are we really parts of the same whole held together by consciousness? "Separation is an illusion," says Russell Targ.

If consciousness is awareness of self, others, past, present, future; and, in altered states, other worlds, then higher consciousness is the awareness of interconnectedness and the sense of compassion for all living things. Out of this grows altruism, a caring for one's communities, local, regional, national, and global.

Astrophysicist Frank Drake, the founder of SETI, believes that the basic requirement for anyone traveling to another civilization—the nearest, he believes is a thousand light years away in the Milky Way—is altruism. The technology required to pull off an intergalactic trip, Drake says, requires "individuals who set aside their own desires to support the society as a whole." Anyone we meet coming from the other direction is likely to be altruistic for the same reason, Drake says. The fittest will be the altruistic.

Do scientists believe in God?

Ironically, one year after Max Planck presented his theory of quanta, in an atmosphere still permeated with the belief that the real world was real; the spiritual world, not real, William James gave a series of lectures in Edinburgh that were to be published as *The Varieties of Religious Experience*. James was a scientist himself, a chemist and physician as well as a psychologist and philosopher. Concluding an exhaustive search to understand religious motives around the world, James said simply, "God is real, since he produces real effects."

In effect, James was using the scientific method: collect data, develop ways to measure the data; develop a working hypothesis; then test the hypothesis. Many scientists note that the scientific method itself relies on intuition in creating innovative and imaginative ways in which to measure data, and to create and test hypotheses.

In 1975 physicist Fritjof Capra wrote in *The Tao of Physics*: "Physicists derive their knowledge from experiments, mystics from meditative insights. Both are observations, and in both fields, these observations are acknowledged as the only source of knowledge." Capra continued, "What we need therefore, is not a synthesis, but a dynamic interplay between mystical intuition and scientific analysis."

Capra was comparing Buddhism with modern physics. Trinh Xuan Thuan, professor of astronomy at the University of Virginia, a practicing Buddhist and astrophysicist, voices a similar observation. "To say that religion has discovered everything, and science is useless would be nonsense," Thuan said in a recent interview in *Science and Spirit* magazine. "I also refuse to use science to justify Buddhism. But we can take inspiration from one another, and that's why we need both."

In talking about the peculiar behavior of photons behaving as if they were still together, even though they were separated by seven miles, Thuan said, "The paradox disappears if one has the view that reality is whole, and that there is neither a 'here' nor 'there.' Eastern thought has long defended this concept of interdependence in which reality is not fragmented, but holistic."

The separated photon twin experiment is proof, said physicist Targ, that we live in a non-local, interconnected world. Those photons are "not genetically linked," he said; "they are psychically connected in time and space" because we live in a holistic universe. "We are all connected to a spiritual internet," he continued, "and the Bible, the Bhagavad Gita, the Kaballah, the Koran are the software packages."

What happens to us in a quantum world?

As Edgar Mitchell has said, consciousness is the missing link between science and religion. The epiphany he experienced whizzing through space allowed him to relate to Bushmen,

Haitian shamans, Tibetan monks. "This is the core experience which is the root of all religious experience," Mitchell said. Left to its own devices,—"Get rid of the mental garbage!" he advises—consciousness connects automatically with the larger network of which we are a part.

Psi and Consciousness Research and Projects

The Monroe Institute 62 Roberts Mountain Road, Faber, VA 22938-2317. 434-361-1252 (tel); 434-361-1237 (fax). E-mail: monroeinstitute@aol.com; Web site: www.monroeinstitute.org

Located on hundreds of breathtaking acres in the Blue Ridge Mountains, The Monroe Institute (TMI) is a private, nonprofit organization established thirty years ago by the late Robert Monroe, whose alarming and sudden out-of-body experience in 1958 changed his life. A former radio producer in New York City, Monroe developed sound as a way to access altered states of consciousness.

TMI welcomes participants to spend six days in the beginning program, the Gateway Voyage, during which they are sequestered in a darkened cell, given earphones and binaural tapes that quickly elicit deep awareness states in the brain. Throughout a twenty-four-hour cycle, listeners meet with their advisers and other members of the group (limited to twenty-four) to share as much or as little as they choose. Some experience out-of-body travel; others do not. At the end, according to spokeswoman Trina Murphy, "They may not have got what they wanted, but they definitely got what they needed."

Spiritual seekers come from around the world, with the most from North America and Europe, according to Skip Atwater, director of TMI. Ages range between thirty and ninety, (with the majority falling between 40 and 60) with slightly more men than women. "The experience comes from within," says Atwater, emphasizing that the tapes help the physiology, but the personal experience is yours. Others say it accelerates deep meditative states. *You are more than your physical body.*

Start with the Gateway Program and "*Focus 10: Mind awake, body asleep.*" The institute has facilities for several levels after that, including accommodating those who show exceptional abilities traveling to other states. Six-day Gateway Voyage: about $1,700.

Rhine Research Center 402 North Buchanan Boulevard, Durham, NC 27701. E-mail: info@rhine.org; Web site: www.rhine.org

The successor to Duke University's Parapsychology Lab, the nonprofit Rhine Research Institute is one of the oldest parapsychology centers in the country. They welcome psi-related experiences by E-mail or slow mail, but they cannot reply. Ask for information on their eight-week summer study course for anyone interested in psi abilities.

Boundary Institute P.O. Box 3580, Los Altos, CA 94024. E-mail: info@boundaryinstitute.org; Web site: www.boundaryinstitute.org

This nonprofit scientific research organization is investigating quantum mechanics as pure mathematics, and not physical reality; and looking at "poorly-understood psi phenomena"— "not your father's ESP research."

Click on their Web site and sign up for their online psi tests, designed to gather a database of precognition—predicting what will happen in the immediate future.

Consciousness Research Lab E-mail: info@PsiResearch.org; Web site: www.psiresearch.org

Consciousness Research Lab conducts controlled laboratory studies of poorly-understood psi phenomena, "mind-matter interaction, distant healing, clairvoyance, and precognition." They work on the hypothesis that scientific understanding of "mind, matter, space, and time may be incomplete, possibly in fundamental ways." They investigate areas as diverse as fluctuations in casino and state lottery winnings, as well as the effects of environmental changes on the psyche, such as tides and the phases of the moon. The organization does not offer training or counseling, but welcomes your personal ESP experiences by E-mail. Due to heavy volume, they don't promise a response. Director Dr. Dean Radin's book, *Conscious Universe,* provides further insight.

Cognitive Sciences Laboratory   Web site: www.lfr.org

Part of the Laboratories for Fundamental Research, Cognitive Sciences Laboratory was the center for government-sponsored parapsychology research known as Star Gate. It still sponsors research to determine which psi phenomena can be validated in the lab, to understand their mechanisms, and to find practical applications for them. A current study in the West Los Angeles area accepts volunteers to join a study of how the "nervous system can automatically predict the future."

The Global Consciousness Project   Web site: http://noo sphere. princeton.edu

Click to the *Current Results* page of this site and see the products of several random event generators throughout the world. The Global Consciousness Project at Princeton is an ongoing study to measure "scientifically" the effects of interconnected consciousness using nonrandom patterns of numbers generated in its random event generators. So far, the events of 9/11 show compelling evidence that concentrated attention *does* affect machines, as did Princess Diana's funeral, various earthquakes, and other events.

Institute of Noetic Sciences   101 San Antonio Road, Petaluma, CA 94952-9524. 707-775-3500 (tel); 707-781-7420 (fax). E-mail: info@noetic.org; Web site: www.noetic.org

The baby of Willis Harman and Edgar Mitchell, Institute of Noetic Sciences (IONS) is a membership organization that calls itself "a global wisdom society in which consciousness, spirituality, and love are at the center of life." The institute takes these words very seriously and sponsors research in frontier science, such as the Global Consciousness Project at Princeton (see above). It also sponsors symposiums. A recent one focused on quantum holography and drew on researchers from around the world. "Holography refers to the indications we have from the structure of nature that every part contains the whole," said Director of Research Marilyn Schlitz. "While gravitation holds the universe together, it is possible that the quantum hologram helps it self-organize." Annual awards are given to people nominated for their special acts of altruism.

Esalen Center for Theory & Research E-mail: fpoletti1@attbi. com; Web site: www.esalenctr.org

In a joint program with the Institute of Noetic Sciences (IONS), the Esalen Institute has formed an alliance to promote research "to explore the further evolution of human nature." Their research focuses on the "natural history of extraordinary functioning," including supernormal human capacities, and the effects of transformative practices such as meditation.

American Society for Psychical Research Inc. 5 West 73rd Street, New York, NY 10023. 212-799-5050 (tel); 212-496-2497 (fax). E-mail: aspr@apr.com; Web site: www.aspr.com

The venerable American branch of the even more venerable British Society for Psychical Research, ASPR has been around for many years, doing research and sponsoring major lectures. They welcome accounts of your spiritual experience via E-mail or postal mail, but cannot guarantee a reply. You can also sign up online to participate in current research.

A special near-death experience study is being conducted. Contact: William Roll, PhD, Dept. of Psychology, State University of West Georgia, Carrollton, GA 30118.

Danah Zohar Workshop   57 Bainton Road, Oxford OX27AG, England. +44 (0)1865-311473 (fax). E-mail: dzohar@dzohar.com; Web site: www.dzohar.com.

Danah Zohar is an MIT-trained quantum physicist, now a visiting fellow at the Cranfield School of Management at Oxford. Zohar, with psychiatrist Ian Marshall, is the author of *SQ Spiritual Intelligence, the Ultimate Intelligence and The Quantum Self*. She has proposed that the individual personality follows the laws of quantum physics and is subject to the same unpredictable flux.

Zohar and Marshall's SQ and Servant Leadership in the Himalayas invites twenty-five participants to daily supervised meditation and dialogue on the ten qualities of "SQ servant leadership": self-awareness, spontaneity, reflective questions, being led by visions and values, learning how to reframe problems and opportunities, nurturing inner power and learning how to use failure, setbacks, and mistakes. Spend a half day hiking in the Himalayas, two days visiting sacred sites in Kathmandu. Discuss Eastern philosophy and western science (quantum physics). Add two days of white water rafting on the Trishuli River, and you have a smashing trip. Ten days: about $5,000, including airfare from London to Kathmandu.

Mount Baldy Institute for Resonant Viewing   1942 Broadway, Suite 409, Boulder, CO 80302. 303-440-7393 (tel); 303-4440-8620 (fax). E-mail: simeon@mountbaldy.com; Web site: www. mountbaldy.com

Dr. Simeon Hein, director of Mount Baldy Institute, teaches graduated weekend courses in remote, or resonant, viewing, designed to train people to intuit information about events, people, or places separated by time or space. Many interesting projects, including a forum for graduates. Limited to eight people per class. Three days: tuition, about $400.

Web Sites

www.parapsychology.org is the site of the Parapsychology Foundation in New York City. They sponsor research on impartial scientific inquiry. Click on the Lyceum for information on their clearinghouse and courses.

www.ssq.net is the site of Science and the Spiritual Quest at the Center for Theology and Natural Sciences in Berkeley, California. They sponsor workshops and conferences on the scientific and the spiritual quests.

www.iiihs.com is the site of the International Institute of Integral Human Sciences in Montreal, Canada. A non-governmental organization associated with the United Nations, the institute sponsors programs, conferences, and courses in science and spirituality, and interreligous and intercultural understanding.

www.consciousness.arizona.edu is the site of the University of Arizona Center for Consciousness Studies.

www.templeton.org The John Templeton Foundation sponsors research programs and seminars; also gives generous awards for research in science, religion, spirit, and health.

www.issc-taste.org Read scientists' psi phenomenal experiences.

www.ehe.org The site of the Exceptional Human Experience Network, where you can share psi experiences.

www.mbmi.org is the site of the Mind/Body Medical Institute that sponsors regular conferences on spirituality and health.

Spider webs, like the web of the universe, are fragile and stable at the same time. (*Roger Archibald*)

www.unlimitedloveinstitute.org Based at Case Western Reserve University in Cleveland, the Institute for Research on Unlimited Love hopes to find support for the study of unselfish "delight in the well-being of others."

www.jse.com is the site of the *Journal of Scientific Exploration.*

http://onebehindthemany.tripod.com/clouds.htm is the site for an exhaustive list of books on consciousness.

www.artbell.com has lots of interesting items.

www.edgarmitchellapollo14.com Edgar Mitchell's home page.

www.hubblesite.org is the entrance to the universe.

www.opus-net.org is the site of the Organization for Paranormal Understanding and Support.

www.ciis.edu/comserv/sen.html is the site of the Spiritual Emergence Network for those in need of help in their spiritual journeys.

http://home.hiwaay.net/~jalison for artistic renderings of alien portraits.

> In ancient Native American tradition, Grandmother Spider is the knower of all things and the spinner of the web of the universe that holds everything together. Anything alighting on the web, such as a butterfly, causes the whole fabric to tremble. Anything done to one part of the earth affects another part, as the butterfly in Vietnam that flaps its wings and creates a wind that moves around the world.

Chapter 8
Spirituality and the Earth

Nature is a wizard.
—Henry Thoreau, *Journal*

FLOWER ESSENCES

In folk tales throughout Europe (in a theme that might be derived from the first-century writer Apuleius's story, *The Golden Ass*), an angry woman puts a curse on a man and changes him into an ass. For years he is forced to carry sacks of the miller's flour from the mill to market. One day, as he lumbers back to the mill for more flour, he passes by the local witch's house and overhears her say that the stupid ass doesn't realize that all he needs to do to release himself from enchantment is to eat a lily or a rose. Finding the flower in a garden, he eats it, and presto! He is a man again—naked, and with some explanations to make to the startled villagers, but fully human.

Jung's colleague Marie Louise von Franz used this story to explain the alchemical transformation that happens when the psyche is released from the dominance of animal instincts on the road to becoming a complete human being.

The story also illustrates our deeply ingrained belief in the healing power of flowers and plants, which are able not only to cast off the burden of our curse, but also to refine our out-of-balance spirits.

Findhorn Flower Essences Wellspring, The Park, Findhorn Bay, Forres, Moray, Scotland IV36 3TY. +44(0)1309 690129 (tel); +44(0)1309 691300 (fax). E-mail: info@findhornessences.com; Web site: www.findhornessences.com

Edward Bach, a Scottish physician and intuitive, was the first modern person to develop essences from flowers, by incorporating folk techniques. Using Scottish field flowers, Dr. Bach developed a sun-infusion method that extracted the essence which, mixed with pure water from "sacred healing wells," could be bottled and sold. He developed thirty-nine essences designed to release specific negative emotional conditions, from homesickness to creative blocks, to bring us back "to our true selves," according to his student Elyse Furlong (www.essentialharmony.com).

At Findhorn, you can work in "cocreative contact with Nature," in three courses: Healing with Flowers, a weekend workshop; Nature, Spirit, and Life Force, an advanced weekend workshop, designed to help you attune to the kingdoms of the devas; and Practitioner Training, a five-day intensive.

Alaskan Flower Essence Project Education & Research, P.O. Box 1369, Homer, AK 99603. 907-235-2777 (tel/fax). E-mail: alida@alaskaessences.com; Web site: www.alaskaessences.com

Working from the Twin Creeks Trailhead Lodge, near Homer, Alaska, this summer Practitioner Training Program introduces you not only to Alaskan flowers, gems, and environmental essences and their therapeutic uses, but also to a deeper communication with nature. Much of each day is spent in the field; the rest at lectures on profiling the essences, therapeutic care of the soul, working with special populations such as children and animals, space-clearing (both director Steve Johnson and Jane Bell are Feng Shui practitioners), and certification requirements. Go earlier and enjoy some of the Alaskan countryside. Lodging is in a housekeeping apartment, bunkhouse, or tent; ranges from $500 to $160 a week; tuition is about $1,900.

One Heart Box 517, Goodwood, SA 5034, Australia. +61 (0)8-8297-6223 (tel). E-mail: oneheart@senet.com.au; Web site: www.oneheartbe.com

One Heart Academy's annual Mystical French Adventure is an unusual combination of flower essences, yoga, energy healing, and esoteric sacred sites in La Val Dieu (the Valley of God), Languedoc, France. Once a stronghold of the Knights Templar, Cathar ruins and a fortress remain. This region is also the center of the Mary Magdalene legend, and the cave, water sources, and church at Rennes-le-Chateau that are sacred to her. Was she an Egyptian priestess of Isis? Is this where the Holy Grail is buried?

Carol Asher, who, with Robert March, has been leading seminars to La Val Dieu for many years, says the goddess energies permeate the region. Incorporating these feelings of nurturing and healing, Carol and Robert give course work in some of the twenty-three local flower essences that Carol has developed from the flowers and Spanish broom whose perfumes are redolent in the air. Robert begins each day teaching yoga and meditation classes with Bridget Lytton-Miner, a yoga instructor. Then the day is yours to learn Languedoc Flower Essence Therapy, Sekhem Reiki, anointment massage, or to hike and explore some of the intriguing sites.

During the eleven days, more than forty hours are spent in course work; fifty hours in sacred-site visiting. It pays to be in good shape before you go, and to learn a little French. Lodging is in the village, some private, some dormitory rooms. Eleven days: about $1,800, airfare not included.

Migliara No.7, 94 Crescent Road, Toronto, ON M4W 1T5, Canada. 416-323-1133 (tel); 416-323-0204 (fax). E-mail: lucem@ican.net; Web site: www.dallaluce.com

This is not a flower essence course, but it incorporates flowers, the earth, and the feminine spirit in Italy. Migliara is a restored five-hundred year-old farmhouse in Tuscany, about an hour south of Florence, where summer days are vibrant with the smell of field flowers and the sound of distant waterfalls. Lucinda Vardey offers The Flowering of the Soul, a one-week retreat for women "of all ages and beliefs," in which you can explore new images of the divine feminine through prayer and contemplation and relaxing with Mother Earth."

Perelandra, Center for Nature Research P.O. Box 3603, Warrenton, VA 20188. 800-960-8806 (toll free); 540-937-2153 (tel); 540-937-3360 (fax). Web site: www.perelandra-ltd.com

Machaelle Wright, founder of Perelandra, believes in "co-creative science," working in partnership with nature. For almost three decades, Wright has developed her hundred-foot circular garden, located on forty-five acres in northern Virginia, with the advice of nature spirits. Perelandra's flower essence health program has evolved a concept called "soil-less gardening," which is the application of nature's wisdom to other aspects of life, such as work or home. "Change bombards us now," she recently observed. "No mistakes are allowed. With co-creative science, you get it right the first time."

Honeysuckle vines (*Roger Archibald*)

Wild roses. (*Roger Archibald*)

Perelandra is open to visitors only three afternoons a summer. It's free; because of the high demand, register in advance. The essences and much more are contained in the free catalog. Perelandra gives discounts for first-time buyers, and a 5 percent additional discount if you buy online.

NATIVE AMERICAN HERBS

Journeys into American Indian Territory P.O. Box 575, Eastport, NY 11941. 800-458-2632 (toll free); 631-878-8655 (tel); 631-878-4518 (fax). Web site: www.indianjourneys.com
For more than fifteen years, Robert Vetter has been hosting journeys to Native American communities to better understand the ancient culture preserved in oral tradition and rituals. In the

Mohawk Valley, New York, you can study herbology with Native American elder Jan Longboat from the Turtle Clan in Six Nations Reserve, Ontario. She teaches you to identify the plants, to prepare them, and to understand their most effective uses. Two days: $375, includes everything. (Many other Native American programs, as well.)

Mepkin Abbey, a Trappist Monastery in Monck, South Carolina, makes *Earth Healer Compost Tea*. The compost is made from laying-hen manure and kiln-dried white pine shavings and comes in a large "tea bag." Soak the tea bag overnight, then water your houseplants. Divinely effective, the tea bags come in half-pound, one- and two-pound bags. Web site: www.mepkin abbey.org.

NATURE SPIRITS

For a view of nature spirits, consider some of Ireland's famous fairies (the *aes aidhe*); the *Pooka,* a shape-shifting, generally bad-spirited gnome who demands a tithe of the harvest—or else; the *Merrows,* beautiful sea creatures, whose webbed hands and big feet do not turn away Irish men. They occasionally marry, but before long, the Merrow returns to the sea. *Leprechauns* are wizened, drunken little men who guard treasure, including piggy banks; *changelings* are fairy children exchanged for human babies. They screech, are usually unpleasant, and often are really old men in disguise or wooden models of babies. *Grogochs* are half human and half fairy, and resemble wild men wearing twigs and leaves. *Banshees* can be a seductive young woman, a middle-aged matron, or a tiny old woman; whatever form they take, Banshees foretell death. A *dullahan* instills fear because he carries his head in one hand as he speeds by on a reckless steed, usually on lonely roads on foggy nights. Take a look at www.Irelandseye.com.

THE MYSTERIOUS EARTH

Whatever sensitives and intuitives are able to evoke magically from the earth, the fact remains that the earth itself is mysterious. Once subject to merciless bombardment from asteroids, the earth finally settled down. Some scientists speculate that the moon flew into orbit as our satellite, after it was wrenched from one of the deep trenches in the Pacific Ocean. Held in space by the tensions of the orbits of the near planets and the distant planets, Earth gradually cooled, keeping its molten core, as hot as the Sun, and pushing up a mantle of minerals beneath a crust of solidified matter.

Earth never stops moving. It revolves on a daily and an annual cycle around the Sun. The planet tilts on its axis, is subject to periodic wobbles, and is gradually moving the focus of its north pole from Polaris to Vega (in 11,000 years). This polar shift already affects the angle of the spring equinox, which, 2,000 years ago, was oriented to Aries, is currently in Pisces, and in a thousand years will be in Aquarius.

Aside from these uneven tilts in space, Earth, which is 71 percent water, is subject daily to the pull of the lunar tides which causes the sea to breathe in and out every six hours. Tidal forces from the Moon and Sun keep us in constant flux: the speed of Earth around the Sun changes (El Niño, for example, can slow Earth's rotation); and our geomagnetic poles shift daily by several miles.

The Delphic Oracle's Secret

Then there are the changes *inside* Earth. The mantle responds to the hot inner core and produces bulges and an uneven surface of the crust, as much as forty miles thick on land, but only three to six or seven miles thick under the oceans. The unstable crust is subject to cracks, through which minerals seep. Recently, archaeologists working in league with chemists and geologists, discovered a fissure beneath the Delphic Oracle, consulted by every ancient Greek from Plato to Alexander the Great.

The "Oracle," a priestess sacred to Apollo, sat in a room with a tripod enveloped by vapors. The vapors actually were gases from petrochemicals escaping through the fissure, the scientists theorized. Among the gases was ethylene, often used as an anesthetic and which, in light doses, produces a feeling of euphoria. The priestess hired to be the Oracle, archaeologists now be-

Delphi was sacred to the god Apollo, shown here in a drawing from a drinking cup, dated to about 470 B.C.E. in the Delphi Museum. He makes an offering to the sacred earth, watched by a raven. (*Delphi Museum*)

lieve, would have been prone to "seeing" the future after breathing ethylene vapors.

The Bulges

Moving bulges in the crust affect not only the movement of the tectonic plates (the cause of many earthquakes), but also the gravitational field, which changes its place and size around the planet according to the mass of the bulge. Less mass equals low gravity.

Only satellites are able to identify these pockets of changing mass that affect gravity levels: changes in the magma movements inside volcanoes, or the "bulges" in the Pacific Ocean, for example, that produce the warm eastward flowing swell that

When volcanoes explode, Earth speaks. They rumble from within, lie dormant for years, and then one day, erupt, their dust and smoke covering the Sun, sometimes for weeks. (*FEMA*)

becomes the El Niño, or the flow of water into and out of aquifers. Add to all this natural flux and uncertainty the sub-tle—and sudden—effects of global climate change, such as warmer winters in the north and huge shelves of ice that plunge into the Antarctic seas, and it becomes clear that the only immutable law of the earth is change.

Do we need to worry?

These are things that, as the average person in the street, we might know and not know at the same time. What we need to know, we know. What we don't know will affect us sooner or later.

Years of perpetual wisdom dipensed by the *Old Farmer's Almanac* illustrate some of the nuts-and-bolts understanding of the earth that comes from working in harmony with it to sur-vive. Contemporary pagans, who seek to live in spiritual union with nature, see themselves, not unlike shamans, as deeply wed-ded to the earth. Nature is central to pagans, says Graham Harvey in *Contemporary Paganism*. Pagans view Earth, he says, as "a person with rights, responsibilities, desires and dislikes, problems and pleasures."

Wiccans incorporate respect for the earth through annual rit-uals, and they "sense an 'aliveness' and *presence* in nature," writes Margot Adler in *Drawing Down the Moon*. Sensitive to lunar changes and geomagnetism, the Wicca religion incorpo-rates Earth as a living thing in their practices. "They tend to view humanity's 'advancement' and separation from nature as the prime source of alienation. They see ritual as a tool to end that alienation," says Adler.

In *The Spiral Dance* fellow Wiccan Starhawk says, "Nature knows best. Magic is part of nature; it does not controvert nat-ural laws. It is through study and observation of nature, of the visible, physical reality, that we can learn to understand the workings of the underlying reality."

From another area, a Tai Chi teacher once said, talking about the subtleties of human interaction with nature, "When you learn what gravity is not, you can do anything."

DOWSING

As we struggle to understand some of the puzzling things going on around us, dowsing has become increasingly popular over the last few decades. Farmers, going back to the Neolithic period, probably always dowsed to find sources of water; and dowsers still are called in to find water, especially by well-reliant homeowners during drought. Some dowsers even correct bad water situations: People who can't sleep, or whose lives are emotionally distraught, are helped by finding, for example, that they are sleeping over sources of *contaminated* water.

But few people actually need to find underground water anymore. Dowsing now focuses on finding and converting negative energies in your environment, balancing chakra energy, healing by finding the diseased tissue and changing the DNA.

According to dowsers, almost everyone can be taught to dowse, to find the subtle energies that hover over and around us, and the magnetic energy lines that we sense under our feet. The humble, naturally Y-shaped twig that points toward hidden sources of water has been replaced by Y- and L-shaped dowsing prosthetic devices and pendulums. Some dowsing teachers teach a kind of psychic dowsing, without any tangible tools. The thrill of feeling the rod in your hands actually bend as if under some ethereal control when it senses a source of energy is, however, unforgettable.

More and more, dowsers are exploring the invisible in much the same way that shamans visit the spirit world to find out the cause of disruption in their community. Veteran dowser and British physician Aubrey Westlake said he thinks the rediscovery of dowsing by so many people "has been vouchsafed to us by providence." Dowsing to find the worlds of subtle energies, according to Westlake, acts like training wheels until we have evolved enough to do it naturally.

"Dowsing should be regarded as a special and peculiar sense, halfway between our ordinary physical senses, which apprehend the material world," Westlake said, "and our to-be-developed future occult senses, which in due course will apprehend the supersensible world directly."

One Dowser's Technique

In an explanation of his technique, Geomancer Sig Lonegren, formerly of Vermont, now of Glastonbury, England, echoes Machaelle Wright at Perelandra in her understanding of earth spirits or devas. Lonegren believes that labyrinths attract underground water. To build a labyrinth, he says, you must "dowse from the center" of where the labyrinth will be. Then "communicate with the spirit of the place," by bringing a gift.

"Now calm down and tell this spirit what you have in mind, and ask it to work with you to make this a place of meditation. Now, using a pendulum or an L-rod, stand somewhere on your lawn and ask, 'What direction is the best place for me to put the center of this labyrinth?' It will show you a line." Repeat this, says Lonegren until you have triangulation; where the two lines cross is your center. Lonegren also dowses for Bach flower essences to find the best remedy.

"The purpose of a geomancer," Lonegren said in an interview in *Spirit of Change*, "is to work for harmony in the earth, fertility of the earth, and to create spaces that enhance the possibility that whatever you're trying to do there happens. Geomancers," he said, "are what I would call spiritual ecologists."

To get to know more about dowsing, take courses, attend conferences, follow new directions in dowsing, and become a certified dowser, you can join the nonprofit **American Society**

of Dowsers P.O. Box 24, Danville, VT 05828. 802-684-3417 (tel); 802-684-2565 (fax). E-mail: ASD@dowsers.org; Web site: www. dowsers.org

The School of Mid-Atlantic Geomancy was founded by Sig Lonegren, who now resides in Glastonbury, England. +44 (0) 1458-835-818 (tel). E-mail: sig@geomancy.org; Web site: www. geomancy.org

ANAM Holistic Center Manor Kilbride, Blessington, County Wicklow, Ireland. E-mail: joe@anamspirit.com; Web site: www. anamspirit.com

Joe Mullally invites anyone in Ireland or thinking of vacationing there to ANAM for his weekend courses in divining (or dowsing), Bach flower essences, and nature spirituality. Stay in local B and Bs. He will also connect you with Irish tour guides for a holiday. Weekend dowsing courses: EU 160.

Http://members.tripod.com/~Reid_ J is the site of Digital Dowsing, with lots of links.

FENG SHUI

Technically, a geomancer is a diviner of lines; and in China, a geomancer practices Feng Shui. The union of wind and water, Feng Shui is the practice of achieving harmony with nature, built structures, gardens, roads, and the people who use the area. The central idea is the flow of chi—the life force or energy present in all living things. Blocked chi causes illness, lack of career success, disagreement in families, sheer bad luck. A person in a blocked chi situation has the uneasy sense that something is not right, but often does not know why. A good practitioner can spot the trouble by using a combination of technical knowledge (windows that open out, rather than up or in, for example, are better for the flow of chi), and intuition. Solutions involve everything from placing plants in certain areas to getting rid of antique furniture because of its negative energy to actually moving somewhere else.

Like dowsing, Feng Shui works with nature and subtle energies. Many practitioners join the Black Hat Sect Feng Shui tradition, which blends mystical and wisdom teachings. Others use Feng Shui to unblock other types of problems, such as inability to get a job or to overcome nightmares.

Center for Applied Feng Shui Research Kappvest InfoServ Pte Ltd., 110 Gerald Drive, #01-45, Singapore. E-mail: events@ge omancy.net; Web site: www.geomancy.net

This Web site is full of information about Feng Shui. Robert and Cecil Lee give an online certification course Applied Feng Shui, which gives a basic foundation ($188); and Flying Star or Xuan Kong Fei Xing, which is for professionals learning house analysis ($288).

Feng Shui Designs, Inc. P.O. Box 399, Nevada City, CA 95959. 800-551-2482 (toll free); 530-470-9215 (tel). E-mail: info@feng shuidesigns.com; Web site: www.fengshuidesigns.com

Feng Shui Designs gives practitioner certification courses with Helen and James Jay, who trained with Feng Shui Grand Master Lin Yun, as well as popular writer on the subject, Lillian Too. Six-day courses are held in Nevada City. Tuition: $1,200; lodging is extra, in local houses, B and Bs, or hotels.

Geomancy/Feng Shui Education Organization 2939 Ulloa Street, San Francisco, CA 94116. Contact: Steven Post: 415-753-6408 (tel). E-mail: joe1080@aol.com; Web site: www.geofeng shui.com

Steven Post, Dr. Edgar Sung, and Barry Gordon—all Black Sect Feng Shui masters—offer a three-year professional training program in San Francisco and at the Open Center in New York City (212-219-2527, x 135). Each year includes three four-day workshops, and a five-day summer intensive with room and board: $4,100. Dr. Edgar Sung also guides Feng Shui and I Ching trips to China.

Visionary Villages

Spiritual life is the bouquet of natural life.

—Joseph Campbell

Take Feng Shui harmony to the extreme, and you get places like Ecovillage, a Findhorn experiment that brings together as many as two-thousand people "united by a common goal" based on shared "ecological, social, and/or spiritual values." Ecovillage, in Scotland, currently composed of four hundred people from forty countries, grows its own organic food, has renewable energy systems, holistic health care, ecological building that honors the earth, and family support systems, including rituals and celebrations. To take a visual tour visit www.findhorn.org/ecovillage/display.html.

Arcosanti   HC 74, Box 4136, Mayer, AZ 86333. 928-632-7138 (tel). E-mail:tminus@arcosanti.org; Web site: www.arcosanti.org
   The vision of Italian architect Paolo Soleri, Arcosanti is a cluster of preformed concrete buildings in the Arizona desert that offer sustainable living space, commercial centers, and a cultural arena for five thousand people. No cars eliminate bad air; giant greenhouses provide food and winter heat; wind and sun provide energy. Soleri and his staff use the earth as forms for the concrete structures, and in the making of tiles and bronze bells for which Arcosanti has become famous.
   You can spend a week learning about Soleri's theory of arcology (architecture and ecology); or take a tour any hour from 10:00 A.M. to 4:00 P.M. The seminar week includes everything: $450.

The Rocky Mountain Institute 1739 Snowmass Creek Road, Snowmass, CO 81654-9199. 970-927-3851 (tel). E-mail: recept@ rmi.org; Web site: www.rmi.org

The Rocky Mountain Institute's headquarters building bears out the research that this organization has conducted for a couple of decades on finding corrections to some of the wrong ecological turns we have made. Located north of Aspen, Colorado, the institute's north side is built into a hill, and has an earth-sheltered roof. A central greenhouse provides passive solar heat; and the sixteen-inch thick walls are a double course of masonry filled in the center with polyurethane foam. Lots of other ways to learn about relating to the earth here. Free one-hour guided tours are offered on Fridays at 2:00 P.M.; or drop in on weekdays from 9:00 A.M. to 4:30 P.M. and take a self-guided tour.

LEY LINES

What is the meaning of the super straight lines that cross Great Britain and seem to be connected with ancient stone sites as well as churches? What is the meaning of the *ceques,* the straight lines that extend south of Cusco, Peru, and go to Nazca? What is the meaning of the straight roads built by the Anasazi? Or others, around the world?

A "ley" is an ancient word for a cleared strip of land. Paul Devereux, who has been a student of ley lines for several decades, developed a theory of their origin about ten years ago, after intensive scholarship and hands-on testing. Past president of the Society of Ley Hunters, Devereux could not resist making the comparisons with other long straight tracks or roads around the world. In Great Britain, he suggested that the roads *preceded* the building of Stonehenge or any of the other major Neolithic sites.

Working from the observations made by anthropologist Marlene Dobkin del Rios in Peru, that the brain "sees" designs

Lines have been etched and carved into the earth for millennia, some meandering, like these natural and man-made ones in British Columbia; others straight as an arrow, called ley lines, are possibly routes to the Spirit World. (*Stephanie Ocko*)

and patterns in the beginning of trance, shortly after being affected by hallucinogenic herbs, such as ayahuasca or peyote, ("grids, dots, webs, spirals . . . arabesques, nested curves, lines, and so on"), and that, as the effects deepen, the shaman "flies," Devereux suggests that the long straight lines, or ceques in Peru, are in fact a map of the spirit world, the physical anchor of the ecstatic flight the shaman makes in trance. Devereux also points out that in most cultures of the world, the dead are taken from the living via a straight path, in many places, called the "death route," on the way to the spirit world.

Presented at a conference in Germany in 1996, Devereux's theory that ley lines are maps of the spirit world has only added to the intrigue surrounding ley lines.

Ley lines were first uncovered in 1921 by a local Herefordshire businessman and amateur photographer, Alfred Watkins, who followed the dots of prehistoric features of the land, and, in a flash, saw that they were connected by what he called The Old Straight Track. Prehistoric monuments follow the paths, probably as ancient religious centers; and Christian churches were often built near pagan sites, sometimes with stones from old circles.

A year after Watkins died in 1935, ley lines, or the straight track, took an ethereal bent when a novelist, Dion Fortune, wrote a book in which she suggested ley lines were "lines of force." Local dowsers interpreted the force as being cosmic in origin, and by 1960, mapmakers placed reported Unidentified Flying Objects landing sites on ley lines (some, erroneously), and proposed that they were magnetic vortices bringing in cosmic rays, visions, and beings.

Proponents of the cosmic force theory of leys persist among some New Agers, even though geologists, minerologists, archaeologists, and others have tested and retested rocks and sites that are thought to be "hot," and found no unusual energies. The adventure continues, because the mysteries of geomagnetism are ongoing: Do we underestimate Earth as being a real player in some of the peculiar forces we experience?.

For more on the theory of shamanic spirit routes, see Paul Devereux's Web site, www.acemake.com.

For information on the Society of Ley Hunters, try: www.leyhunter.com.

Note: Most tours of Stonehenge and other stone monuments mention ley lines and even include maps.

Goddess Tours

England, Ireland, Egypt, Crete, and Malta are the main sites for worship of *The Goddess*, a multi-form deity who encompasses the aspects of the Earth Mother: the young woman, the forgiving mother, and the wise old crone. She is sometimes called Isis, Astarte, Artemis, Demeter, Persephone, Aphrodite, and other ancient goddess names, as well as Celtic feminine deities, Paleolithic representations of a fecund "goddess," and the great maternal Neolithic goddess on Malta. In Hawaii, the great earth goddess Pele makes her presence known in an eter-

Where do gods and goddesses go when the people who worshiped them move away? They linger in surprising places, like this golden Diana as a huntress, in a park in Washington, D.C. (*Roger Archibald*)

nal volcano whose unceasing flow of magma is giving birth to another in the Hawaiian chain of islands.

Anthropologist Marija Gimbutas author of *Goddesses and Gods of Old Europe* gathered many proponents when she traced "the Goddess" in ancient civilizations. Goddess worship has become popular with the rise of paganism and the Wicca religion, which recognizes the goddess and the horned god in ceremonies that mark the seasons throughout the year.

Not everyone who goes on goddess tours is Wiccan, however; some just experience being in the presence of the goddess as comforting and inspiring, and find the healing they seek in pure feminine energy.

Please note that some goddess tours are exclusively for women. Men are not excluded on *all* tours; call first.

Shamanic Journeys, Ltd. P.O. Box 5025, Eugene, OR 97405. 800-937-2991 (toll free); 541-484-1099 (tel); 541-686-5960 (fax). E-mail: nscully@shamanicjourneys.com; Web site: www.shaman icjourneys.com

"As we become more aware of who we really are, we naturally gravitate to the practice of conscious evolution," said Nicki Scully, an author, lecturer, and healer who has been leading tours to Egypt since 1978. "When we learn to perceive the world from our heart, instead of our will . . . then we will be in alignment with divine will." Join Scully with author and translator of the *Egyptian Book of the Dead* Normandi Ellis on a sixteen-day tour of Egypt. "There is no place like Egypt, and no doorway like the one we will enter together," says Scully. Explore the Goddess Isis mysteries, engage in mystery school initiations, and ceremonies. Egyptologist guide, five-star accommodations on land and on the Nile. Sixteen days: about $4,400, includes airfare from New York City.

Ancient Sacred Sites Tours Ann Maher; +61 (0)3-9718-2651 (tel in Australia). E-mail: maherram@bigpond.com

Ann Maher is a licensed aromatherapist and Reiki master who is studying to become a Druidess. Your Inner Quest for the Grail is a spiritual and physical experience of the "powerful, sacred land" of Southwest England. Start at Glastonbury's Chalice Well, sacred to the Great Goddess, go to Stonehenge, King Arthur sites, and rarely visited stone circles in Cornwall and Devon. Druidic rituals are held when appropriate; evening group meditation deepens the connection.

Sacred Sites Tours 3420 Pillsbury Avenue S, Minneapolis, MN 55408. 612-823-2442 (tel). E-mail:info@sacredsitestours.com; Web site: www.sacredsitestours.com

This company offers "intentional travel for women and girls," to experience the sense of awe and exploration that accompany the goddess experience. The Realms of the Goddess tour centers in a small market town in Wiltshire, near Stonehenge, and stays in a renovated, three-star hotel built in 1599. From there, day tours range to Stonehenge, the Uffington White Horse, and Glastonbury. Eight days: about $2,300.

Sacred Journeys for Women P.O. Box 8007, Roseland Station, CA 95407. 888-779-6696 (toll free). E-mail: alaura@sa credjourneys.com; Web site: www.sacredjourneys.com

Sacred journeys are for women "longing for a deeper meaning and purpose in life," who are eager to travel and explore the spirit. Among many global adventures, Gayle Lawrence offers a Pilgrimage to the Goddess Pele. Immerse yourself in the real Hawaii by swimming with sea turtles and dolphins at a resort with forty-two acres of tropical foliage. Then make the pilgrimage to Volcanoes National Park, picnic on the rim of a crater, and invoke the great goddess. Daily circle and workshops. Seven days: about $1,500, airfare not included.

Purple Mountain Tours 34 Purple Mountain Road, Putney, VT 05346. 802-387-4753 (tel/fax). E-mail: hshik@sover.net; Web site: www.purplemountaintours.com

Psychic healer Helene A. Shik and Willow LaMonte, an American Malta-resident who publishes the newspaper, *Goddessing Regenerated*, are your guides on Purple Mountain's *Goddess Tour to the Sacred Sites of Malta* at the spring equinox. Malta is the site of some of the most beautiful Neolithic temples and carved figures of the Mother Goddess in Europe; in the spring, wildflowers bloom in profusion. Spend two days exploring Malta and the Tarxian Temple complex with its famous spirals, then move to the small island of Gozo for tours with a local guide, then back to the Mnajdra Temple for a ceremony with the solar alignment. Fourteen days, about $3,500, includes airfare from Boston.

Feminine Matrix   Danica Anderson, 7638 58th Avenue, NE, Olympia, WA 98516. 360-455-4701 (tel). E-mail: danica_kolo@ yahoo.com; Web site: www.femininematrix.com

The sun is captured for a moment in the trees. (*Roger Archibald*)

Danica Anderson is a therapist specializing in feminist arche-typal psychology. With that theme, she offers spirituality travel tours—"deepening circles that house women's experiences." Anderson guides women's work/study sacred pilgrimages to Malta, where she does "intensive breakthrough therapies on-site on related topics associated with the site." She also offers ap-proved CEU home-study courses in understanding violence, post-traumatic stress, and women's issues. Your participation helps fund her work on trauma with Bosnian women refugees. Starting about $1,800. Her pilgrimages are on demand.

Goddess Tours 2601 NW 29th Drive, Boca Raton, FL 33434. 561-999-0903 (tel); 561-558-0209 (fax). Web site: www.goddess unlimited.com

Every woman is a goddess. Release the goddess within! tours, are designed for women traveling alone, and for women who need "time to themselves . . . with like-minded companions." Try a cruise that leaves Lisbon, Portugal, goes to the Canary Islands, then crosses south to Barbados. Ten days: about $2,400. Or celebrate the arts at the Sundance Film Festival, the Edin-burgh Arts Festival, or New York City theater.

Chapter 9
Prayer Groups, Consciousness Communities, and Mystery Schools

Peace comes within the souls of men
When they realize their oneness with the universe.
—Black Elk

On September 11, 2001, forty global random event generators, which produce a continuous stream of numbers, fed each second over the internet to Princeton University, recorded an unusual event. The previously randomly generated numbers took on a "structure" that analysts at the Global Consciousness Project at Princeton were able to correlate in graphs that matched the sudden attacks of September 11. (http://noo sphere.princeton.edu.)

It was not the first time (although it was the most widespread) that the random numbers had coalesced into a structure, as a result, say researchers, of "resonance and coherence of focus"; other events that altered the data at the Global Consciousness Project have been Princess Diana's death, the first few minutes around New Year's Eves, several major earthquakes, and "a variety of global meditations."

Human attention through prayer and concentration creates a critical mass that is a well of potential power. Laboratory studies have identified changes in a string of DNA brought about by feelings concentrated on the DNA by the researchers: happiness encouraged it to relax and thrive; anger caused it to grow rigid.

The recent study from the Russian Academy of Sciences that witnessed free-flowing photons (light cells) taking on the shape of the DNA placed in the same container, and continuing to hold that shape after the DNA was removed, further emphasized the power of the fabric of our living composition. Our cells renew themselves moment to moment; we heal others at great distances.

Why not pray for peace?

A visitor to the Franciscan chapel at the top of Mount Nebo, Jordan, thought to be the resting place of Moses, lights a candle in prayer. (*Roger Archibald*)

"Prayer is, to us, as water is to the seed of a plant," said Gregg Braden, in response to the question, Why do we have prayer? A former earth scientist, now author, Braden said in *The Isaiah Effect*, "We are like those seeds. We come into the world whole and complete unto ourselves, carrying the seed of something even greater."

Elizabeth Lesser in *The New American Spirituality* says that we pray to connect to something bigger. "Prayer," she says, "is an expression of our thirst for connection, for peace, for compassion. It is our longing for God."

And if we *all* pray together?

Braden says, "Multiply the effects of . . . one individual, empowered through a specific mode of prayer, by even a fraction of the six billion or so people in our world, and we begin to get a sense of the power inherent in our collective will. It is the power to end all suffering and avert the pain that has been the hallmark of the twentieth century."

The internet can change the way we affect the world. By creating a group—from everywhere—and focusing on good: peace, love, healing, resolutions to conflicts, prayer can bring changes.

Some groups gather online and agree to pray at a certain hour of a certain day to establish an arena of positive change. Others encourage concentration throughout the day. Some of the following groups are working toward global evolution in other ways.

Prayer Groups

Global Renaissance Alliance   Web site: www.renaissance alliance. org

Pause daily for ten minutes of silent prayer, opening to the "wisdom and love of God." West Coast: 9:00 A.M.; East Coast: 12 Noon; London: 5:00 P.M. The Renaissance Alliance was founded by Marianne Williamson and Neale Donald Walsch.

Findhorn Foundation Web site: www.findhorn.org

The Network of Light Meditations for Peace is held daily with the following meditation in: London at 12:15 P.M. and on the East Coast of the United States at 7:15 A.M.

Let us each come into our heart center, that place of deep inner peace in the center of our being, setting aside all that has occurred during the day in order to be here and to be fully present in this sanctuary.

Let us connect with everyone else at the heart level.

And with everyone else in our community.

And raising our consciousness to just above the crown of our heads, let us connect with our soul, seeing it in its beauty and truth and knowing we are all part of the one great soul.

And from that soul level, we align ourselves to the network of light, to all those groups and individuals meditating in service to this planet. And we see the network of light as a glowing web surrounding and protecting our planet with light.

We align ourselves with the spiritual hierarchy, with the masters of compassion and wisdom, and with the Christ at the heart of humanity.

We align ourselves with the angelic realms and we welcome the presence of Michael and Raphael, those two great angelic beings who guard and ward humanity.

And we align ourselves to Shambhala—the center where the will of God is known.

And having created a group vessel to receive the divine qualities of love, light, and power, we open ourselves to act as channels to receive these energies and to ground and anchor them in the sanctuary.

[A twenty-minute period of silence.]

Now it is time for us to radiate out to the planet the divine qualities of love, light, and power which we have anchored in this sanctuary. . . .

As we sound the first OM, let us visualize the quality of love radiating out from this sanctuary to touch the hearts of every human being and especially those who are suffering or oppressed—no matter what race, color, or creed. Let us also see love transmuting the thought forms of fear, hatred, and violence.

As we sound the second OM, let us see the quality of light flowing out from this sanctuary to the whole planet, and especially to the military, political, and spiritual leaders, so that enlightened decisions may be made.

Finally, as we sound the third OM, let us visualize the quality of power radiating out from our sanctuary, so that the divine plan for the earth unfolds for the highest. . . .

Let light and love and power restore the plan on earth.

James and Salle Merrill Redfield Web site: www.celestinevision.com

The Redfields' World Prayer Project publishes *Alerts* with suggested prayer-visualizations to hold "throughout the day whenever possible." With their prayers, they counsel to think of yourself as a "Peace Mover" to channel love wherever it is needed.

Contemplative Outreach, Ltd. P.O. Box 737, 10 Park Place, Suite 2B, Butler, NJ 07405. 973-838-3384 (tel); 973-492-5795 (fax). E-mail: office@coutreach.org; Web site: www.centering prayer.com

Centering Contemplative Prayer, a non-denominational, Christian prayer method modeled after contemplative prayer practices of the Desert Fathers and Mothers of the first centuries C.E. was organized in the 1970s by three Trappist monks, William Meninger, Basil Pennington, and Thomas Keating. The recovery of ancient prayer is to regain the practice, active for the first sixteen centuries of the Christian church, that guides the soul to a deeper connection to God. Contemplative or "centering" prayer requires "choosing a sacred word as the symbol of our intention to consent to God's presence and action within." The single word, which can be anything you consider sacred—God, peace, love, grace—is repeated at will during a twenty-

A nun in Choroni, Venezuela, stands before her painting of her historic town. (*Roger Archibald*)

minute period of prayer, practiced ideally twice a day. The Lectio Divina, is a direct conversation with Christ, based on the scriptures.

Contemplative Outreach creates a spiritual network of individuals and small communities, and sponsors weekend retreats. Father Keating suggests committing to six weeks of daily centering prayer to lock in the practice. (They hope to expand retreats to five days.)

Emissary of Light: James Twyman Web site: www.emissary oflight.com

Twyman, the "Troubadour of Peace," who travels to hot spots around the world to give peace concerts, holds a Beloved Community in Joshua Tree, California. If you can't attend, read the peace prayers on his Web site.

Dolphin Energy Club Shirley Bliley, DEC Coordinator, The Monroe Institute, 62 Roberts Mountain Road, Faber, VA 22938-2317. 804-361-9132 (tel); 804-361-1611 (fax). E-mail: DEC1pd@ aol.com; Web site: www.monroeinstitute.org

This unusual "club" enlists people who are willing to join a healing pool to be called from time to time to focus their consciousness for two weeks on a person in need of healing. Healers prepare by using Monroe Institute's Hemi-Sync tapes, based on frequency patterns of brainwaves of talented healers. Results are spectacular. Club dues are $50 for nonmembers of the Monroe Institute; $35 for members. The healing is free.

Web Sites

www.beliefnet.com has links to prayer groups of all religions. It also hosts prayer circles, a gathering of internet people who pray on behalf of a person, group, or cause.

www.jesuit.ie/prayer/ the site of Sacred Space, run by Irish Jesuits, is an on-line invitation to pray at your computer for ten minutes a day.

www.worldprayers.org is the site of the World Prayers Project, which gives viewers the choice of four different types of random prayers from all faiths.

www.childrenoflight.com Organizes periodical worldwide meditations online.

Global Consciousness Communities

Pathfinding Project   The Institute of Noetic Sciences Web site: www.noetic.org/Ions/community/pathfinding.asp

Members of the Pathfinding Project: 1) seek to understand the present state of the world; 2) create positive images of the future to pull us in the direction we desire; and 3) identify specific paths to develop a "just, compassionate, and sustainable society." Their attention lies in a variety of areas, from a search for the meaning of life to environmental sustainability to equitable distribution of resources. Visit their Web site and become a Pathfinder.

Foundation for Conscious Evolution   Web site: www.con sciousevolution.net

Barbara Marx Hubbard believes in establishing communities for cocreation of our next evolution, Homo Universalis. Through creating core groups, we "can weave together a shared vision to guide humanity across the quantum jump." Her Peace Room serves as a resource center for healing projects around the world.

New Planetary Consciousness   *Tikkun,* 2107 Van Ness Ave, Suite 302, San Francisco, CA 94109. 415-575-1200 (tel); 415-575-1434 (fax). E-mail: community@tikkun.org; Web site: www. tik kun.org

Author and popular speaker Michael Lerner, editor of the progressive Jewish monthly, *Tikkun,* is the author, with Cornell West of *Jews and Blacks: Let the Healing Begin.* He and others who recognize that "our well-being depends on the well-being of every single person on the planet," founded the New Planetary Consciousness, which is committed to finding equality and "a recognition of the spirit of God in each other."

Center of Cocreation   Web site: www.centerofcocreation. com

Dedicated to a "co-creative planetary culture," the Center of

Cocreation in Boulder, Colorado, believes "humanity is being called by Spirit to participate in the greatest adventure of all time—birthing a new world." Offers opportunities for global and local projects.

Conference Groups' Web Sites

www.greatmystery.org site of the Prophets' Conference.

www.bizspirit.net site of the Message Company.

www.eomega.org site of Omega Institute in Rhinebeck, New York.

www.hollyhock.ca site of Hollyhock, on Cortes Island in British Columbia.

Mystery Schools

Unlike ancient mystery schools, which selected a few members of the community to share in a pool of esoteric knowledge, modern schools are open to everyone. Because the purpose is to build a bridge between our often forgotten deep sources and our often confusing daily lives, contemporary mystery schools are unique in the way they construct a curriculum that draws on the rich resources available from a variety of global ethnic, religious, and philosophical traditions, ancient and modern.

In these intensive programs, participants dance, sing, play musical instruments, compose poetry, and experiment in mind-body-soul learning from shamanic and other practices, ranging from ancient Greece to modern Africa .

Typically, the schools form groups that meet regularly over several months, (or twice, separated by several months), and often continue for more than a year. Alumni stay in touch, and create a new community that reinforces the learning. Participants report that they feel empowered and deeply connected to their communities in a more self-confident and ethical way.

Nine Gates Mystery School   437 Sausalito Street, Corte Madera, CA 94925. 800-995-4459 (toll free); 707-779-8236 (tel). Web site: www.ninegates.org

Gay Luce, a transpersonal psychologist, has been running Nine Gates since 1985, with co-facilitator Ilona Ireland, and a host of master teachers from around the world who challenge you "to go to your edges." The program is given in the spring and fall in two sequential and seamless nine-day sessions in Santa Barbara, California, and Joshua Tree, California. Part One, Foundation, strengthens connection with the earth and self; and Part Two, Expansion, explores intuition and spirit. Two sessions: about $4,000; room and board extra.

Pathways Institute Mystery School   800-647-4132 (toll free). E-mail: mail@pathwaysinstitute.com

With centers in San Francisco and Washington, D.C., Pathways, founded in 1986 as "a lifelong learning academy in the human arts," is a graduated program, beginning with the Basic Workshop, a twelve-week conference held at various locations throughout the year. The Mystery School's Hall of Priests and Priestesses is spread over four years. The first year comprises a weekend and four separate weeks of specialized study—archetypes, myth and symbol, life-shaping forces, and, in week four, the natural elements, on the Big Island of Hawaii. Tuition: about $3,500.

Mystery School   Dr. Jean Houston, PMB-501 2305-C, Ashland Street, Ashland, OR 97520. 541-488-1200 (tel). E-mail: info@mysteryschool.info; Web site: www.mysteryschool.info

In nine successive weekends at sites in Pomona, New York, or Ashland, Oregon, popular author, lecturer, and philosopher Jean Houston offers cross-cultural mythic and spiritual experiences that focus on the "ways different cultures activate different parts of the brain, the body, the mind, the emotions, and the soul." Themes include Aboriginal dreamtime, North American abundance, Peruvian shamanic ecstacy, Mediterranean art of happiness, and lots more. Nine weekends, including tuition, room, and board: about $3,800.

Web Sites on Mystery Traditions

www.spiritual-path.com the Spiritual Path for the Evolution to Higher Consciousness.

www.open.ac.uk/HST/SHAC the publishers of *Ambix,* and for anyone interested in alchemy and chemistry.

www.hermeticgoldendawn.org the Order of the Golden Dawn, located in Florida, continuing the tradition from nineteenth century mysticism.

Dreams are where it begins. (*Roger Archibald*)

www.Kabbalah-web.org the World Center of Kabbalah Studies.

www.webcom.com the Gnostic Society, located in Los Angeles.

www.bota.org the site of the Builders of the Adytum, an organization that studies the Kabbalah and the Tarot.

www.phanes.com Phanes Press, publisher of classical and new studies of mystical traditions.

www.hrpub.com the site of Hampton Roads Publishing Company "for the evolving human spirit."

Chapter 10
Labyrinths

By coming and going, a bird weaves its nest.
—Ashanti proverb

"I am ashamed to confess my first thought was that I was walking through a brain," whispered a man after he finished walking the labyrinth at the historic Old Ship Church in Hingham, Massachusetts. "It has the same convolutions." In the solemn atmosphere, lit by dim lamps, about a dozen people walked, then meditated, then walked again the replica of the labyrinth of Chartres Cathedral.

"But, it's like a runner's high!" he said, outside and under the stars. "I only walked a circle, but everything seems changed. I feel as if I have had a spiritual workout."

The magic of walking the labyrinth affects people in different ways. Basically a walking meditation, labyrinths seem to encourage faster healing among the sick, and self-understanding among criminals. For these reasons, several hospitals and prisons currently use labyrinths for rehabilitation purposes.

In climates like California, homeowners are installing garden labyrinths made of stone or tile, with trees, fountains, or a table and chair for study in the middle. Labyrinth manufacturers are hiring designers to create new and artistic configurations, based on the fundamental concept of weaving to the center and back.

It is possible to buy "finger labyrinths," to do at your desk.We've come a long way from the Minotaur.

Labyrinths, unlike mazes, are unicursal, which means there is one path to follow through its twists and turns to the center, and you never find yourself in a cul de sac.The labyrinths you are likely to walk have either seven (the "Cretan" labyrinth) or eleven courses (the "Classic" Chartres labyrinth).

When you reach the center, the only place left to go is back, via the other path.You are never lost, but exactly *where* you are internally is up to you. Some walk it as if it were a kabbalah, murmuring praise to God at each turning; others say the rosary or walk on their knees; some untangle the knots of problems as if they were pacing back and forth in a classroom; others go slowly as if each step were their last.

Sara Hopkins-Powell, president of Southern Oregon University, walks the labyrinth at Grace Cathedral, she says in an article in *Spirituality and Health*, as a "pilgrimage of purgation (the walk in), illumination (the center), and union (the walk out)." Some advise using it as a rite of passage to begin or end a new chapter in your life, or to say goodbye to someone (hug him or her in the center, then wait while he or she leaves).

LABYRINTHS: BIRTH AND REBIRTH

The Reverend Lauren Artress, rector of Grace Cathedral, San Francisco, walked the labyrinth in Chartres Cathedral a few years ago and was so surprised and transformed by the quiet ritual that she installed a labyrinth in her own church. Concurrently, she created a nonprofit,Veriditas, to introduce people to the "healing, meditative powers of the labyrinth," which she called "symbolic of the path of life."

In promulgating the word, Reverend Artress met Robert Ferre of the Saint Louis Labyrinth Project. Ferre, whose field is the sacred geometry of twelfth century Gothic cathedrals, among them, Chartres, had been giving tours to France for a

This unusual labyrinth, called The Man in the Maze, is an a ancient icon of the Tohono O'odham Native Americans living south of Tucson, Arizona, near the Mexican border. Titoi, the man in the maze, is Everyman, taking the turns as life presents them. The photo is of wall painting at Cathedral of St. Xavier, in Tucson, Arizona. (*Roger Archibald*)

decade. He helped Artress organize a pilgrimage tour to Chartres, and today, describes himself as a "full-time labyrinth maker and part-time tour director." He creates "portable" labyrinths made of fabric, usually canvas, and still gives sacred geometry tours in France in the summer, now, with "more emphasis" on labyrinths.

Reverend Artress, with Veriditas, accompanies an annual tour to Chartres, hosts a candlelit labyrinth walk with music twice a month at Grace Cathedral, and schedules regular labyrinth-walk facilitator trainings to spread labyrinth-walking around the world.

Labyrinths Are Everywhere

If there isn't already a labyrinth in your community, there probably soon will be. Until then, you can do a virtual seven- or eleven-course labyrinth at www.labyrinthonline.com, a very beautiful site. If you want a three-dimensional labyrinth, do a switchback walk up any hill (or, if you are in England, Glastonbury Tor); or visit the Guggenheim Museum in New York or the Hirshhorn Museum in Washington, start at the top, and wind your contemplative path down.

How-to

Most labyrinths have posted rules of etiquette, as the courses can get crowded at certain times of day, with as many people working toward the center as toward the exit.

Experienced walkers advise approaching the labyrinth as you would a sacred site:

- Begin with a meditation.
- At the entrance, perform a private ritual before you cross the threshold. Take a few cleansing breaths, acknowledge its beauty, ask for permission to enter, and focus on your private intention.
- Walk at your own speed—Artress says a labyrinth will teach you "the discipline of finding your own natural rhythm."
- Don't talk; avoid distractions. Respect others on the paths.
- When you reach the center, pause and let the spirits come in. Be with your intention. If it is to slay your private mon-

ster, remember Theseus. If you believe *you* are the Minotaur, feel what it is like to be trapped in the center for a few minutes.
- Walk back as reverently as you began.
- At the exit, cross the threshold and turn to the center to give thanks.
- Sit silently for a few minutes and let whatever happened sink in.

Ancient Courses

According to ancient writers, Daedalus, the clever architect, was charged by King Minos of Crete to build a suitable containment for the bull-headed boy that his wife had given birth to after a

A spiral carved on a rock deep inside the Saguaro National Park, Arizona. (*Roger Archibald*)

wild fling with a bull. Daedalus designed a labyrinth that imprisoned the Minotaur in the middle, and was so complex that Theseus, the hero from Athens, needed the help of Ariadne's golden thread to find his way back out after he had slain the monster.

Later, according to another legend, when King Minos had lost patience with the creative Daedalus, the King imprisoned both Daedalus and his son Icarus in the labyrinth, but they managed to escape by fashioning wings of feathers and wax. Together, they flew up and away from Crete, until Icarus became hypnotized by the sun and flapped his wings feverishly to be able to embrace the sun, until feathers floated out of the melting wax, and Icarus fell helpless into the sea.

Ancient writers list at least five built labyrinths scattered throughout the Mediterranean in the first century C.E., from the coast of present-day Turkey to Italy. Exactly what labyrinths were used for is not clear, but there were lots of them. Some scholars believe the labyrinth was a stage for initiation of youths and maidens who leapt and sang and danced along the courses.

The Mysterious Labrys

The word *labrys,* which was the double ax used in Crete as a building and ceremonial tool, is an ancient word, according to linguists, that, like other Mediterranean words, wine and gold, is so old that its roots can't be traced. Because of the connection of the word for double ax and labyrinth, some scholars have wondered if the labyrinth was used for initiates into a building trade, perhaps a secret society, in a ritual carried by artisans around the Aegean and Mediterranean coasts.

Medieval builders installed labyrinths in cathedrals in Europe, which were considered ways to work through the wrong turns you had taken in life. Pilgrims traveled far to find them, and walked them in reverence.

For psychologist Carl Jung, the centers of labyrinths (and

mandalas) were symbols of the Self, reached by a labored journey through the monster-ridden dark. The Self can also sit like the spider in the middle of the labyrinthine web, spun on Ariadne's golden thread of Spirit.

Jung might be able to explain the vigorous interest in labyrinth walking in the last decade. Today around the world, newly created public and private labyrinths draw skeptics and believers alike, who find them challenging because they are both exotic and strangely familiar, puzzling and transparent, troubling and peaceful, like many other spiritual experiences.

One Heart Tours 128 Slocum Avenue, Saint Louis, MO 63119. 800-873-9873 (toll free); 314-968-5557(tel); 314-968-5539 (fax). E-mail: Robert@labyrinthproject.com; Web site: www.labyrinth project.com

In addition to producing eleven- and seven-circuit portable fabric labyrinths, Robert Ferre runs two pilgrimages a year to France, which begin and end in Paris and spend the middle of the week at Chartres, Amiens, and Mont St Michel, studying the sacred geometry of Gothic cathedrals. Ferre has special permission for his pilgrims to enter Chartres Cathedral after closing to walk the labyrinth there. Seven days: about $1,300, airfare not included.

Veriditas 1100 California Street at Taylor Street, San Francisco, CA 94108. 415-749-6358 (tel); 415-749-6357 (fax). E-mail: Veriditas@gracecathedral.org; Web site: www.kirstimd.com

The Reverend Artress runs annual seminars in spirituality to Chartres Cathedral in France. They are usually held in May, "Mary's month," she says. The rector of Chartres Cathedral invites her pilgrims to walk the labyrinth after closing hours. Housing is in the adjacent seminary. About $900, airfare not included.

Women who are seeking to grow their spirituality are invited to partake in Dream Quest, an overnight in Grace Cathedral,

Spiders spin the web, then sit in the center, which can be the center of the universe or the Self. (*Roger Archibald*)

San Francisco, with song, drama, and lots of labyrinth walking by candlelight. The Women's Dream Quest is held three times a year, about $100. Bring your sleeping bag. For information, call or contact chris@gracecathedral.org.

Web Sites

www.labyrinthproject.com Robert Ferre's site, has links to an exhaustive list of everything to do with labyrinths, including labyrinth locations.

A natural spiral, the golden mean, in slow motion. (*Roger Archibald*)

www.thehealingspectrum.com lists labyrinth books and products.

www.labyrinthos.net is the site of British enthusiast Jeff Saward.

www.geomancy.org is Sid Lonegren's site.

www.lessons4living.com has lots of advice about how to relate to a labyrinth.

The Labyrinth Society, Inc. P.O. Box 144, New Canaan, CT 06840-0144. 877-446-4520 (toll free). E-mail: labsociety@aol. com; Web site: www.labyrinthsociety.org

"Dedicated to supporting all those who create, maintain, and use labyrinths," the society is a membership organization that publishes a newsletter and sponsors annual conferences.

Chapter 11

It's a Mystery: Crop Circles and Alien Abductions

There is more day to dawn. The sun is but a morning star.
—Henry Thoreau, *Walden*

CROP CIRCLES

It was an unnaturally sultry late spring evening in 1990, wind-less, and beautifully gold as the sun began to set. Gary and Vivienne Tomlinson went for a walk across the wheat fields in Surrey, in the south of England, to a nearby hill, where they sat and enjoyed the view until twilight. Then, on the walk back down, clouds rolled suddenly across the sky, and the wind sprang up. By the time they reached the path next to the wheat field, the wind was unnaturally strong. A band of shimmering "mist or light fog" surged through the field, spinning into a vortex.

As the wind plowed through the wheat, it gave off a "high pitch like a set of Pan-pipes," the Tomlinsons told Lucy Pringle (in *Crop Circles*). The wind pushed them down from above with a tremendous pressure. Then, as the shimmering mist engulfed them, feeling "tingly all over, like pins and needles from head to foot," the wind shuttled them from their path into the center of the wheatfield. There they saw "a circle being formed" by the band of mist that split in two; then, as it softened, became a series of small whirlwinds, "like watery glass with a quivering line inside."

The Tomlinsons went home in a state of shock, they said, and for a day or so, felt tired and nauseous. Vivienne was treated for a punctured ear drum. The entire event, they calculated, took about seven minutes.

Ancient Messages

No one knows how long crop circles have been carved into growing fields in Great Britain. There are very few contemporary accounts like the one above, and only scattered reports of memories from decades beginning in the 1920s. One woodcut from 1687, showing "The Devil" wreaking havoc in a wheat-field, might be a frustrated farmer's attempt to explain his violated crop. Crop circles, in fact, might have been around forever, like the tree that fell in the forest with no one to hear it.

They make a lot of noise these days, however. As interest in them grows, the circles themselves have taken on more elaborate geometrical and mathematical designs that are breathtaking in their elegance, beauty, and complexity, let alone whatever techniques are involved in producing them. Most are large, some super sized: more than two hundred feet in diameter. Since the late 1980s their number has grown exponentially, from one or two to 102 in 2001. The season begins in April and lasts as long as the crops, until late August or September.

Researchers as well as hoaxers make their own crop circles; researchers, to find out what differences exist between man-made and whatever-made circles; hoaxers, to pollute whatever "messages" crop circle makers might be sending. A pair of hoaxers known as Doug and Dave claimed authorship for every English crop circle when there were only a few a season, boasting that it is a whiz to make one in a couple of hours in the dark. Now other hoaxers' claims are severely challenged by the increasing number and sheer complexity of the designs. So far, however, no one has been able to claim the reward by the National Farmers Union for the apprehension of a person caught in the act of creating a crop circle.

Advertisers from around the world, representing Japanese car manufacturers or national computer companies happy to profit from the phenomena, requisition fields from farmers, and fly in their own crop-circle makers who spend days creating designs that look good in shiny magazines.

Skeptics fuel the confusion. For every Web site that "analyzes" the latest circle is one that refutes the analysis. The British media dismiss crop circles and crop circle researchers as foolish; governments ignore the fuss; faithful researchers beg for financing.

British wheat or other vegetable fields are not the only places circles have appeared: they have shown up in anywhere from twelve to seventy countries (depending on the source), from the United States to the Czech Republic to Israel to China. India might top the scale in the number reported; but the UK is the most organized in its reception of them. Nor are they confined to fields: records exist of circles occurring (without any telltale makers' footprints) in snow, sand, ice, and mud.

Unlike the Nazca lines in Peru, or the giant chalk horses on English hills or the giant fertility god in Cerne, which were carved two millennia ago and meant to last, crop circles are temporary, like beautiful summer romances. They happen suddenly, last a short time, create a lot of excitement, and linger in the memory, never-to-be-reclaimed.

Seeing them at all is problematical. From eye level, the circles appear to be simply some kind of disruption in the field. One farmer walked past his field one morning at 5:00 A.M., and when he returned at 7:00 A.M., saw that a circle had been added. Although walking through a circle may enable a person to map its shape, how could anyone but a pilot ever fully view a crop circle? If they are meant to be seen, it is from above.

Reports of physical reactions are fairly common. Pringle has witnessed her own and others' episodes of healing. Pringle had thrown a shoulder into disarray playing tennis the night before she visited a freshly made circle with a friend. Not only was Pringle's shoulder cured; her friend who had suffered for many years from a chronic circulatory condition lay down for twenty minutes and rose up feeling better than she ever had.

But many others report feeling nauseous, or more often, lethargic and gloomy, which lasts for a day or so. Some find their knees buckle under; others faint. Some suffer short-term memory loss or have "new" feelings, either bad or good. One man reported having an erection that simply would not go away.

As researchers get better at what they do, several have noticed that not all circles are made with equal precision. Some are perfect, so perfect the music of the spheres comes to mind. Others are sloppy, irregular, like the work of an apprentice or another group.

Some hear a "roaring" while a circle is being made. In freshly made circles, visitors sometimes hear "crackling," like static. One researcher recorded sound at 5kHz, which translates into human hearing as a kind of "trilling."

A farmer who witnessed men in gray walking through his crop circle before they vanished said that for two or three days, he could not get rid of the taste of almonds.

And crop circles go on, new and temporary, each summer. They last only as long as it takes the bent-over wheat to rise back up to the sun. And that is one of the major differences between man-made and other circles. Humans break the wheat stalks when they make paths; the powers from elsewhere gently bend and "weave" the wheat into patterns, and somehow miraculously keep the seeds in place. Human circle makers shake the seeds loose.

A Biophysical Analysis

William Levengood, a biophysicist from the University of Michigan analyzed samples from a circle and found tiny areas at the nodes of the stalk that he called "explusion cavities." Levengood believes these mark where the water in the cells of the stalk, heated "by microwave energy in a spinning plasma vortex," was forced out. Seeds from the samples taken from the center of the circle and regenerated in the laboratory had a 111 percent mean growth rate, far more vigorous than non-circle seeds. Levengood also found higher concentrations of magnetic iron particles in the soil of the circle.

Other researchers who regularly test the circle wheat find electromagnetic and radiation gauges occasionally go off the scale.

For information on other experiments, consult http://home. clara.net/lucypringle.

Are crop circles a cocreation?

Who knows where or when another will appear? In 1998, intuitive Louise Olivi did an experiment with seven other attendees at the Midwest Crop Circle Symposium. Together they designed a shape, and asked the "intelligence who makes crop circles" to manifest it. That was in April. On May 3 of the same year, Louise gathered seven people at her home in Connecticut and asked them to meditate on the shape with the same intention.

Amazingly, in what appears to have been a simultaneous manifestation, the Beltane Wheel, an almost exact copy of the shape Louise and her group had imagined, appeared in a field near Silbury Hill in England.

Did Louise Olivi and her meditators create the circle? Did they have a kind of group precognition? Did the circlemakers demonstrate that they can pick up our focused concentration? Did Louise Olivi and her group *cocreate* the circle, with the makers? (The design, Louise said, was based on a button she was wearing at the conference.)

Similar experiments are being conducted at the Mount Baldy Institute in Boulder, Colorado (www.mountbaldy.com).

Familiar shapes occasionally appear. In 1996 a long serpent was carved in a field near Barbary Castle. Its general shape and egg-motif at its head very closely matched the famous 1,300-

foot long serpent earth mound in Ohio, dating from two millennia ago.

A Dutch Example

Circle researcher Nancy Talbott, one of a group of American researchers known as BLT Research, which includes Dr. William Levengood, was investigating Dutch crop circles in Hoeven, the Netherlands. She had spent the better part of two weeks with Dutch crop circle investigator Robbert van der Broeke and American parapsychologist William Roll, carrying their night-vision camcorders and flash cameras every night into the fields to wait. Nothing had happened.

Talbott was ready to quit, feeling as if she had wasted time better spent elsewhere. Giving up on the fields, she went to bed to read. About 3:00 A.M., she heard the neighbor's cattle braying. From her window, she had a clear view of a string-bean field. She felt uneasy. Cattle sleep at night. They brayed again; then suddenly her room was ablaze with light. Outside over the bean field, Talbott witnessed a "tube" of brilliant light about eight inches to one foot in diameter flash for one second. Then all was dark for one second. Again, the flash. Again, darkness. A third flash, and then Talbott tore downstairs to meet van der Broeke tearing upstairs. He, too had witnessed the light display. In the morning light, they were able to see an ellipse, about thirty-five by twenty feet, "with a twenty-foot long pathway," Talbott said, "which ended in a crossbar (like the capital letter 'T')."

Who are these masked artists?

Are crop circle makers one step ahead of us, playing with our minds? Being distantly witty? Are we on the verge of real communication with a higher intelligence?

Researcher Lucy Pringle points out that a circle called the

The "Julia Set" crop circle that appeared July 1996 in a field across the highway from Stonehenge. Named after the fractals of its design, the Julia Set refers to a mathematical term. (© *Colin Andrews, 1996*, www.CropCircleInfo.com)

Julia Set that appeared in July 1996 in a field on the other side of the highway across from Stonehenge appeals to a multiplicity of disciplines. In *Crop Circles* she wrote: "To the mathematicians and geometers, it is a representation of the computer-generated fractal image, the Julia Set; to a musician, it is a base clef; to a marine biologist, a perfect example of the cross-section of a nautilus; and finally, to the medical fraternity, it constitutes a mammalian skeleton with precisely the correct number of vertebrae. Alternatively," Pringle adds, "the formations could be manifestations of our own subconscious."

Chilbolton Radio Telescope and the Arecibo Message

If crop circles are codes, which so far have gone right over our heads, two pictograms that appeared next to the Chilbolton radio telescope facility in Hampshire, England, in August 2001 have challenged the best. One was a human face composed of the kind of dots that make up newspaper photographs, set in a framed rectangle. It was a blur from the ground, chillingly in focus from above.

The second appeared a week later, another framed rectangle, covered with dots and dashes, that is a mirror image of the pictographic information sent from the Arecibo Observatory in Puerto Rico in 1974 by the late Carl Sagan and Frank Drake, now chairman of the board of SETI. Their target: Star Cluster M13 in the constellation Hercules, 23,000 light years away. The message, to be received in the year 47,000, describes us here on Earth: our binary system, our DNA chemical composition and structure, the chemical composition of our atmosphere, where we are in the solar system, our population, a human stick figure that indicates how tall we are, and a graphic shape of the Arecibo transmitter.

The Chilbolton figure caught everyone by surprise. For one thing, it was made over a weekend in a privately owned field next to an area restricted to the public. For another, the data it contains, both the subtle changes in our message, and new data added, are hard to dismiss as a hoax.

Paul Vigay, director of the Independent Research Center for Unexplained Phenomena, was the first to identify it. The DNA double helix has an added string, or one million extra sequences. The human stick figure has a greatly enlarged head. Silicon is added to the human chemical composition. The population numbers are greatly expanded, as is the number of planets in the solar system, from nine to eleven. Added to the area where the 1974 message carried the symbol for the Arecibo transmitter was what Vigay believed to be a representation of a previous geometric crop circle at the same location.

SETI sent analysts and, before the summer was out, declared it a hoax. If the aliens are sending a message about having received our 1974 radio message, then it makes sense to leave the pictogram next to a radio antenna, they said. But why reply in such a "crude" way by carving pictures in a wheat field? Why not send a radio signal? (See www.eionews.addr.com/psyops/chilbolton_1999.htm.)

American researcher Dr. Brian Crissey argued (on www.5thworld.com) that the message received was in "the exact same order of complexity as the message sent—simple, direct, easy for common folks to understand," he said. "It is basically saying, 'Copy, Roger! Do you read me?'"

SETI further argued that it was a hoax because the aliens depicted on the reply looked like us. "Visit the local zoo, and you'll find critters that share a lot of your DNA."

Crissey replied: "If we can genetically engineer corn . . . then surely ExtraTerrestrials (ETs) can mold local life-forms to reflect their own chosen characteristics."

SETI argued that the beam from Aricebo was narrow and probably hard to intercept. "The chances that it has hit another solar system in the twenty-seven years since its broadcast are one in fifty thousand," they said.

"ETs have been with us on earth," Crissey countered, "probably since our conception as human beings." Perhaps they saw the message printed in Sagan's *Cosmos,* he said.

SETI asked why the alien's biochemistry, except for the changes in DNA and the addition of silicon, matched ours so perfectly.

Crissey said that if our genetics had been altered by "ancient space travelers," then, of course, we would have the same genetic makeup—"similar to that of our parent ETs." To Crissey, the silicon addition remains a mystery and worthy of further examination. To him, there is little doubt that the message in the field near Chilbolton is from "off-planet."

SETI analysts chided, "We can expect better from true extraterrestrial intelligence."

The Thrill of the Search

Undeterred and even inspired by the skeptical opposition, crop circle investigators prepare each spring for the new year. The internet allows them to keep on top of global sightings, and to stay in touch.

Summer nights are filled with sky watchers, looking for any unusual lights or aircraft in the area especially of Wiltshire. Many people sleep in the fields, hoping to be there when one comes. But many wake up surprised to find a magnificent one only a few yards away. Researchers continue their scientific analyses with the latest technology, and psychic experiments with group meditation, music (as in the film, *Close Encounters of the Third Kind*), and flashing lights.

"The crop circle phenomenon excites, intrigues, surprises, and ultimately still surpasses us," says researcher Chet Snow.

Is this another intelligence, a more advanced civilization trying to communicate with us, sending messages that some are trying desperately to decode? Are they playing with us? Or gently responding to us when we ask questions? Do we imagine, while they explicate? Louise Olivi's button was transformed into the so-called Beltane Wheel.

Or is it some elaborate government project designed to deflect our attention from UFOs?

Is this another manifestation of our new consciousness? And does that make us ready to accept messages that might have been around for millennia?

Find out for yourself.

Ron Russell, Director, Midwest Research P.O. Box 460760, Aurora, CO 80046. 303-400-1322 (tel); 303-400-1341 (fax). E-mail: ron@cropcircles.org; Web site: www.cropcircles.org

Ron Russell was a successful professional artist and photographer (and still is) before he accepted the challenge of crop circles. Now his research group engages in conferences and experiments with scientists, including Dr. Simeon Hein of the Mount Baldy Institute for Resonant Viewing.

Ron offers two tours a year, both are educational and fun. One is Sacred Sites and Circles, which is a week-long overview of circles and admission to the Glastonbury Crop Circle Conference, private visit to Stonehenge, visits to Silbury Hill and sites in Glastonbury, and lots of guest lecturers, including Lucy Pringle, Colin Andrews, Busty Taylor, and John Michell. Join other "croppies" at the Barge Inn Pub, which maintains a room full of the latest crop circle information. Seven days, lodging, meals, ground transport, but no international airfare: about $2,500. Gives a good background in crop circles.

Then you can move on to a more intensive research experience and join Russell's Energy Team. This is a solid week of crop circle investigation, "intense and fun." You need to know how to shoot video tape. The group makes a test crop circle and keeps nightly sky watches. In the process, you will learn a lot from Russell about fractals, sacred geometry, and be able to discuss the telepathic aspects of crop circle makers. Seven days: $3,000, entirely tax deductible. Does not include hotel or international airfare. Ground transport provided.

Louise Olivi   E-mail: lolivi2001@yahoo.com; http://home.att. net/~1.olivi

Louise Olivi has been studying and conducting summer tours to England, including the annual Glastonbury Crop Circle Conference, for several years. A minister of the Spiritualist Church, intuitive, teacher, and healer, Olivi also is the channel for Maasaw, a Hopi Great Spirit (www.home.att.net/~lovili/maasaw. htm).

Her nine-day crop circle tour includes admission to the conference, a one-day tour of the circles with local researcher Lucy Pringle, and lodging at a B and B in Wiltshire, where 75 percent of crop circles occur. You also visit Avebury by van, have private time at Stonehenge, and find out the latest at the Barge Inn Pub.

Nine days, about $1,800 to $2,000; international airfare not included.

Chet Snow P.O. 1738, Sedona, AZ 86339. 928-204-1962 (tel). E-mail: chetsnow@sedona.net

Dr. Snow, an author, lecturer, and regression therapist, and his wife Kallista have been hosting trips to crop circles since 1992. This interesting couple have photographed one of their crystal skulls inside a freshly made circle, and found "pure pink energy spiraling up from the bent-over crop." Snow believes crop circles originate from different makers. For seven days you can join their small group, visit the white horse chalk formations, Avebury, Salisbury Cathedral, have private time inside Stonehenge, attend the Wiltshire Crop Circle Conference, and take a flight over the circles. Seven days, ground transport in a van, B and B lodging, about $1,800; international airfare not included.

Center for the Study of Extraterrestrial Intelligence: CSETI Ambassador to the Universe Trainings and Expeditions
P.O. Box 4556, Largo, MD 20775. 888-ET-CSETI (toll free); 301-249-3915 (tel); 877-92-CSETI (toll-free fax); 501-325-8328 (fax). E-mail: Coordinator@cseti.org; Web site: www.cseti.org

"Every year or two," according to CSETI coordinator Debbie Foch, CSETI takes paying volunteers for one week to study crop circles as well as sacred sites in England. The program consists of daily discussions and lectures, with fieldwork at night "initiating contact with extra terrestrial (ET) intelligence," often in the circles or nearby fields.

With Dr. Stephen Greer, expect to be introduced "within the framework of Universal Peace" to remote viewing and remote vectoring of extraterrestrial spacecraft. "Participants also train with ET communications systems, including lasers and electronics, as well as thought interaction with machines." Those trained are encouraged to form their own research groups. Foch says, "We frequently have very close encounters with ET craft during these trainings." Seven days, about $2,200, including lodging and brunch, access fees, and ground transportation; international airfare not included.

Web Sites

www.cropcircleinfo.com is the sight of twenty-year researcher Colin Andrews.

www.cropcircleresearch.com Paul Vigay, a computer expert and crop circle investigator, got interested when he realized an electro static charge indicator that he had invented was giving unexpected energy readings in wheat stalks taken from crop circles. Vigay has the most comprehensive crop circle Web site, publishes a newsletter, lists the many crop circle conferences scheduled around the world, and provides a forum for online interactive discussion as well as links to other groups.

To sign up for the free newsletter, send a blank E-mail with "Subscribe" in the subject line, to: cclist@cropcircleresearch. com

www.paradigmshift.com is an excellent compilation of various crop circle theories.

www.earthfiles.com is an excellent site for sources and a scientific research overview by writer and TV producer Linda Moulton Howe.

www.5thworld.com is the site of Granite Publishing and Dr. Brian Crissey's analysis of the Chilbolton Code.

http://home.clara.net/lucypringle is the British researcher and photographer Lucy Pringle's site.

www.lovely.clara.net is Crop Circular, Freddy Silva's informative site.

www.cropcircleconnector.com is Mark Fussel and Stuart Dike's international clearinghouse for pictures, books, films, recordings, and videos relating to crop circles.

www.mountbaldy.com the site of the Mount Baldy Institute for Resonant Viewing, posts their results with precognition and focused meditation and crop circles.

ALIEN ABDUCTIONS

More than four decades since the term "flying saucer" was first spoken, the UFO phenomenon has revealed considerably more about our nature than about theirs.

—Keith Thompson, *Angels and Aliens*

"M" woke up one night next to his deeply sleeping fiancée, "vibrating and paralyzed." A few months before, he had had a "vivid/lucid/realistic 'dream'" and was not happy about it. This night he said, "Hello" to the darkness, and something in the room responded, "Good."

His body stiff with fear, he felt something move—like a cat, but he didn't own any pets—on the end of his bed. Only when the presence straddled his legs and arms did he open his eyes. "Jesus Christ! You look like an enormous bug!" he whispered into the dark. The creature's huge black eyes were two inches away from his face. It had a gigantic head on a segmented, stick-like neck.

But before M's critical and panic faculties could take over, the creature "went inside my mind, and . . . simultaneously gave me as much information as it took from me. And there was this unbelievable sensation of love. The purest thing I have ever tasted in my life. . . . It was a moment with the Creator," he said in a let-

These are the clouds that resemble UFOs. Lenticular clouds over Death Valley, California. (*Roger Archibald*)

ter published in *PEER Perspectives*, the newsletter of psychiatrist John Mack's Program for Extraordinary Experience Research.

This experience is one of hundreds reported by two-hundred alien abductees, or experiencer participants, as Mack prefers to call them, whom he has interviewed and helped in the past dozen years. Initially, a reluctant participant himself, he gradually found that he was moved by the "intensity of feeling," recounted in the experiences he listened to, as well as by something innately genuine in the experiencer. "It's as if the person is touched by the divine. It seems almost unethical to question what they say," he said. The experience is different than our reaching out to the spirit world. "When *it* comes to *us*, it's tough and hard. We've protected ourselves from it over the years. We're insulated."

The amazing similarity among the recounted stories that he has collected from around the world, from children and the aged, from ordinary people to shamans, has led Mack to believe that there is some kind of "crossover experience" leading to nonordinary states of consciousness, that might reflect "laws of the universe or subtler energies that we do not yet comprehend." Matter becomes energy, energy becomes matter.

The basics of alien abduction experiences involve pity and terror. They are all:

- vitally real, not dreamlike. They shock, sometimes physically painfully. Objects are inserted into cranial cavities, ears, nose, eyes, the sinuses. Needles are thrust into veins, joints, sexual and internal organs. Afterward, there is a feeling of love, an expansive, encompassing, forgiving kind of divine love.
- accompanied by blinding beams of light, and
- intense vibration. Some say the vibration seems to change cells (see Dolphins, chapter four.)
- in the present time. The passage of time recounted later is "lost" time.
- in altered states of consciousness that manifest as if "something's not right about the light, shadows are wrong"; people and objects perceived out of the sides of the eyes are different than when looked at straight on. A woman on a train sat next to a man who was an insect out of the corner of her eye, perfectly normal when she looked at him.
- involved with floating. Abductees are taken from wherever they are and floated through walls or ceilings to the "spaceship" or alien medical facility or surgical room.
- involved with a different definition of traveling: Things come to you. "You don't have to travel," said one experi-

encer. "You just are right there." Others use the word, "delivered."

- the same in the message that the earth is dying, and we are hastening its demise.
- marked by a sense of mission, usually involving "saving" the earth. Experiencers often report special psychic abilities after an abduction, such as being able to channel knowledge and "read" people's feelings before they can.
- give a sense of the interconnectedness of everything. "They [aliens] actually *are* us, a piece of us," said one experiencer.

At the end of *Passport to the Cosmos*, Mack relates the aliens as they have been described to him:

- the Grays, small, with large black eyes, who can shape-shift especially into animals, and who have been around for thousands of years.
- luminous beings, who have translucent bodies.
- reptilians, who "play rough."

Why are they coming to us? Mack believes "something went wrong" in their evolution or technological invention, and "aliens seem to have lost their bodies." One experiencer described it as, "They've lost their home inside themselves; they've evolved into something that's not quite right, that has something lacking." Another said they have "a sense of longing for something we have."

Mack believes they lost their bodies but have maintained a connection with the Divine Source; whereas humans have lost their connection with the Divine Source but maintained their sexual, sensual, nurturing, caring bodies. Aliens' desire for "hybrids," Mack believes, are their—and our—stake in the future, creating a breed of creatures well-adapted to a greatly altered earth.

Ants are worth looking at closely, if some aliens take on their shape. This ferocious one is in Tasmania. (*Roger Archibald*)

Meanwhile, while they try to identify exactly how we are able to care and to nurture (with their own "scientific methods"), we can do with a dose of the spirit world in our daily lives to mitigate our out-of-control materialism.

The Official Denial

Few discussions divide people more than the whole thicket of so-called alien visitation. The "military," the "government"—whoever, whatever—have been blamed as the source of disinformation and the labeling of believers as "crazy" since 1947, when news of a crashed space ship and some surviving aliens in New Mexico went through the air waves and, not long after, the cover up. The National Aeronautics and Space Administration (NASA), the story goes, wants to break the news that extraterrestrials exist gently and gradually to an otherwise stunned population.

Today, the public disavowal of extraterrestrial contact has created an underground of people who have had experiences that are considered socially unacceptable. The underground is also a breeding ground of people with false memories of having been abducted, as well as of stories of conspiratorial governmental interference with personal lives.

In addition to trying to make sense out of their sometimes horrific experiences, alien experiencers must contend with feeling marginal, if not insane. Most are not.

Added to this is the cat-and-mouse game played by aliens, themselves. The crop circle phenomena, for example, intrigue, seduce, and confound. SETI researchers complain that they carve their messages in wheat fields rather than send straightforward radio messages; experiencers wonder why, if aliens are so worried about the future of Earth, they don't do something about it themselves. "It's as if the agent or intelligence at work here," says Mack, "were parodying, mocking, tricking, and deceiving the investigators, providing just enough physical evidence to win over those who are prepared to believe in the phenomena, but not enough to convince the skeptic."

Mack believes that our denial of extraterrestrial intelligence transcends government denial and, instead, meets a bedrock resistance because it challenges our worldview. Tulane philosopher Michael Zimmerman calls extraterrestrials "agents of cultural deconstruction," that threaten our real, tangible, material world. How can we explain and live easily with beings who slip effortlessly between the physical and the invisible; and who change shapes to suit (or not suit) the occasion? And, worse, with beings whose psychosocial, emotional, and intellectual make-up might be radically different from everything we have known, catalogued, and studied?

We meet, and then?

Hollywood usually ends its "ET" movies in tearful joy, with the moment of alien/human interaction. Some go off into the great ship. Or if the aliens are not mean and blowing up our public buildings, they are exemplars of wonderfulness, with access to a niceness which we can't imagine maintaining forever. Humans work with that grain of sand that produces the pearl; friction defines us.

As Brian Crissey suggests in his rebuttal of SETI's criticisms of the Arecibo crop circle pictogram, when one more advanced civilization overtakes another, it has to be done slowly to be successful. Therefore, he argues, their wheat circle response to our message to the stars was at the "same order of complexity as the message sent." In other words, it was a real and gentle attempt to communicate. Similarly, the strong emphasis on mathematical and geometrical shapes of the crop circles is loaded information aimed at certain segments of the population.

Mack's experiencers often report a stronger-than-human love coming from the aliens, whose eyes—big, black, pupil-less, and with an engulfing gaze—transmit the transformative message. To describe the experience, abductees use words like "intoxicate" and "mesmerize"; some said they felt dizzy. One woman said it was as if "they're deeply in love with us."

The Star Nation Peoples

Extraterrestrials are called Star Visitors among native North and South Americans, and it is from Star Visitors that these tribes acknowledge having received their cultural knowledge, healing practices, stories of origin (from the stars), and future prophecies. "When the Eagle flies with the Condor" marks the so-called End Times, when a series of environmental and political disasters will force great refugee movements from the mid-latitudes to the Equator and the mountains, and people will move from the Fourth to the Fifth World. The Fifth World will see a changed Earth environmentally and geologically, and survivors will pick up the pieces and start again. The date is 2012.

In this time of transition, Native Americans have been called upon by Star Visitors to reveal the prophecies entrusted to them many years ago, to warn people that they can still turn away from complete disaster. To this end, representatives of tribes from the Americas, as well as Finland Laplanders, New Zealand Maoris, and Australian Aborigines have convened in several Star Knowledge conferences (see www.spiritweb.org/Spirit/star-family-gathering.html).

Native Americans are buoyed by the presence of Star Visitors, because they give hope. There is still time to save the earth from dying, by reconnecting with each other and by listening to the earth when it speaks.

Some believe Star Seeds have been planted in some children, producing a race of people who will be able to carry the weight of reconstruction involved in the Fifth World.

Who are the Star People?

"All who walk on two legs are our brothers and sisters," said Iroquois Elder Paula Underwood. "We come from the Unity of the Universe." Some Native Americans believe Star People are *us*, from the future, at a higher level of consciousness. Or they project mental images of themselves, constantly shape-changing, to communicate with us.

Lakota medicine man Floyd Hand was visited by an extra-terrestrial eight-feet tall, with big eyes and gills. Star People accompanied Black Elk while he was on a vision quest. Some extraterrestrials are like ants, with big black eyes, long fingers, and toes. The Grays answer questions, and are the easiest to access. Among the Ogala Sioux, White Buffalo Calf Woman is a Star Visitor who came to prophesy thousands of years ago and is expected to return soon, preceded by signs of a white buffalo being born, whose skin changes to red, black, and yellow. Crop circles are Star Visitors' primary means of communicating with us now.

Sorting out ways in which you can communicate positively and fruitfully takes time and concentrated thought. We might be humbled, we might be separated from our egos, we might wonder what we can possibly give in return.

"Alien abductions," said Mack, "are an outreach program from the cosmos to the consciousness-impaired."

CSETI Ambassador to the Universe Trainings and Expeditions P.O. Box 4556, Largo, MD 20775. 888-ET-CSETI (toll free); 301-249-3915 (tel); 877-92-CSETI (toll-free fax); 501-325-8328 (fax). E-mail: Coordinator@cseti.org; Web site: www.cseti.org

To get closer to the phenomenon, the Center for the Study of Extraterrestrial Intelligence, (CSETI) led by Dr. Stephen Greer, is open to volunteers who would like to pay to spend a week in the field after learning how to recognize and respond to extraterrestrial contact. Committed to the "thoughtful, long-term development of bilateral extraterrestrial intelligence (ETI) human communication and exchange," CSETI also supports open public education of the results of their research.

CSETI researchers maintain that Earth has been visited "for decades, if not centuries, and that this contact has intensified since 1947." Topics in their trainings and workshops include human-initiated contact, understanding where extraterrestrials come from, and what their motives are; peaceful applications of their technology; and "world peace and unity as a prerequisite for extensive ETI contact."

Training involves meditation and remote viewing, and skywatching for contact from dark to somewhere around midnight. Sites are where previous sightings have taken place recently in the United States. Seven days: $595, for the first participation; $500 a week thereafter. Price includes materials and tuition.

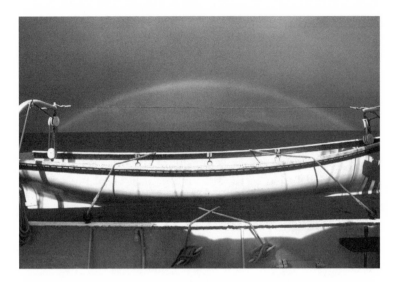

Life boat with a rainbow: fair winds and [following] seas.The passage will be smooth. (*Roger Archibald*)

PEER P.O. Box 398080, Cambridge, MA 02139. 617-497-2667 (tel).Web site: www.peermack.org

The Program for Extraordinary Experience Research, a nonprofit research and educational organization, sponsors forums and dialogues, and publishes a newsletter and articles. If you would like to share with Dr. Mack your alien abduction experience, or access a referral to an appropriate therapist in your area, please write or call for more information.

Web Sites

www.spiritweb.org/Spirit/star-family-gathering.html is the site of summaries of Star Knowledge Conferences by Dr. Richard J. Boylan, a psychologist who works with extraterrestrial and anomalous experiencers. Many links to other sites.

www.star-knowledge.net is the site of Lakota spiritual leader Standing Elk.

www.dreaman.org is the site of National UFO Sightings Database and the United States UFO Information and Research Center. Sponsors an annual conference, is building a database on all anomalous experiences.

www.centerchange.org is the site of the Center for Psychology and Social Change, the parent organization of PEER, which sponsors several programs, some dedicated to mind-body healing, as well as medicine and spirituality training.

www.cfree.org the site for the Center for Extraordinary Exploration, is a helpful site with many links.

www.ufoabduction.com is the site of Dr. David Jacobs, a psychiatrist and experiencer.

Chapter 12
Staying Healthy, Traveling Safely

All will be well. And all will be well.
—Abbess Hildegard of Bingen

While travel for spiritual enlightenment or renewal may have a different set of motivations, it is pretty much the same as any other kind of travel, and the same rules apply.

Passports and Visas

Start with www.travel.state.gov for general passport information. For visa information, click on "Visas for U.S. citizens to go to other countries." *Passport* information is also available from a 35-cent-a-minute automated line, 900-225-5674. *Visa* information is at 202-663-1225.

Make sure your passport is up-to-date and will not expire while you are away. Check with your travel company or with the State Department for visa information on the countries you will be visiting. Very often your travel company arranges visas in advance; or, if the country is eager to promote tourism, it is a simple process of getting them after you go through customs. You can pay with dollars.

Before you go, make copies of your passport, visa, if you have one in advance, and tickets, and keep them separate from the original. It's helpful to write down the numbers in a daybook or diary, or any clever place you can contrive, in case—worst scenario—your *copies* are stolen or lost, too. Also leave some copies at home.

If your passport is lost or stolen, you will need a copy of it, as well as other identification, such as a driver's license, to present to the American Consulate to get a temporary passport.

Country Information

For links to Consular Information sheets go to www.travel. state.gov. They give useful information, warts and all, about countries. Click on "Travel Publications for useful Tips for Travelers" booklets that give more extensive data on areas.

Money

Before you go, try to exchange a few dollars at a bank that deals in international currency. Then memorize how the new currency translates into dollars so you don't wind up undertipping a French waiter or overpaying for a twenty-foot Buddha for the front hall.

In Europe, most countries have converted to the Euro which can be used across borders. There are eight Euro coins, in value from 1 to 50; and seven notes, from 5 to 500. Great Britain maintains its pound.

Once you arrive, your tour director should be able to direct you to the best place to exchange money. It may be at the airport or your hotel, or, in some countries, from a guy on the street. He's legitimate; he just eliminates the middle man.

Money belts that slip around your waist may make you feel pudgy, but they are an excellent safety measure. Take some American dollar bills, as well.

Expect to pay an *exit tax* in many countries. It is usually about $15. Keep it set aside so you don't forget; otherwise, you have to go to a bank, and that can take hours.

If you carry a wallet, choose a slim style and keep it in a *front* pocket (jacket or shirt pocket, or pants pocket) rather than your back pocket. Clever thieves take the whole back pocket as well as the wallet.

Women sometimes feel safer slinging a shoulder purse across their body. Remember, thieves with pocket knives can easily slash most straps. Watch it if you carry it over your shoulder, as it also can be easily lifted off in a crowd or by someone passing by on a motorbike.

Flying

Time is the key. Plan on spending as long as it takes. If that's the whole day getting across this country, then go with the flow. Do arrive two hours before a domestic flight, three hours before an international flight. You may want to consider going a day or two before you meet your group, to get acclimated and relax. Before you go, make sure you know where and when you are to meet your group, and have relevant telephone numbers for contact there.

Expect airport delays if there are any glitches in security. Some airlines have increased security to such a level that they make you go through twice. Don't wear or carry any metal object that might set off the detector. If you have to remove your shoes for a security check, make it easy for everyone by wearing some kind of slip-on. Before you go, make sure your shoes don't have metal shanks.

Don't be embarrassed if you are singled out for a special shakedown; it's done on a random basis. Leave sharp objects, including nail files, at home. If security guards remove "dangerous" items from your suitcase, kiss them goodbye unless you come prepared to mail them home or to your hotel. Some travelers carry pre-addressed envelopes to meet that eventuality.

Seriously consider taking only a carry-on, the size that fits into the container that many airlines use as a model. In some cases, for example, doing a vision quest, a carry-on should be all you need. It cuts down on time and possible angst.

After you arrive, expect to wait for your checked luggage. If you're making a connecting flight outside the United States, stay on top of the situation with an eagle eye on the carousel, grab your luggage as soon as it appears, then go, swift as the wind. You usually go through customs and baggage-check only once per country.

Remember to lock your suitcase or your carry-on, and to cover your identification tag.

Hotels

When you check in, do what you can to keep your room number from being advertised in the lobby. Better hotels disguise the number in a foldover card, which is for your eyes only.

Put your valuables in the hotel safe, which is probably safer than the little safe in your room closet.

Check fire escape routes; lock your door.

Study whatever maps you have to understand where you are in relation to the places you plan to visit. Ask at the desk what to expect for fair taxi rates.

Watch Your Back

Check the State Department's country guides to learn a little about how local crowds behave and what kinds of crime are prevalent. Rely on your intuition to guide you away from things that don't "feel" right.

Keep as anonymous as you can. Dress blandly, blend in, don't look lost, don't get into arguments.

Avoid crowds and places where Americans are known to congregate.

Limit contact with friendly strangers, and don't accept food or drink from them as it might be laced with a powerful sedative.

Be careful in traffic; look both ways when you cross a street. On the road, be extra careful and pray a lot.

Petty thieves are everywhere, and tourists are as the sheep to the wolves. Street thieves usually work in pairs. Street vendors sell illegal artifacts, overpriced local goods, and things that actually are made elsewhere (at Petra, in Jordan, for example, vendors hawk camel-bone goods made in India). Generally your guide will lead you to cooperatives or shops where you can buy genuine crafts or souvenirs and support local artists and artisans.

Jet Lag

Some travelers take small doses of melatonin, available in vitamin stores, before they travel, to avoid having that feeling of fatigue and why-did-I-ever-come-here? that accompanies sudden changes in the biological clock. Other over-the-counter medications are available.

As a general rule, drink a lot of water on the plane; avoid alcohol; don't overeat. Exercise on long flights. When you arrive, try to find a spot of sunlight where you can sit for a little while: it alleviates jet lag.

Some practice the feast-fast-feast rule three days before you depart. Then fast on the flight day, and break your fast with breakfast in the new country.

Health

Contact the Centers for Disease Control www.cdc.gov; or call 877-394-8747 (tel); or 888-232-3299 (fax). Get a printout for the countries you will visit, then check with your doctor about booster shots or one-time inoculations. In Peru, you may need a yellow fever certificate. In Saudi Arabia, (if you can get a transit visa), you need proof of a meningitis vaccination. Keep a record of the dates of your inoculations and vaccinations for your own edification.

Centers for Disease Control recommends getting shots or boosters for the following. Because some are given over the course of a few weeks, start early.

Hepatitis A
Hepatitis B
Rabies (if you will be around animals)
Typhoid
Polio
Tetanus/diphtheria/measles

Anti-malaria medication (choose the right one based on discussions with your doctor). Malaria mosquitoes don't buzz, and they alight on the wall with their rear ends sticking up. Wear light-colored clothing; cover as much skin as you can; avoid perfumes; sleep under netting; wear DEET. Expect them in any and all rainforests, especially between sunset and sunrise.

Generally:

- AIDS virus is transmitted by unprotected sexual contact and contaminated blood. It does not live long on surfaces, such as door knobs.
- Pneumonia and tuberculosis are prevalent throughout the world, and are fairly contagious. Wash your hands often, keep them away from your nose and mouth.
- Cholera is present in many coastal communities, and it pays to stay away from uncooked fish. The rule is: Boil it, cook it, peel it, or forget it.
- Think twice before plunging into the Nile: the tiny snail-borne larvae that cause bilharzia are prevalent there.
- Generally, travel with some kind of diarrhea medicine, such a Immodium or Pepto Bismol, and make sure you re-

hydrate often. You should be able to buy bottled water everywhere.

- Don't brush your teeth with the tap water. The microbes that you pick up will wreak havoc while you are there, and in some cases may stay with you for weeks to come.
- Wash your hands often.
- Take aspirin or Tylenol.

High Altitude

> *If you are meant to do something,*
> *it will be the easiest thing in the world to do.*
> —Jock Archibald, *Going to Peru*

If you are flying in from sea level, give your body a chance to rest before taking the train up to Machu Picchu or going on to Mt. Kailash. If you can, prepare for altitude before you go, or do the ascent slowly, in parts. Above 9,000 feet, unacclimated travelers experience headaches and lethargy. Drink lots of water, expect sleeplessness. Sleep below 9,000 feet if you can.

The plane introduces you to high altitude, especially if you start from sea level. Cabins are pressurized to between 7,000 and 8,000 feet, at a flying altitude of about 30,000 feet.

In Peru, guides give you coca leaves (it's not cocaine) to chew on, which alleviate the strain of heights.

Some people adjust quickly, others never do. It depends on a lot of other factors, too.

Insect Bites

Take insect repellent, which is at least 35 percent DEET. This is toxic to just about everything, but it might prevent serious disease, such as dengue fever, from insects you encounter in the tropical jungle or on river banks. Apply it about every four hours if you are on a trek through the rainforest, and put it on your shirt sleeves and pants and socks as well. Also take along anti-itch lotion.

Sun Protection

Always apply protective lotion and reapply often. Skin cancer rates are growing exponentially these days. High altitudes and oceans are high UVA and UVB areas; but even if you are in a northern climate on an overcast day, slather on the lotion, no matter what color your skin is. Many doctors say a lotion with SPF 15 is enough; make sure it is renewed every few hours.

Clothing

Long-sleeved shirts and pants may seem a counterintuitive choice for the jungle, but it saves you from insect bites, prolonged fevers, and later pain.

The same clothing advice applies to high altitudes, along with a brimmed hat to protect your face from the sun.

Moist jungle air is home to fungi, and fungi love to eat leather, so consider alternatives to leather in belts, shoes, and bags.

Insurance

First check your own health insurance to see what it covers when you are away from home.

The following companies offer insurance that covers travel- and health-related problems. Look for coverage of:

- pre-trip cancellations, as well as trips that are cancelled when underway, for whatever reason;
- delays beyond twelve hours en route;

A boatman in Venezuela keeps watch on the passage. (*Roger Archibald*)

- loss of luggage or documents;
- loss of baggage that traveled on another flight and is delayed.

Also, find coverage for any health-related problems, including:

- finding a doctor or hospital;
- emergency evacuation;
- accidents;
- death, related to accidents (bear in mind that traffic-related accidents happen frequently among tourists).

Many companies offer coverage, but it pays to shop around; you can start with the following three:

Travel Guard International
1145 Clark Street
Stevens Point, WI 54481
800-826-4919 (toll free)
Web site: www.travel-guard.com

Global Travel Insurance
#202-585 16th Street
West Vancouver, BC V7V 3R8 Canada
800-232-9415 (toll free); 604-913-1150 (tel).
E-mail: info@globaltravelinsurance.com
Web site: www.globaltravelinsurance.com

Travel Insurance Services
2950 Camino Diablo, Suite 300
Walnut Creek, CA 94596-3949
800-937-1387 (toll free); 925-932-1387 (tel)
Web site: www.travelinsure.com

BIBLIOGRAPHY

Adler, Margot. *Drawing Down the Moon.* Boston: Beacon Press, 1986.

Atwater, F. Holmes. *Captain of My Ship, Master of My Soul.* Charlottesville, VA: Hampton Roads Publishing, 2001.

Bear, Jaya. *Amazon Magic: The Life Story of Ayahuascero & Shaman Don Agustin Rivas Vasquez.* El Prado, NM: Colibri Publishing, 2000.

Braden, Gregg. *The Isaiah Effect.* New York: Three Rivers Press, 2000.

Brennan, Barbara Ann. *Hands of Light: A Guide to Healing Through the Human Energy Field.* New York: Doubleday, 1993.

Brown, Michael F. *The Channeling Zone: American Spirituality in an Anxious Age.* Cambridge: Harvard University Press, 1997.

Burl, Aubrey. *A Guide to the Stone Circles of Britain, Ireland, and Brittany.* New Haven: Yale University Press, 1995.

Capra, Fritjof. *The Tao of Physics.* 4th ed. Boston: Shambhala, 2000.

Chopra, Deepak. *Ageless Body, Timeless Mind: The Quantum Alternative to Growing Old.* New York: Three Rivers Press, 1998.

Cousineau, Phil. *The Art of Pilgrimage.* Berkeley, Calif.: Conari Press, 1998.

Cumes, Carol, and Romulo Lizarraga Valencia. *Journey to Machu Picchu: Spiritual Wisdom from the Andes.* St. Paul, Minn.: Llewellyn Publications, 1998.

Christ, Carol P. *Rebirth of the Goddess.* New York: Routledge, 1998.

Diallo, Yaya. *The Healing Drum: African Ceremony and Ritual Music.* n.p.: Inner Traditions International, 1994.

Dong, Paul and Aristide H. Esser. *Chi Gong, The Ancient Chinese Way to Health.* New York: Paragon House, 1990.

Drury, Nevill. *Exploring the Labyrinth.* New York: Continuum, 1999.

Duffy, David G.P.R. "Santiago di Compostela," *The New York Times,* 5/30/99, *www.nytimes.com/library/travel/europe/ 990530sant. html*

Eck, Diana L. *A New Religious America.* San Francisco: Harper, 2001.

Engel, Klaus. *Meditation.* Frankfurt am Main: Peter Lang, 1997.

Gimbutas, Marija. *Goddesses and Gods of Old, 6500–300 B.C.* Berkeley and Los Angeles: University of California Press, 1990.

Gould, Stephen Jay. *The Structure of Evolutionary History.* Cambridge, Mass.: Belknap Press, 2002.

——. *Wonderful Life: The Burgess Shale and the Nature of History.* New York: W.W. Norton, 1990.

Graff, Dale E. *Tracks in the Psychic Wilderness.* Boston: Element Books, 1998.

Grof, Stanislav. *Psychology of the Future.* Albany: State University of New York Press, 2000.

Grauds, Constance. *Jungle Medicine.* San Rafael, Calif.: Citron Bay Press, 2001.

Guenther, Margaret. *Holy Listening: The Art of Spiritual Direction.* New York: Cowley, 1992.

Harner, Michael. *Way of the Shaman.* San Francisco: Harper, 1990.

Harvey, Graham. *Contemporary Paganism.* New York: New York University Press, 1997.

Houston, Jean. *Jump Time: Shaping Your Future in a World of Radical Change.* New York: Jeremy P. Tarcher, Putnam, 2000.

James, William. *The Varieties of Religious Experience.* New York: New American Library, 1958.

Kabat-Zinn, Jon. *Wherever You Go, There You Are: Mindfulness Meditation.* New York: Hyperion, 1995.

Kaku, Michio. *Hyperspace. A Scientific Odyssey Through Parallel Universes, Time Warps, and the Tenth Dimension.* New York: Oxford University Press, 1994; New York: Doubleday, 1995.

Kalweit, Holger. *Shamans, Healers, and Medicine Men.* Boston: Shambhala, 1987.

Keating, Fr. Thomas. *Open Mind, Open Heart: The Contemplative Dimension of the Gospel.* New York: Continuum, 1994.

Kelly, Jack and Marcia. *Sanctuaries: A Guide to Lodgings in Monasteries, Abbeys, and Retreats.* n.p.: Bell Tower, 2001.

Krippner, Stanley, ed. *Dreamscaping: New Techniques to Understand Yourself and Others.* New York: McGraw Hill, 1999.

Lesser, Elizabeth. *The New American Spirituality.* New York: Random House, 1999.

Lorie, Peter, and Julie Foakes, comp. *Buddhist Directory: The Total Buddhist Resource Guide.* Boston Tuttle, 1997.

McMoneagle, Joseph. *Mind Trek.* Charlottesville, VA: Hampton Roads Publishing, 1997.

Mack, John E. *Passport to the Cosmos.* New York: Three Rivers Press, 1999.

Mitchell, Edgar. *Way of the Explorer: An Apollo Astronaut's Journey Through the Material and Mystical World.* New York: Putnam, 1996.

Myerhoff, Barbara. *Peyote Hunt: The Sacred Journeys of the Huichol Indians.* Ithaca: Cornell University Press, 1976.

Myss, Caroline. *Sacred Contracts.* New York: Harmony, 2001.

Narby, Jeremy and Francis Huxley. *Shamans Through Time.* New York: Jeremy P. Tarcher/Putnam, 2001.

Newberg, Andrew, Eugene D'Aquili, and Vince Rause. *Why God Won't Go Away.* New York: Ballantine Books, 2001.

Ocean, Joan. *The Dolphin Connection: Interdimensional Ways of Living.* n.p.: Dolphin Connection, 1989.

Ostrander, Sheila and Lynn Schroeder. *Psychic Discoveries.* New York: Marlowe, 1970, 1997.

Perkins, John and Shakaim Mariano Ijisam Chumpi. *Spirit of the Shuar.* Rochester, Vt.: Destiny Books, 2001.

Plotkin, Mark. *Medicine Quest.* New York: Viking Penguin, 2000.

Pringle, Lucy. *Crop Circles.* London: Thorsens, 1999.

Radin, Dean. *Conscious Universe: The Scientific Truth of Psychic Phenomena.* New York: HarperCollins, 1997.

Redfield, James. *The Celestine Prophecy: An Adventure.* New York: Warner Books, 1997.

Regalbuto, Robert J. *A Guide to Monastic Guesthouses.* Harrisburg, Penn.: Morehouse Publishers, 2000.

Ricard, Matthew and Trinh Xuan Thuan. *The Quantum and the Lotus: A Journey to the Frontiers Where Science and Buddhism Meet.* New York: Crown, 2001.

Sarangerel. *Chosen By the Spirits: Following Your Shamanic Calling.* Rochester, VT: Destiny Publishing, 2001.

Selke, Ilona and Angelika Hansen. *Journey to the Center of Creation: Entering the World of Dolphins and the Dimensions of Dreamtime.* n.p.: Living From Vision, 1997.

Sheldrake, Rupert. *Dogs That Know When Their Owners Are Coming Home.* New York: Three Rivers Press, 1999.

Smith, Huston. *Why Religion Matters.* San Francisco: Harper, 2001.

Smith, Penelope. *Animal Talk: Interspecies Telepathic Communication.* Hillsboro, Ore: Beyond Words Publishing, 1999.

Starhawk. *The Spiral Dance.* Tenth Anniversary Edition. San Francisco: Harper, 1989.

Suzuki, D.T. *Zen Buddhism. Selected Writings of D. T. Suzuki.* Edited by William Barrett. New York: Doubleday, 1956.

Targ, Russell and Jane Katra. *Miracles of Mind: Exploring Nonlocal Consciouness and Spiritual Healing.* Novato, Calif.: New World Library, 1999.

Thompson, Keith. *Angels and Aliens.* New York: Fawcett Columbine, 1991.

Tompkins, Peter. *Secrets of the Great Pyramid.* New York: Harper & Row, 1971, 2d ed., 1978.

——— and Christopher Bird. *Secrets of the Soil.* New York: Harper & Row, 1989.

Torrance, Robert M. *The Spiritual Quest.* Berkeley: University of California Press, 1994.

Villoldo, Alberto. *Shaman, Healer, Sage.* New York: Harmony Books, 2000.

Vitebsky, Piers. *The Shaman.* Boston: Little, Brown and Co., 1995.

Watts, Alan. *Way of Zen.* New York: Pantheon, 1958.

Weil, Andrew. *Breathing: The Master Key to Self-Healing.* Sounds True, 1999. Compact disk.

Weil, Andrew and Jon Kabat-Zinn. *Meditation for Optimum Health: How to Use Mindfulness and Breathing to Heal Your Body and Refresh Your Mind.* Sounds True, 2001. Compact disk.

Westbury, Virginia. *Labyrinths.* Principal photography by Cindy A. Pavlinac. Sydney: Landsdowne, 2001.

Waterfalls always self-regulate. (*Roger Archibald*)

Whiteley, Richard. *The Corporate Shaman*. New York: Harper-Business, 2002.

Wood, Nicholas. *The Book of the Shaman*. New York: Barron's, 2001.

Wuthnow, Robert. *After Heaven: Spirituality in America Since the 1950s*. Berkeley: University of California Press, 1998.

Zohar, Danah and I.N. Marshall. *Quantum Self: Human Nature and Consciousness Defined by the New Physics*. New York: Quill/William Morrow, 1991.

INDEX